Dr. Maria Alpers
Dr. Herbert Voges
Dr. Gerhard Weiß

Britain and America

Neue Ausgabe
Oberstufe

Cornelsen-
Velhagen & Klasing

BRITAIN AND AMERICA
Englisches Unterrichtswerk für Gymnasien
Neue Ausgabe
Oberstufe · Textband

von Dr. Maria Alpers, Hannover, und Dr. Herbert Voges, Einbeck

in Zusammenarbeit mit
Dr. Gerhard Weiß, Kaiserslautern

und unter Mitwirkung von
OStD Otto Hagemann, Bad Salzuflen, und
StD Hans-Joachim Strunz, Berlin

Für Beratung bei der Textauswahl
und wertvolle Hinweise
danken Herausgeber und Verlag
folgenden Damen und Herren:

StD Dr. Rudolf Amann, Ulm
Elizabeth Daymond, B.A. (Oxon.)
OStR Paul Finck, Hannover
Dr. Richard L. G. Flower, M.A. (Cantab.)
OStR Annemarie Kampermann, Hildesheim
Colman Kraft, M.A. (Yale)
OStR Franz Schmidt, Bielefeld

Verlagsredaktion:
Dr. Annelore Naumann und
Martin Rosenthal

Arbeitsbuch für den Schüler: Bestellnummer 478
Lehrerbuch: Bestellnummer 5615

6. Auflage – 4. Druck 1980
Bestellnummer 460

© Velhagen & Klasing, Berlin, 1969
Alle Rechte vorbehalten.
Die Vervielfältigung und Übertragung auch einzelner Textabschnitte, Bilder oder Zeichnungen ist – mit Ausnahme der Vervielfältigung zum persönlichen und eigenen Gebrauch gemäß §§ 53, 54 URG – ohne schriftliche Zustimmung des Verlages nicht zulässig. Das gilt sowohl für die Vervielfältigung durch Fotokopie oder irgendein anderes Verfahren als auch für die Übertragung auf Filme, Bänder, Platten, Arbeitstransparente oder andere Medien.
Druck: CVK-Druck, Berlin
ISBN 3-464-00046-x

Vertrieb: Cornelsen-Velhagen & Klasing Verlagsgesellschaft, Bielefeld

Contents

Only an Ocean between (Lella S. Florence) 7

I Great Britain—The Land

The Beauty of Britain (John B. Priestley) 10
London (John Gunther) 12
Oxford and Cambridge—Two Famous University Cities (Norman St. John-Stevas and
    John Summerson) 15
Seeing Stratford (John B. Priestley)... 18
Scotland is a State of Mind (James Doyle).. 20
Northern Ireland—Compromise and Good Will..................................... 21

II The British People and their Institutions

The Chosen People (John Milton).. 24
Distrust of Logic and General Ideas (William R. Inge) 24
Cant (George Bernard Shaw) 25
A Gentleman Ideal (John H. Newman) 25
The English Pedigree (Dorothy L. Sayers) 27
The Queen 28
The House of Lords (H. W. Howes)... 29
The Working of the House of Commons (Peter Bromhead) 30
The Citizen and Law and Order (H. W. Howes) 32
Law in England (Egerton Smith).. 33
The Education System in England and Wales (Elizabeth Daymond) 36
Secondary Education (Anthony Sampson).. 38
What's new in British Universities? (Margaret Likierman) 40
The English Press (Karl E. Meyer).. 41
The National Health Service (Peter Bromhead).................................... 44
Sport as a Social and an Individual Phenomenon 46
Sport is War minus the Shooting (George Orwell) 46
A View of Young People in Britain today (Rosalind Priestman) 47
The Position of Women in Britain (Rosalind Priestman)............................ 49
Britain's Changing Anatomy (Anthony Sampson) 51

III The U.S.A.—The Land

Climate in Britain and America (Lella S. Florence)................................ 54
Sweet Land of Liberty (Archibald MacLeish) 55
New York (Richard J. Whalen) 57
Chicago 59
Los Angeles.. 61
Niagara Falls (Rupert Brooke) 63
The New Conservation (Stewart L. Udall) 65

IV The American People and their Institutions

Analysis of the American Character (Henry St. Commager) 67
Blending Many Strains into a Single Nationality (John F. Kennedy)................. 69
Condition and Fate of the American Indian (Calvin Kentfield) 72
The First Vote against Slavery 73
For Freedom and Equality (Martin Luther King).................................. 75

Black Power (James Baldwin)	76
Excerpts from the National Advisory Commission's Report on Civil Disorders	79
Principles of American Higher Education (Earl J. McGrath)	80
American Colleges and Universities (Howard E. Wilson)	81
Television in the U.S.A. (Lee Graham)	83
America—A Sports-loving Nation (Ivan T. Sanderson)	86
American Women (Malissa Redfield)	88
The Macbeth Murder Mystery (James Thurber)	90
Living in 2000	93

V British Politics

Excerpts from Magna Carta, 1215	95
Excerpts from the Habeas Corpus Act, 1679	95
Excerpts from the Bill of Rights, 1689	96
Of the Beginning of Political Societies (John Locke)	97
Conciliation with the Colonies (Edmund Burke)	98
The Victorian Age in Retrospect (George M. Trevelyan)	99
Government by the Party System	101
What is British Socialism? (Harold Wilson)	103
Principles of Liberal Policy (Donald Wade)	104
The Philosophy of the Conservative Party (Geoffrey D. M. Block)	106
Into Europe, andante	109

VI Commonwealth Problems

Why Great Britain survived her Rivals (John R. Seeley)	110
The Commonwealth and Britain (H. W. Howes)	111
Requiem for a Commonwealth (Anthony Lejeune)	113
Canada discovers itself	114
Australia	117
New Zealand—Country at the Cross-roads (Enid Bloomfield)	119
The Passing of Mahatma Gandhi (Clement Attlee)	121
The Problems of India today (Harford Thomas)	122
The Challenge of Africa (Kofi A. Busia)	124
The World watches Kenya (Kuldip Sondhi)	126
Arrival in Liverpool (William Conton)	128
Britain's Coloured Population (Anthony Lester)	129

VII American Politics

The Mayflower Compact, 1620	131
Excerpts from the Declaration of Independence, 1776	131
Excerpts from Lincoln's Emancipation Proclamation, 1863	132
Abraham Lincoln, The Gettysburg Address, November 19, 1863	133
Baron von Steuben (William H. Taft)	133
The New Deal (Alan P. Grimes)	134
TVA (Tennessee Valley Authority)	135
The Written and the Unwritten	136
The American Two-Party System (Abraham Ribicoff/Jon O. Newman)	139
Elections in the U.S.A. (Abraham Ribicoff/Jon O. Newman)	141
The Future of American Labor Unions (John Herling)	143
John F. Kennedy, Inaugural Address, January 20, 1961	144

VIII Science

Natural Selection (Charles Darwin)	147
Lamps are lighted (William A. Simonds)	148
Science, Technology, and the Human Spirit (David E. Lilienthal)	150
Work and the Automatic Factory (Max Lerner)	151

Are Machines getting smarter than Men? (From an interview with Norbert Wiener)	153
A New Era in American Agriculture	156
"Open Skies"—Satellites in the Sixties (Arthur C. Clarke)	157
Promise and Menace of the Nuclear Age (Edward Teller/Albert L. Latter)	159
Landing on the Moon (Wernher von Braun)	161
The Laser's Bright Magic (Thomas Meloy)	163
Genetic Intervention (Joshua Lederberg)	165
Sketches of the Future (John Davy)	167

IX Arts

The Norman Abbey of Tewkesbury (John Moore)	169
The Spire of Salisbury Cathedral (Darcy Braddell)	170
England at the Time of Queen Elizabeth (John D. Wilson)	172
An Inspiring Painter of Atmosphere (A. G. Dumfries)	173
J. M. W. Turner's "The Fighting Téméraire" (William M. Thackeray)	174
Modern English Sculpture (See colour plates, Nos. XIII–XVII)	
Henry Moore (Anne Symonds)	174
The Edinburgh Festival (Rita MacDonald)	175
"Punch" in the Sixties (Bernard Hollowood)	177
American Architecture (Thomas H. Creighton)	180
Minoru Yamasaki (Paul Heyer)	183
A Real American Style of Music (Leonard Bernstein)	185
The New Jazz	186
The Comic Strip—A Mirror of the American Way of Life	188

X Literature

Standard English (Andrew Wilkinson)	190
The Cultural Background of Shakespeare's Time (John D. Wilson)	191
The Shakespearian Theatre (John D. Wilson)	193
Shakespeare, the Poet of Nature (Samuel Johnson)	195
Human Relationships in Shakespeare (Victor G. Kiernan)	195
On Poetry (Percy B. Shelley)	196
On Books (John Ruskin)	197
The Modern English Play (Penelope Gilliatt)	198
American Literature now stands in its Own Right (John Steinbeck)	200
The Contemporary American Short Story (Danforth Ross)	201

XI Religion

The Church of England (Peter Bromhead)	204
The English Bible (George M. Trevelyan)	205
The Common Prayer Book (John Elton)	206
Puritanism in England (Richard H. Tawney)	207
The Quakers (Eric Priestman)	209
New England Calvinism and Anglicanism (Leo Pfeffer)	210
Protestantism in the U.S.A. (Denis W. Brogan)	211

XII Humanity

The Unity of European Culture (Thomas Stearns Eliot)	213
Individuality (John Stuart Mill)	215
The Indestructibility of the United Nations (Walter Lippmann)	217
Excerpts from the Universal Declaration of Human Rights, 1948	219
Excerpts from the UNESCO Constitution	220
Excerpts from J. F. Kennedy's Message on the Peace Corps, March 1, 1961	220

The symbol ° indicates an abridgement of the original text.

Only an Ocean between

Yes, but what an ocean! Three thousand miles of cold grey water whipped into seasickening turbulence by cold relentless winds. It's a mighty fierce barrier to lie between two great countries and two great peoples. That damp expanse of waste space is to be blamed for most of the misconceptions and the quaintly inaccurate ideas prevailing on either side of the Atlantic about the people across the way.°

But some of the differences are fundamental and profound, and must be understood to be tolerated. They are the natural outgrowth of the shape and age and size of the country, the kind of soil and climate, the indigenous resources—in fact, the whole contour of the environment within which the people of Britain and America have built their respective cultures and developed their respective national characteristics. These are the kind of differences, nourished on customs and traditions through many generations, which are hard to change and will just have to be accepted by both sides. For instance, America is convinced that all her institutions and achievements are the *biggest* and best in the world; and no one could convince an Englishman that his are not the *oldest* and best. Because England is a small place, he scorns size as a measure of merit. Because the United States is big, size looms large in the American's measure of values. Because England is old, the Englishman lays great store by tradition. Because America is young, the American rejects tradition and goes in for innovation and experiment. So what? Both sides are guilty of a too long cherished insularity, for which that grim old Atlantic can mostly be blamed. It's not the mere distance, because the 3,000 miles which separate London from New York is about equal to the space between New York and San Francisco. Yet the New Yorker and the Californian understand each other far more sympathetically than the Briton and the New Yorker. But the ocean *can* be bridged—and the sooner the better!

In 1620, when the Pilgrim Fathers packed their hopes and their haversacks into the *Mayflower* and set out on their grand adventure, they bade farewell to some six or seven million of their kith and kin, scattered over some 88,000 square miles of the green sea-girt island which is Great Britain. When they cast anchor on the rocky coast of the New World there were, all told (including the Red Indians, the Spaniards, the French and the earlier English settlers in Virginia), a mere handful of human beings. But they had millions of square miles to play about in—millions of miles of primeval forest and steaming swamp, of endless plains and towering mountains, of fertile valleys and arid deserts.°

When the Pilgrim Fathers turned their backs on their Mother Country in 1620, she was already hoary with age, as time goes. She already had centuries of history behind her—"1066 and all that," which to an American seems almost the beginning of time, was a fairly recent date in her affairs. (British schoolchildren begin the study of *modern*

◀ Land's End

1 Yorkshire Dales, Yorkshire

history with the year 1485.) Already England had an established culture. The Universities of Oxford and Cambridge were centuries old. Chaucer, Christopher Marlowe, Shakespeare, Ben Jonson, had lived and died, leaving the imperishable beauty of their work for future generations. All over England great cathedrals stood in massive majesty, strong and mighty against the ravages of time, linking one generation to the next. Americans who have had the good fortune to visit Britain begin to understand the pride of the British in these age-old achievements of their forbears. They begin to appreciate the Briton's reluctance to accept any change—his resistance to any departure from the deep-rooted traditions of his long-established customs.°

The conception of space is quite different in the mind of a Briton and an American. To the Briton the 600 miles from Land's End to John O'Groats is a prodigious distance. It is, in fact, the longest trip you can take in Britain without getting your feet wet. A motor trip from the Midlands to Cornwall (about 200 miles) is a major undertaking, and so is a railway journey to almost any place in Scotland. I don't suppose one out of a hundred has ever even contemplated taking a sleeping-car for a night's journey. In most cases travelling from one point to another in Britain is a matter of only a few

2 Seward County, Nebraska

hours on the train. After that you tend to run into the sea. I've lived half my life in England and I've got around quite a bit. But I've never seen the inside of a sleeping-car, although they run to Cornwall, Wales, the North and Scotland. To the American, who has to travel five days and four nights by railroad to get across the continent, a few hundred miles are just no impediment to speak of.°

The country in America is vast and robust and far-flung. It has grandeur (and sometimes monotony), but it lacks the charm of the English scene. When I first saw England I was enthralled by the small green neatness of everything. The fields under cultivation looked so beautifully tailored, and I felt that if I could turn them upside down I should find all the seams perfectly finished.°

The Americans have their broad highways streaking from coast to coast, often visible straight ahead as far as the eye can reach. That is the road for high-powered cars, and that is what the American likes.

But the Englishman loves his twisting country lanes with their promise of pleasant surprises just round the corner.

Lella S. Florence in "America and Britain", 1946

I Great Britain—The Land

The Beauty of Britain

We live on one of the most beautiful islands in the world. This is a fact we are always forgetting. When beautiful islands are mentioned, we think of Trinidad or Tahiti. These are fine, romantic places, but they are not really as exquisitely beautiful as our
5 own Britain. Before the mines and factories came, and long before we went from bad to worse with our arterial roads and petrol stations and horrible brick bungalows, this country must have been an enchantment, designed by God to be the earthly paradise of wandering water-colourists. Even now, after we have been busy for so long flinging mud at this fair pale face, the enchantment still remains. Between the cities, away from
10 the main roads, there are still bright tracts of this earthly paradise. Sometimes I doubt if we deserve to possess them. There can be few parts of the world in which commercial greed and public indifference have combined to do more damage than they have here. We have been hard at it fouling our nest for a long time now. The process continues. It is still too often assumed that any enterprising fellow after quick profits has a perfect
15 right to destroy a loveliness that is the heritage of the whole community.

It is not that the ordinary Briton is completely insensitive. I believe that he has a better sense of beauty than most aesthetes imagine. The trouble is, he is too mentally lazy to make quick effective protests. He grumbles privately, knowing very well that the favourite local bit of countryside now spoilt has been lost to him for ever, but he
20 does no more. I am certain, however, that he misses what is gone.°

I shall be told that the newer generations care nothing for the beauty of the countryside, that all they want is to go rushing about on motor-cycles or in fast cars. Speed is not one of my gods; rather one of my devils; but we must give this devil its due. I believe that swift motion across a countryside does not necessarily take away all appreciation
25 of its charm. It depends on the nature of the country. With some types of landscape there is a definite gain simply because you are moving so swiftly across the face of the country. There is a certain kind of pleasant but dullish, rolling country, not very attractive to the walker or slow traveller, that becomes alive if you go quickly across it, for it is turned into a kind of sculptured landscape. As your car rushes along the rolling
30 roads, it is as if you were passing a hand over a relief map. Here, obviously, there has been a gain, not a loss, and this is worth remembering. The newer generations, with their passion for speed, are probably far more sensitive than they are thought to be. Probably they are all enjoying aesthetic experiences that so far they have been unable to communicate to the rest of us. We must not be too pessimistic about young people if they
35 prefer driving and gulping to walking and tasting.

The beauty of our country—or at least all of it south of the Highlands—is as hard to define as it is easy to enjoy. Remembering other and larger countries, we see at once that one of its charms is that it is immensely varied within a small compass. We have here no vast mountain ranges, no illimitable plains, no leagues of forest, and are de-
40 prived of the grandeur that may accompany these things. But we have superb variety.

A great deal of everything is packed into little space. I suspect that we are always faintly conscious of the fact that this is a smallish island, with the sea always round the corner. We know that everything has to be neatly packed into a small space. Nature, we feel, has carefully adjusted things—mountains, plains, rivers, lakes—to the scale of the island itself. A mountain 12,000 feet high would be a horrible monster here, as wrong as a plain 400 miles long, a river as broad as the Mississippi. In America the whole scale is too big, except for aviators. There is always too much of everything. There you find yourself in a region that is all mountains, then in another region that is merely part of one colossal plain. You can spend a long, hard day in the Rockies simply travelling up or down one valley. You can wander across prairie country that has the desolating immensity of the ocean. Everything is too big; there is too much of it.

Though the geographical features of this island are comparatively small, and there is astonishing variety almost everywhere, that does not mean that our mountains are not mountains, our plains not plains. Consider that piece of luck of ours, the Lake District. You can climb with ease—as I have done many a time—several of its mountains in one day. Nevertheless, you feel that they are mountains and not mere hills.°

With variety goes surprise. Ours is the country of happy surprises. You have never to travel long without being pleasantly astonished. It would not be difficult to compile a list of such surprises that would fill the next fifty pages, but I will content myself with suggesting the first few that occur to me. If you go down into the West Country, among rounded hills and soft pastures, you suddenly arrive at the bleak tablelands of Dartmoor and Exmoor, genuine high moors, as if the North had left a piece of itself down there. But before you have reached them you have already been surprised by the queer bit of Fen country you have found in the neighbourhood of Glastonbury, as if a former inhabitant had been sent to Cambridge and had brought his favourite fenland walk back from college with him into the West. The long, green walls of the North and South Downs are equally happy surprises. The Weald is another of them. East Anglia has a kind of rough heath country of its own that I for one never expect to find there and am always delighted to see. No doubt it is only natural that East Lincolnshire and that

3 River Avon in Hampshire, Southern England

4 Cumberland, Lake District

South-eastern spur of Yorkshire should show us an England that looks more than half Dutch, but the transition always comes as a surprise to me. Then, after the easy rolling Midlands, the dramatic Peak District, with its genuine steep fells, never fails to astonish me, for I feel that it has no business to be there. A car will take you all round the Peak
5 District in a morning. It is nothing but a crumpled green pocket-handkerchief. Nevertheless, we hear of search-parties going out there to find lost travellers. Again, there has always been something surprising to me about those conical hills that suddenly pop up in Shropshire and along the Welsh border. I have never explored this region properly, and so it remains to me a country of mystery, with a delightful fairy-tale
10 quality about its sugar-loaf hills. I could go on with this list of surprises, but perhaps you had better make your own.

John B. Priestley in "The Beauty of Britain", 1962

London

London has changed a good deal in the past few years—in architecture, street scenes, the attitude to Queen and country, food, the look of the people (it's better, particularly
15 their teeth), political and social structure, urban development, clothes, and youthful folkways. This huge conurbation (a fashionable new British word meaning "the coming together of built-up areas") is not standpat, but distinguished by a lot of taut experimentation. The mood is up.

But first let us glance at this magnificent and copious city in the large, before de-
20 scribing details of what's going on.

London, a triple capital (of England, the United Kingdom, and, in a manner of speaking, the British Commonwealth), has a population slightly over eight million, which puts it second among the world's cities, a bit ahead of New York, but behind Tokyo. The area of Greater London is 620 square miles, almost twice that of New

York City (319.8 square miles). The Thames bisects it in a series of loops like an intestine. It contains roughly a third of all taxable value in the British Isles, and holds one-sixth of the total population of Great Britain.°

Today this colossus of cities is the third port in the world (after New York and Rotterdam), as well as one of the greatest financial, industrial, mercantile, and trading centers. But it is rich in a good many other respects as well. Few other cities have given so many geographical metaphors to the language—Downing Street, Rotten Row, Fleet Street (which was once a river), Whitehall, Harley Street, Petticoat Lane, Savile Row, and London Bridge, which today is actually falling down—more precisely, slipping further into the muck of the Thames a few inches every year. Names grow into abstraction and become fixed in common speech all over the world—like Sherlock Holmes, Old Vic, Mother of Parliaments, Wimbledon, Mr. Pickwick, Covent (originally "Convent") Garden, Big Ben, Greenwich Time, Scotland Yard.°

We come now to "Swinging London". This is a misnomer, because only a small element of youthful London swings. Most Londoners profess to be bored by the subject, and tend to dismiss it as an aberration. But they cannot deny that the youngsters have given parts of the metropolis a new look, and that London is, as a result, the brightest city in Europe at the moment.

5 The City of London

6 London, Tate Gallery and Vickers Building

Young people swarm into the pubs and discotheques, dance with mechanical frenzy, and make a place fashionable for a week—then move on to another. They have little interest in public affairs, think that the "angry young men" of the John Osborne epoch are as dated as Moses, and never talk politics, as one said to me, "except to a new
5 acquaintance". They have washed their hands of taking care of the world, or of being the world's bellwether or watchdog. Some who do not live at home have no regular place to sleep and go about with three possessions—a bedroll, a toothbrush, and a guitar—with which they camp on any friend's doorstep.

What mostly distinguishes them is their dress, as a walk down King's Road in Chelsea
10 will amply show. I saw one young man who, I thought, must be an actor who had

arrived from some Shakespeare performance without changing his costume—a peach-colored velvet jacket with lace cuffs and sequined pants. But no; this was his "ordinary" wear.

How can the London youngsters afford their evening forays? For one thing, most—both boys and girls—earn quite good salaries for Europe, as much as £18 a week, and, since they are young enough still to be living at home when they "live" anywhere, they have no rent to pay. Girls usually pay their share on a date. Clothes are relatively cheap at the bright new boutiques which are a madly flourishing business all over the place. It is not fashionable to drink much, or to gamble, and this too saves money.

At least four main reasons help account for the rise of the swingers: 1) reaction against the conservatism and conventionality of their parents; 2) an impulse to release after long years of austerity; 3) more earning power; 4) a sense that the world is doomed and that they might as well have a fling while they can. The whole movement is rooted in protest.

Frightened elders, particularly emigrants from the Continent, are much shocked by this ball-before-Waterloo atmosphere, and even go so far as to say that London today reminds them of Berlin before Hitler, with its insane vortex of corruption. But today's high jinks in London are mild—almost innocent—by comparison. Berlin was vicious, which London is not, and the swingers in their plumage are a sign of vitality, in their own peculiar British way, rather than of decay.

John Gunther in "Harper's Magazine", 1967

Oxford and Cambridge—Two Famous University Cities

I never realized when I first decided to go to Oxford *and* Cambridge the seriousness of the step I was taking. One might have gone to Eton *and* Harrow and got away with it. Oxford and Cambridge, however, are a national passion. Father is divided against son, mother against daughter, aunts against nephews and nieces, by a fierce emotional conviction that they are "Oxford" or "Cambridge". This feeling seems stronger amongst those who have not attended them than with those who have. The crowds that throng the tow-paths of the Thames on Boat Race Day show that.

Let us try to survey both the universities from an inner standpoint. Similarities, of course, are many. An ancient tradition of centuries is shared by both, and the threat of modern scientific education is equally felt. Scientists throng "King's Parade" in Cambridge as much as they do "The High" in Oxford.

If similarities exist, the differences are deeper marked. The most striking contrast is the difference in ethos between the two. Cambridge is a matter-of-fact, down-to-earth, sensible university. It is still defiantly progressive. Oxford is very much the city of dreaming spires, and conservative in its deepest roots. Eccentricity is frowned on at Cambridge; at Oxford it is a cult. Poetry flourishes at Oxford; philosophy finds its home in Cambridge; Oxford undergraduates have a certain brilliance; their conversation sparkles; they are intimately concerned with their inner reactions and feelings. Cambridge undergraduates are more concerned with their relations with their fellow-men; they get on with the job.

Generalizations are inevitably faulty. Oxford types may be found in Cambridge and vice versa; individuals exist who defy any classification; yet, generally speaking, the distinction is true.

Are Oxford and Cambridge romantic? Well, yes, that is the only word. Romantic to the outsider because of their long history, their exquisitely beautiful buildings, and the sense that within those buildings something timeless and beneficent lives in spite of all changes in the world at large.

Oxford and Cambridge form two of the most wonderful groups of buildings in the world, and it is no use pretending that, if Oxford or Cambridge were re-housed in efficient, modern structures, they would still be Oxford and Cambridge. They would not.

They would remain great institutions, yes; but just that essence which makes them precisely what they are would have been lost. Oxford today leads a peculiar sort of double life. Down the famous High Street roar trucks and buses. They roar between the glories of English architecture: University College, Queen's College, Magdalen College, etc. The buses are bound for the Morris Works, one of the biggest motor-car plants in Europe, in full swing there, just outside the old city.

The other Oxford exists now like an island in a flood, cut in two by the main stream. But what an island! Leave the High Street, and in a moment you are in a city of wonderful, stately silence, not a city of free squares and open places, but a city of enclosures. For the colleges of Oxford look inwards. Each has one or two, or perhaps, three, grass-

7 Aerial View of Oxford

8 King's College Chapel, Cambridge

covered quadrangles into which no wheeled traffic goes. Round these beautiful quadrangles are the chapels and halls and libraries of Oxford, and the rooms of the undergraduates of the colleges.

Among this network of quadrangles, the life of the university goes on. All day, during term-time, undergraduates in their queer, scrappy little gowns—tokens of a seventeenth-century style of dress—thread their way through this Gothic labyrinth, or come streaming in and out of it on bicycles, with the automatic familiarity of bees round a bee-hive.

The colleges may be small or large, but whether they are small or large, they are never—or very rarely—grandiose. But here and there rise the great gestures of Oxford architecture—the soaring fourteenth-century steeple of St. Mary's, the elegant tower of Magdalen, and the bulk of Tom Tower at Christ Church.

Those are the messengers, sky-messengers of Oxford, seen for many miles round. This grandeur of silhouette is unique to Oxford. If Oxford leaves the impression of enclosure and skyward aspiration, Cambridge leaves the impression of horizontal space. I think this is partly due to the overpowering, horizontal splendour of King's College, the most conspicuous of the colleges, and one of the few which is visible all at once from the street. The quadrangle—a very large one—is screened from view by a light, low, pierced stonework screen. The college itself spreads broadly across the background, which, on one side of the quadrangle, is a building which I think, without doubt, is one of the great architectural spectacles of Europe: King's College Chapel.

9 Hall of Christ Church, Oxford   10 Modern College in Cambridge

There is nothing you can compare that building with, except buildings so utterly different in climate and purpose as to make the comparison absurd—the Parthenon, perhaps, or Chartres Cathedral. But why compare? The complete and unruffled nobility of King's Chapel is one of those things which make comparisons meaningless.

At evening service, with only the fading daylight above you and the sparkle of candles on the choristers' desks, you feel that space has been mastered in a way that has never been achieved at any other time or place.

As to architecture, Cambridge is to Oxford what Paris is to Rome. In Cambridge, as in Paris, everything is on show, and the whole is laid out to the best advantage. Oxford, like Rome, abounds in beauty, but it is a hidden beauty that must be sought for.

Norman St. John-Stevas and John Summerson, 1951

Seeing Stratford

"You must admit you haven't been there," they said. I told them that I had been *through* the town more than once. But that was nothing, they retorted, because I hadn't *seen* anything there, didn't know where Shakespeare was born or buried or where Anne Hathaway lived, had never sat on the edge of the second-best bed. I told them I didn't care. "We know you don't care for the sight-seeing part of it," they confessed, "but that won't last long. It's a delightful run, and look what a lovely morning it is."

The real literary shrine is, of course, a library. For the rest you may at times come close to an author's spirit in various odd places and atmospheres, it may be in an autumn wood, on a bare moor, in a bar-parlour, within sight of a palm reef and a line of breakers. But the official literary business, with its documents of birth, marriage and death, its museums and antique-shop airs, its array of beds and pens and desks and chairs, its visitors' books and picture postcards and glib custodians, is simply so much solemn nonsense. The persons who really enjoy this cultured and hushed-voiced sight-seeing are never people who care very much about books and authors. Stratford is their Mecca. I hope Shakespeare himself knows all about it, that he is keeping an immortal eye on his birthplace. How he must enjoy the fun! I can hear him roaring with laughter. I can see him bringing other immortals (probably Cervantes among them, for if those two are not hand-in-glove, then there is no friendship among the shades) to see the local branch of the Midland Bank, which tries to look Elizabethan and romantic and even has some scenes from the plays drearily depicted round its walls. He will show them how everything in the place is conscientiously thatched and beamed. He will watch us paying our shillings in this place and that, to gape at an array of articles that have really nothing to do with him, rooms full of Garrick and Hathaway relics. His attitude towards all solemn and pompous official persons and bores was always touched with a light malice and his own irony, and he must delight in the fact that he contrived to leave behind him so few facts about his life and so few things to admire. He must enjoy watching his biographers compiling their works, when they know only too well—poor fellows—that all the facts could be set down on two or three sheets of note-paper and that they will have to write page after page beginning, "We

11 Tourists in Stratford-upon-Avon

can imagine the young Shakespeare," or "No doubt the poet at this time," or "Is it not likely that the dramatist,"—feverishly padding.

Having left little or nothing of his own behind him, he must take a malicious pleasure in the efforts of his townspeople to provide visitors with Shakespeare museums. I hope he watched them ransack every corner of the place and dubiously install documents relating to the wood of his mulberry-tree and portraits of the mayor of 1826.

Yes, Shakespeare himself would laugh all right if he spent a day in his little town now. He would be amused at the solemn arts-and-crafts persons who have set up shop in the kindly shadow of his great fame; at the expensive hotels that try to delude Missouri and California into the belief that they are hostelries lately removed from Eastcheap; at the Shakespeare This and the Hathaway That meeting the eye everywhere; at the transformation of his bustling little town into a shrine where Justice Shallow guides the feet and eyes of Judge K. Shallow. He would laugh but he would understand, too. He would turn wise yet wondering eyes upon the little yellow man from Cathay who was looking down upon that flat tombstone in the old parish church. He would understand the middle-aged American woman (she had that curious dried look that comes to some American women and suggests they have been specially prepared for export, like dried fruit) who walked up to the curator of Anne Hathaway's cottage and cried: "Well, I've had a lovely time in there and I wouldn't have missed a minute of it." He would understand this, although he himself probably did not have a lovely time in that cottage. He would laugh but he would go down at once to the precious human stuff that is lying underneath all these solemn antics and mummery.

And there was one moment, the other afternoon, when I did really feel I was treading upon his own ground. It was when we were in the gardens of New Place, very brave in the spring sunlight. You could have played the outdoor scenes of *Twelfth Night* in them without disturbing a leaf. There was the very sward for Viola and Sir Andrew. Down that paved path Olivia would come, like a great white peacock. Against that bank of flowers the figure of Maria would be seen, flitting like a starling. The little Knott Garden alone was worth the journey and nearer to Shakespeare than all the documents and chairs and monuments. It was a patterned blaze of tulips, the Elizabethan gentlefolk among flowers. The white ones, full open and very majestic, were the great ladies in their ruffs; and the multi-coloured ones, in all their bravery of crimson and yellow, were the gentlemen in doublet and striped hose. The little crazy-paved paths added a touch of pride and fantasy and cross-gartering, as if Malvolio had once passed that way. And then, to crown all, there were tiny rows of sweet-smelling English herbs, thyme and sage and marjoram, and misty odorous borders of lavender. I remember that when we left that garden to see the place where Shakespeare was buried, it didn't seem to matter much. Why should it when we had just seen the place where he was still alive?

John B. Priestley, "All about Ourselves and Other Essays", 1928

Scotland is a State of Mind

Scotland is a small country, comprising roughly the northern third of Great Britain. It is noted for its scenery, for its fishing and hunting, for tweeds, and for the skill of its distillers. It has a population of a little more than 5,200,000 people, about a million of them concentrated in its largest city Glasgow, which still refers to itself as the "second city in the British Empire," ignoring the existence of such places as Bombay and Sydney, and the fact that it's now the Commonwealth of Nations.

This is one Scotland, but there's another; for Scotland is a state of mind as well as a geographical and political entity. This second Scotland is the Scotland in which every true son of Wallace lives; and although it bears no perceivable relation to anything on earth, past, present, or future, it is the only real Scotland. This Scotland is the greatest country in the world; upon its capital, Edinburgh, have descended the mantles of both Athens and Rome; it produces the most ferocious warriors, the loveliest ladies, the greatest scholars, and the best golf players that ever wore shoes; its king is the ruler of the Commonwealth; its sons have gone forth to the far corners of the globe to run the world's steam engines, quench its thirst, and exert a gracious and civilizing influence upon the rest of Britain.

A Scot is Scottish first and British second, and no matter how far he may wander, his heart never really leaves the Highlands. He is fully conscious of the merits of his country, and glories in the great contributions it has made to Britain and to the world. The discovery of Scotland almost always comes as something of a surprise to the traveller, probably because all of Great Britain is the same colour on the map, and the foreigner is easily beguiled into putting all of its people together. Actually, nothing could be more misleading. Although they are governed by the same Parliament and pay allegiance to the same king, England and Scotland display the differences that might be expected on crossing any international frontier.

The Scot's deep loyalty is rooted in the ancient past, where the dividing line between history and legend is indistinct, before Scotland was unified, and when the Highland chieftains waged ceaseless and savage war upon each other. The rivalry between clan and clan is still strong, even if it finds expression today in words instead of warfare.

The Highland tradition is seen at its colourful best in the clan gatherings which take place throughout the summer and autumn in Scotland. As might be expected, they are pretty robust affairs. The Highland games, which have been a feature of them for more than 900 years, take plenty of muscle as well as skill—one traditional event is "tossing the caber," which is simply seeing how far you can throw a telegraph pole. Another is Scottish wrestling, which might be described as seeing how far you can throw a Scot. By contrast, the dances are marvels of grace, and the spectacle of a six foot, 200 pound Highlander going through the intricate steps of a sword dance with a ballerina's deftness has to be seen to be believed.

The music of the pipes intensifies any emotion the Scot may be feeling at the moment. In one mood, they evoke a sentimental tear, in another, a blood-curdling war-cry.

No one who has ever heard the pipes in Scotland has quite escaped their magic. The place to do it is the misty, mysterious town of Inverness. During the summer, the pipes are always with you in Inverness, from earliest morning until the beginning of the eerie half-light that is as close to night as these northern latitudes ever come. There's quite an air about Inverness, anyway, an air that makes it easy to believe in fairies and ghosts—and Scotland. Inverness calls itself the capital of the Highlands, and that is what it has been—long before Lady Macbeth had trouble getting to sleep there in 1040 A.D., but it is not strictly a Highland city. Rather it is the point of contact between the Gaelic culture of the Highlands and the tamer lowland tradition.

It has one of the most picturesque settings of any city in Britain, and in the autumn, when its surrounding hills are purple with heather, Inverness is the epitome of Scotland. For any traveller, it is the key to the Highlands. Inverness boasts, with some justice, that it has a greater range of scenic beauty, from the pastoral to the precipitous, within a morning's drive than any other city in the British Isles.

There's more to the Scot than picturesque dress, picturesque speech, and robust sports. He is one of the hardest workers in the world, although he never lets toil interfere with an eye for beauty and an ear for music and poetry. He is an individualist, and he builds the "Made in Scotland" stamp right into whatever he does.

James Doyle

Northern Ireland—Compromise and Good Will

MR WHITELAW, Secretary of State for Northern Ireland, made a statement on the White Paper setting out constitutional proposals for Northern Ireland.° He said that under the Government's proposals, Northern Ireland would continue to have a greater degree of self-government than any other part of the United Kingdom. Both the majority and minority communities will (he continued) have an opportunity to play a full part in dealing with issues and procedures of crucial domestic importance to Northern Ireland.

The proposed settlement is devised for the interests of Northern Ireland as a whole. It cannot meet all the wishes of any one section of the community. It requires the cooperation of all the people of Northern Ireland. A heavy responsibility now rests upon their leaders. There can be no excuse for withdrawal of cooperation or resort to violence.

The many problems of Northern Ireland cannot be solved by Government alone but the proposed settlement, given goodwill, provides a fair and reasonable basis for progress. (*Cheers.*)

Mr Merlyn Rees (Labour)—The Opposition have expressed positive views on many of the matters in the White Paper: on the effects of proportional representation, power sharing, the vital need to end the Special Powers Act, an all-Ireland institution, and economic affairs. Would not all of us be wise to follow the advice of the trade unions of Northern Ireland and the Council of Churches and consider carefully the words of the White Paper before giving our firm views?

On the all-Ireland dimension, are not all the indications that the Government of the Republic wish to cooperate? Is there any indication, however, that the Government of the Republic will recognize the three objectives mentioned by the Secretary of State, which I believe were in the discussion paper—particularly the acceptance of the present status of Northern Ireland?

With regard to the changes made in the existing Government of Northern Ireland, will he convey to the Governor and his wife our thanks for a job done well and with courage? (*Conservative cheers.*)

Will he confirm that the White Paper would indicate that apart from the firearms licensing order, which is outstanding for discussion, there are five pieces of legislation that will come before us: renewal of the Temporary Powers Act, Diplock and ending the Special Powers Act, a constitutional Bill, a job discrimination Bill and an order removing the existing discriminatory law and laws of allegiance?

The Opposition will scrutinize these measures carefully and critically with one supreme aim: to have Assembly elections in Northern Ireland at an early date,° in which all can participate. Should not all those who can, especially the leadership, speak clearly against violence and concentrate their minds on Assembly elections?

We believe in a political solution for Northern Ireland; but will he assure the House that if there is any attempt there from any source to erect road blocks and in any other way attempt to bring the province to its knees the security forces will act firmly; in any event, the restoration of law and order and the whole question of the police will be vital subjects to discuss in the months to come.

Is it not the case that the approach of most of us in this House has been based on a belief in the strength of the forces of moderation? Only the people of Northern Ireland can tell us if this belief is well founded. The Government must provide the means for them to speak soon°. In making their choice, the people and leaders of Northern Ireland must face up to the consequences of responsibility.

It is a choice perhaps between cooperation and bloodshed. Is it not the case that if there is no cooperation, there will have to be in the end, and whether we like it or not, a radical reappraisal of Government policy? (*Labour cheers.*)

Mr Whitelaw—I would agree strongly that it would be most helpful if everyone were to follow the advice of the leaders of the Churches and many political and trade union leaders who have urged everyone in Northern Ireland to read carefully what is in the White Paper, and not to be swayed by instant comment or wild allegations. I hope that advice will be followed.

He referred to the question of cooperation with the Republic of Ireland. It is true that in Northern Ireland all the political parties in one way or another wish to see increased cooperation mainly through a Council of Ireland. On his side, Mr Cosgrave recently talked about the need for conciliation and pacification. I believe that these two moves between them, certainly we would hope, would lay a basis for future cooperation.

As for the legislative proposals to which he referred, subject to final checking I think he is correct.

As to the need to have Assembly elections soon, I would strongly endorse that view. It would be most desirable to have these elections at an early date. Until we have had them it is difficult to tell exactly the strength of different feelings in Northern Ireland. When we can have them will depend on many factors—not least the time that it takes us to get legislation through this House on which any such future elections have to be based.

There can be no excuse for violence of any sort arising out of this White Paper. If there is, it will be met by the firmest possible action by the security forces, from whatever side it may come.°

MISS BERNADETTE DEVLIN (Independent Unity)—°There is one question I would like to put, while maintaining my own views on the introduction of the White Paper. It concerns paragraph 118 the latter part of which speaks of "those small but dangerous minorities which would seek to impose their view by violence and coercion"—the next bit is the interesting bit—"and which cannot therefore be allowed to participate in working institutions they wish to destroy". Since I have never had any qualms about my decision and intention to destroy the capitalist system and yet I am allowed to sit here, does it mean that the members of either wing of the republican movement, whose avowed aim is to end British intervention in Ireland, will not be allowed to contest elections at local government or assembly level? If not, what does it mean?

MR WHITELAW—Without prejudging who may be allowed to participate in local government or other elections, the important point in the context of Northern Ireland, which Miss Devlin must face, is that people who resort to violence to press their views, cannot at the same time expect to take part in constitutional advance.°

MR HAROLD WILSON (Labour)—°Our decision to desist from making instant comment or proposing amendments to particular paragraphs of the White Paper stems from the recognition that it must be the responsibility of the Government to put forward these proposals, and only the Government. We recognize that the White Paper is their conclusion of a balanced and fair package after great consideration and consultation. It must now be for the people of Northern Ireland to form their view without steering or guidance from us in this House. Our first preoccupation, and the preoccupation of everybody, must be the avoidance of violence and a settlement based on reconciliation and mutual tolerance.

From the Parliamentary Report on the discussion in the House of Commons about the Northern Ireland White Paper, "The Times", 1973

II The British People and their Institutions

The Chosen People

Lords and Commons of England, consider what Nation it is whereof ye are, and whereof ye are the governors: a Nation not slow and dull, but of a quick, ingenious and piercing spirit, acute to invent, subtle and sinewy to discourse, not beneath the reach of any point, the highest that human capacity can soar to.°

Yet that which is above all this, the favour and the love of Heaven, we have great argument to think in a peculiar manner propitious and propending towards us. Why else was this Nation chosen before any other, that out of her, as out of Sion, should be proclaimed and sounded forth the first tidings and trumpet of Reformation to all Europe? And had it not been the obstinate perverseness of our prelates against the divine and admirable spirit of Wickliff, to suppress him as a schismatic and innovator, perhaps neither the Bohemian Huss and Jerome, no nor the name of Luther or of Calvin, had been ever known: the glory of reforming all our neighbours had been completely ours. But now, as our obdurate clergy have with violence demeaned the matter, we are become hitherto the latest and backwardest scholars, of whom God offered to have made us the teachers. Now once again by all concurrence of signs, and by the general instinct of holy and devout men, as they daily and solemnly express their thoughts, God is decreeing to begin some new and great period in His Church, even to the reforming of Reformation itself: what does He then but reveal Himself to His servants, and as His manner is, first to His Englishmen? I say, as His manner is, first to us, though we mark not the method of His counsels, and are unworthy.

John Milton, "Areopagitica", 1644

Distrust of Logic and General Ideas

A nation which has been "in business" for centuries believes in a "deal," with concessions on both sides, as usually the best way of composing a quarrel; and we think we have observed that the only irreparable mistakes are those which are made by consistent intellectualists or strict logicians.°

This may serve as an answer to the charges of perfidy and hypocrisy. But the English distrust of logic is a deep-seated element of the national character, and a little more must be said about it. The Englishman is constitutionally averse to general ideas and abstract questions. Bishop Creighton was so much irritated by this state of mind that he said: "An Englishman not only has no ideas; he hates an idea when he meets one." This distrust of general ideas has been often shown in our history. Our countrymen were not really stirred by the Crusades; they watched the rhodomontades and vapourings, the heroics and the blood-lust of the French Revolution with mingled contempt and horror. Marxian socialism made few converts among us, and Bolshevism attracts only a few *detraqués* and moral maniacs. We once took up the theory of divine right, and summarily dropped it when it had served our turn. Our pulses do not beat quicker when we hear of Liberty, Equality, and Fraternity. Of the three, we care most about Liberty, but are ready to sacrifice that in an emergency. Our legal system is built up out of precedents, not on any general principles.

William R. Inge, "England", 1926

Cant

The English are a race apart. No Englishman is too low to have scruples: no Englishman is high enough to be free from their tyranny. But every Englishman is born with a certain miraculous power that makes him master of the world. When he wants a thing, he never tells himself that he wants it. He waits patiently until there comes into his mind, no one knows how, a burning conviction that it is his moral and religious duty to conquer those who possess the thing he wants. Then he becomes irresistible. Like the aristocrat, he does what pleases him and grabs what he covets: like the shopkeeper, he pursues his purpose with the industry and steadfastness that come from strong religious conviction and deep sense of moral responsibility. He is never at a loss for an effective moral attitude. As the great champion of freedom and national independence, he conquers and annexes half the world, and calls it Colonization. When he wants a new market for his adulterated Manchester goods, he sends a missionary to teach the natives the Gospel of Peace. The natives kill the missionary: he flies to arms in defence of Christianity; fights for it; conquers for it; and takes the market as a reward from heaven. In defence of his island shores, he puts a chaplain on board his ship; nails a flag with a cross on it to his top-gallant mast; and sails to the ends of the earth, sinking, burning, and destroying all who dispute the empire of the seas with him. He boasts that a slave is free the moment his foot touches British soil; and he sells the children of his poor at six years of age to work under the lash in his factories for sixteen hours a day. He makes two revolutions, and then declares war on our one in the name of law and order. There is nothing so bad or so good that you will not find Englishmen doing it; but you will never find an Englishman in the wrong. He does everything on principle. He fights you on patriotic principles; he robs you on business principles; he enslaves you on imperial principles; he bullies you on manly principles; he supports his king on loyal principles and cuts off his king's head on republican principles. His watchword is always Duty; and he never forgets that the nation which lets its duty get on the opposite side to its interest is lost.

George Bernard Shaw, "The Man of Destiny", 1896

A Gentleman Ideal

It is almost a definition of a gentleman to say he is one who never inflicts pain. This description is both refined and, as far as it goes, accurate. He is mainly occupied in merely removing the obstacles which hinder the free and unembarrassed action of those about him; and he concurs with their movements rather than takes the initiative himself. His benefits may be considered as parallel to what are called comforts or conveniences in arrangements of a personal nature: like an easy chair or a good fire, which do their part in dispelling cold and fatigue, though nature provides both means of rest and animal heat without them. The true gentleman in like manner carefully avoids whatever may cause a jar or a jolt in the minds of those with whom he is cast; — all clashing of opinion, or collision of feeling, all restraint, or suspicion, or gloom, or resentment; his great concern being to make every one at their ease and at home. He has his eyes on all his company; he is tender towards the bashful, gentle towards the distant, and merciful towards the absurd; he can recollect to whom he is speaking; he guards against unseasonable allusions, or topics which may irritate; he is seldom prominent in conversation, and never wearisome. He makes light of favours while he does them, and seems to be receiving when he is conferring. He never speaks of himself except when compelled, never defends himself by a mere retort, he has no ears for slander or gossip, is scrupulous in imputing motives to those who interfere with him, and interprets everything for the best. He is never mean or little in his disputes, never takes unfair advantage, never mistakes personalities or sharp sayings for arguments, or insinuates evil which he dare not say out. From a long-sighted prudence, he observes the maxim of the ancient sage, that we should ever conduct ourselves towards our enemy as if he were one day to be our friend. He has too much good sense to be affronted at insults, he is too well employed to remember injuries, and too indolent to bear malice. He is patient, forbearing, and resigned, on philosophical principles; he submits to pain, because it is inevitable, to bereavement, because it is irreparable, and to death, because it is his destiny. If he engages in controversy of any kind, his disciplined intellect preserves him from the blundering discourtesy of better, though less educated minds; who, like blunt weapons, tear and hack instead of cutting clean, who mistake the point in argument, waste their strength on trifles, misconceive their adversary, and leave the question more involved than they find it. He may be right or wrong in his opinion, but he is too clear-headed to be unjust; he is as simple as he is forcible, and as brief as he is decisive. Nowhere shall we find greater candour, consideration, indulgence: he throws himself into the minds of his opponents, he accounts for their mistakes. He knows the weakness of human reason as well as its strength, its province and its limits. If he be an unbeliever, he will be too profound and large-minded to ridicule religion or to act against it; he is too wise to be a dogmatist or fanatic in his infidelity. He respects piety and devotion; he even supports institutions as venerable, beautiful, or useful, to which he does not assent; he honours the ministers of religion, and he is contented to decline its mysteries without assailing or denouncing them. He is a friend of religious toleration, and that, not only because his philosophy has taught him to look on all forms of faith with an impartial eye, but also from the gentleness and effeminacy of feeling, which is the attendant on civilisation.

John H. Newman, "On the Scope and Nature of University Education", 1852

The English Pedigree

"Take care of yourselves, you hear? Watch out for Angles, Jutes, Saxons, Scots, Picts, Danes and Normans."

The first, most important thing to notice, and the one which gives the clue to all the rest, is that the English are mongrels; and that, alone of all nations upon earth, they pride themselves upon being mongrels. If ever you hear a man boast of his pure English blood, he may be a Bostonian, he may be a Jew; but whatever he is, he is not English.° 5

Ask a man of real English descent whether his people came over with William the Conqueror, and he will probably reply: "Good Heavens, no! We're Saxon; there were Budgeries in the Manor of Budge when Billy the Conk arrived. Of course," he will add, and all his subsequent qualifications will begin with "of course"—"of course, a good deal of Norman blood came into the family afterwards. We're a pretty mixed lot, really. 10
There's a legend that old Sir Gilbert brought back a Saracen bride after the third Crusade. And there was Captain John Budgery, the one that sailed with Hawkins—he married a Red Indian—sort of Pocahontas business, you know. And, of course, there's a lot of Scotch and Irish in me, though my mother's grandfather was pure Huguenot. And I've sometimes fancied there might be a dash of the tar-brush somewhere—there 15
was Robert Budgery who turned up as the missing heir from South America in the eighteenth century, nobody ever knew where his mother came from. The Cornish branch, of course, have a strong Spanish streak in them; the Armada, you know, and all that." So he rambles on, unrolling the history of England along with his family tree, and getting more and more mongrel, and more and more pleased with himself, at 20
every word.

We may disbelieve the legend about old Sir Gilbert and the Pocahontas romance; the important thing is that: that is what the Englishman likes to believe about himself. And one thing we must remember: that before the Conquest there was no such thing as an Englishman. There were Angles and Saxons, Danes, various kinds of British Celt, 25
and probably some people with traces of Roman descent, but the strange compound we call an Englishman had not yet appeared, any more than the English language. The basic Englishman is the compound of Anglo-Saxon and Norman-French; and though he contains elements from both those main sources, his characteristic Englishry is neither of them, but the blend of the two. 30

In this, he is exactly like his own English language. The Anglo-Saxon Chronicle is not written in English: it is written in Anglo-Saxon; the *Tristan* of Thomas is not written in English: it is written in Anglo-French. But the romances written in England in the twelfth and thirteenth centuries are written in what, though antiquated and difficult, is quite definitely and increasingly recognisable as the English speech of to-day; and 35
by the time we get to Chaucer, we are reading something that cannot possibly be called a variety of French or of Anglo-Saxon. It is English; a language in its own right, with its roots in two civilisations, and the most various, flexible, rich and expressive instrument of human speech since the days of Pericles.°

As the language, so the nation. The strength of the English, their adaptability, their 40
strange talent for improvisation, their disconcerting mixture of the practical and the visionary are the virtues of their mongrel breeding. It is not surprising that the English

are dubious about Nordic blood and racial purity. In small and peaceable peoples they consider claims to purity of blood to be harmless and pretty, but rather childish and absurd; in large and ferocious peoples they consider them to be ugly and dangerous, but none the less childish and absurd.

Dorothy L. Sayers, "The Mysterious English", 1940

5 **The Queen**

The Queen is the personification of the State. In law, she is the head of the executive, an integral part of the legislature, the head of the judiciary in England and Wales, Northern Ireland, and Scotland, the commander-in-chief of all the armed forces of the Crown and the temporal head of the established Church of England. In practice,
10 as a result of a long evolutionary process during which the absolute power of the monarchy has been progressively reduced, the Queen acts only on the advice of her ministers which she cannot constitutionally ignore. She reigns, but she does not rule. The United Kingdom is governed by Her Majesty's Government in the name of the Queen.
15 Within this framework, and in spite of the fact that the trend of legislation during the past hundred years has been to assign powers directly to ministers without any necessity for royal intervention, there are still important acts of government which require the participation of the Queen.

The Queen summons, prorogues and dissolves Parliament; as a general rule she
20 opens the new session with a speech from the throne (although this may be read by the Lord Chancellor if the Queen is unable to be present); and she must give Royal Assent before a Bill which has passed all its stages in both Houses of Parliament becomes a legal enactment. The Queen is "the fountain of justice", and as such, can remit all or part of the penalties imposed on people convicted of crime. As "the fountain of honour",
25 the Queen confers peerages, baronetcies, knighthoods and other honours, and makes appointment to all important State offices, including those of judges, officers in the armed forces, governors, and diplomats, and to all leading positions in the established Church of England. The Queen's consent and approval are required before a minister can take up office or a Cabinet be formed. In the realm of international affairs, by
30 virtue of her pre-eminence as head of the State, the Queen has the power to conclude treaties, to cede or accept territory, to declare war and to make peace.

These and similar acts of government involve the use of the royal prerogative which has been defined as "the residue of discretionary authority legally left in the hands of the Crown".°
35 Ministerial responsibility for the exercise of powers by the Crown does not detract from the importance of the participation of the Sovereign in the smooth working of government; for although the Queen has no personal authority and must show complete impartiality in every field, she must be informed and consulted on every aspect of the national life. The Queen holds meetings of the Privy Council, gives audiences
40 to her ministers and other holders of office at home and overseas, receives accounts of Cabinet decisions, reads dispatches and signs innumerable State papers.

Such is the significance attached to these royal functions that provision has been made by Acts of Parliament for a Regent to be appointed to fulfil them if the Sovereign is totally incapacitated, or is under the age of eighteen on accession to the throne. The latest of these Acts—the Regency Act 1953—laid down that the first potential Regent should be The Prince Philip, Duke of Edinburgh, and thereafter those in succession to the throne who are of age.

"Britain, An Official Handbook", 1968

The House of Lords

The House of Lords consists of some nine hundred Lords, Spiritual and Temporal, the majority being there because of the hereditary principle. However, since 1958, when the Life Peerages Act was passed, it became possible for the Queen to confer a peerage—membership of one of the degrees of nobility—upon a man or woman. From 1958 to the beginning of June 1965 ninety-nine life peerages were conferred, some for political reasons and the rest in order to be able to use the valuable experience of distinguished men and women from all walks of life. Thus in the Lords one finds former heads of the Armed Services, leading industrialists, ex-Governors of the Colonies, former diplomats, and scholars, etc. The proportion of those holding hereditary titles who take an active part in the affairs of the House of Lords is comparatively small, and it is noticeable that those holding life peerages are particularly active.

Members of the House of Lords are unpaid. However, they are entitled to reimbursement of travelling expenses from their homes to the House and also expenses for each day of attendance in the House, the maximum for the latter being small. It should not be thought that all this implies that the House of Lords is unimportant. In fact it performs the following functions:
1. It debates and revises Bills brought up from the Commons.
2. It debates general policy usually at a high level on account of the wisdom of the active hereditary peers and the valuable knowledge and experience of life peers.
3. It acts as a legislative chamber. It is possible to introduce Bills in the Lords, though usually they are not controversial ones. Such Bills cannot be about finance or representation.

14 The House of Lords

The Lord Chancellor of England presides over the debates from his position on the Woolsack—a red cloth couch stuffed with wool. He may do something which the man who presides over the Commons, the Speaker, cannot do—leave his official seat and as a peer join in the debate. What is more, he also has a vote. The debates in the Lords are less formal than those in the Commons. °The House of Lords has an additional function as the ultimate Court of Appeal for all Courts in Great Britain and Northern Ireland except for criminal cases in Scotland.

H. W. Howes, "Presenting Modern Britain", 1966

The Working of the House of Commons

Government in Britain is called "parliamentary government" but that expression no longer means the same thing as it did a hundred years ago. Then, it was true to say that the ministers held office only for so long as they continued to be supported by a majority in the House of Commons; now, the possibility that they should be defeated in the House of Commons is so small that we really ought to describe the relationship a little differently. Nevertheless, the whole system still has its centre in Parliament, and can only be described through its working in Parliament.

The two Houses of Parliament, the Lords and the Commons, share the same building, the Palace of Westminster. The present buildings of the Palace were erected between 1840 and 1852, to replace older buildings which had been destroyed by fire in 1834. Parts of the Palace, including the Commons Chamber itself, were badly damaged in an air-raid in 1941, and have been rebuilt since 1945.°

The Commons occupy the north part of the Palace, the Lords the south end.°

15 The House of Commons, State Opening

The Commons debating chamber is only one of the many rooms of the Palace, but is usually called "the House". It has seats for only about 370 of its total membership of 630. The rebuilt chamber is the same size and shape as the old one was, though it has modern air-conditioning, lighting and microphones.

Members do not have special seats. On big occasions the chamber is overcrowded, but most of the time the benches provide more than enough room for all the members who are present. The shape and arrangement of the House are of great political significance. It is rectangular, with the Speaker's chair at one end, and with five straight rows of benches running down one side along its whole length, and five rows on the other side, so that the rows of benches face each other across the floor. This arrangement expresses a fact which is fundamental to the British parliamentary system. One side of the House is occupied by the Government and the members who support it, the other, facing them, by Her Majesty's Opposition—all the Members who are opposed to the Government of the day, and who hope that at the next general election their party will be in a majority so that they can form the Government. The arrangement of the benches in the House of Commons suggests a two-party system, and the Leader of the Opposition receives a salary from state funds.°

The choice of a new Speaker is made by a vote of the House, but normally only after the party leaders have privately agreed beforehand on a particular person. Once a man has been made Speaker he is customarily reappointed to his office in each new Parliament, even if the majority in the House has changed, until he wishes to retire. When he accepts office as Speaker he is expected to renounce all party politics for the rest of his life; this means that the people of his constituency have no normal partisan representative in Parliament. When he retires he is at once made a peer, and goes to the House of Lords.°

The central rule of procedure is that every debate must relate to a specific proposal, or "motion". Some Member moves (proposes) a motion; the House debates it and finally decides whether to agree or to disagree with it. A motion may propose that the House should take some action (for example, give a "second reading" to a bill), or that it should express some opinion. When a motion has been moved, another member may propose to "amend" it, and in that case his proposal is debated. When the House has decided on the amendment it goes back to the original motion, which is now in a new form if an amendment to it has been accepted. A debate ends either (1) when every member who wants to speak has done so, or (2) at a time fixed in advance either by informal agreement between the parties or by a vote of the House (that is, by the Government without the agreement of the Opposition), or (3) when the House, with the Speaker's consent, votes that it shall end. At the end of every debate the Speaker puts the question whether or not to accept the motion that has been debated. If there is disagreement, there is a "division" and Members vote by walking through corridors called "lobbies", being counted as they do so. The names of Members voting are recorded and published. The "Aye" (yes) lobby runs down one side of the outside wall of the chamber, the "No" lobby down the other side. Six minutes after the beginning of the division the doors leading into the lobbies are locked. The practice of allowing six minutes before Members must enter their lobbies gives enough time for them to come from any part of the Palace of Westminster. Bells ring all over the building to summon Members to the chamber to vote. Members often vote without having heard a debate, and perhaps without knowing exactly what is the question; they know which way to vote because Whips (or party managers) of the parties stand outside the doors, and Members vote almost automatically with their parties.°

The life of Parliament is divided into periods called "sessions". At the end of every
5 session Parliament is "prorogued"; this means that all business which has not been completed is abandoned, and Parliament cannot meet again until it is formally summoned by the Queen. Every new session begins with a clean slate.

A session normally lasts for about a year, from late October of one year to about the same date of the next year, though if a general election is held in the spring or summer
10 the normal rhythm of the sessions is interrupted.°

The beginning of a new session, called "the State Opening of Parliament", is a fine ceremonial occasion, though many people who do not understand the rhythm of the sessions cannot understand why Parliament is opened when it was already sitting a few days before. The ceremony takes place in the House of Lords, with a few leading
15 members of the House of Commons standing crowded together at the end of the chamber opposite to the Throne, within the four walls of the room, but technically outside the "House of Lords" itself. The Queen takes her place on the throne and reads out the "Queen's Speech", which is a document, about a thousand words in length, prepared by the Government, in which the Government gives a summary of the things
20 which it intends to do during the Session which is about to begin.

Peter Bromhead, "Life in Modern Britain", °1968

The Citizen and Law and Order

Generally, the British people readily accept the fact that obeying the law is necessary for the smooth running of national and neighbourhood affairs. There is a healthy respect for the officers of the law, and it is realized that the police and the citizen are
25 in partnership to maintain the liberty of the individual. It is probably true to add that this is one of the advantages of having an unarmed police force—a reminder that the policeman is but a civilian dressed in a blue uniform.°

The observance of the law between citizen and citizen is usually accepted, probably without giving the matter serious thought; the right thing should be done and is
30 done. One simple example may be seen daily in any busy London Street. On top of a large box is a pile of newspapers for sale, together with a small box for the money. The newspaper-seller has gone away for a meal. A passer-by picks up a newspaper and puts his money in the small box. When the seller returns he is sure to find that the right money for papers taken during his absence will be ready for him to place
35 in his pocket.

One aspect of the relationship between masses of people and the representatives of law and order can be seen when the police have to keep routes clear for a procession. If the crowd pushes forward the police ask the people to move farther back. Instead of objecting it is not uncommon for the people nearest to the police to lean back in
40 order to help the police. The process will be accompanied by plenty of advice to the police and a suggestion that it was a pity that they had not made up their minds earlier

about exactly what they wanted. Usually, the British crowd is good-humoured, and it is only when a policeman treats a crowd with lack of tact that trouble occurs.°
One of the tests of attitudes towards law and order is the behaviour of people at public meetings. It is extremely rare, even during General Elections, for the police to have to take action against those attending public meetings, although there will always be the odd occasion when a small group tries to break up a meeting violently. One of the characteristics of the British is tolerance, which the majority believe is the secret of happy relationships, neighbourhood, national, and international. Therefore it is common at a public meeting which has become a bit noisy for the chairman to appeal for order, and the appeal is most likely to be effective if he points out that although a number of those present may disagree with what the speaker stands for, he has a right to express his views. There will be an opportunity for questions, and those who have been interrupting the proceedings are assured that they will be able to put questions to the speaker at the end of his speech. In such circumstances even those who do not agree with the politics of the speaker will support the chairman. After all, it shows respect for public order when men can disagree without being disagreeable.

H. W. Howes, "Presenting Modern Britain", 1966

Law in England

In every civilized state the life of the community must be to some degree controlled by rules or customs which in the aggregate are known as the law. In England this was originally unwritten law—a body of custom which was nevertheless well recognized—though occasionally a King, e.g. Alfred, had the most important laws set out in writing, which undoubtedly helped to fix them; but there is no evidence that any code pretending to completeness was ever prepared, or that until the twelfth century or even later there was a single system of law (Common Law) common to the whole country.

When records of proceedings in the King's courts began to be kept (1307 onwards) we find judges declaring what they understood the customary law to be as it was relevant to the cases before them, so that their successors had the advantage of a careful statement of laws which had not previously been preserved in writing. All this is what has sometimes been called *Common Law* as distinct from statute law, i.e. formal laws enacted by the authority of Parliament from 1265 onwards. The term Common Law is, however, also used to include both statute law and the traditional law (originally unwritten), i.e. the whole body of general law applicable to everyone in the realm, as distinct from separate systems of law applicable only to a particular section of the people, e.g. ecclesiastical law, military law, maritime law, etc., or to the system of rules (administered in the Court of Chancery) which grew up under the name of *Equity*.°

Common Law also includes a good deal of what has been called "case law". The language of a statute may unintentionally be ambiguous, and in trying a case a High Court judge declares what appears to be the intention of Parliament. Unless it is reversed on appeal this declaration is afterwards accepted as a statement of the law by judges trying similar cases.

One of the notable characteristics of English law is that it was based on particular rules laying down what was to happen in certain particular circumstances. For example, one of the ordinances which King Alfred caused to be collected and written down was that if anyone plotted against the King's life he should forfeit his life and property; and there were penalties for other misdeeds. There is no original document formulating the various rights of the individual, i.e. nothing like the 1789 declaration of the French National Assembly that men have equal rights of "liberty, property, security, and resistance to oppression". When someone is wronged in a certain way, the wrongdoer must give certain compensation. The law provides remedies for wrongs done; a certain crime shall be punished in a certain way. Our ancestors did not trouble much about stating theories; but if anything was wrong they wanted a practical remedy for it.°

Within the range of the Common Law a fundamental division exists between criminal and civil processes. These are tried in separate courts. Criminal courts deal with crimes, which, though individuals may be the victims, are regarded as offences against the community—murder, burglary, forgery, etc. The state must protect the community. The police therefore arrest criminals, and on behalf of "the Crown" initiate legal action against them, with or without the help of the Director of Public Prosecutions, which commonly results in their punishment if they are found guilty. In theory the action is set in motion by the Crown, and the court was commonly, and is still frequently, called "the Crown Court".

Civil courts deal with offences against individuals—libels, breaches of contract, etc.—and a wrongdoer is usually made to compensate the sufferer by a payment to cover the "damages". Action is taken, not by the Crown, but by one person (or company) against another.

Criminal Trials

British justice has become famous throughout the world; and it is well known that an alleged criminal gets a fair trial and that in particular he is presumed to be innocent until he is proved to be guilty to the satisfaction, not merely of the judge, but of a jury composed of his fellow citizens.

The general conduct of a trial by jury in the Crown Court (i.e. the court for trying criminal charges) at Assizes or at the Central Criminal Court is roughly as follows.

There are certain enclosures in the court room. One small one is "the dock" into which the prisoner is led by warders by a separate entrance from the temporary cells beneath. Another has benches for the jury. Another ("the witness box") is where each witness stands while giving his evidence. Barristers and solicitors are accommodated with seats in the body of the court.

There are seats for a number of spectators; for all criminal trials are to be held in public in order that it shall be seen that justice is being done; but of course space is limited, and many of the public fail to gain admission to a trial which has excited widespread interest.

When the judge in wig and robes has taken his seat on "the bench" (which is in reality a well-padded chair) the prisoner is brought in and the Clerk of Assize reads the indictment (i.e. the charge) and asks him whether he is guilty or not guilty. If he pleads not guilty the clerk reads out the names of twelve jurors (drawn from the list

① The Dock
② Counsel
③ Judge's door
④ Solicitors and Police
⑤ Clerk of Arraigns
⑥ Lord Mayor's chair
⑦ Judge's chair
⑧ Bench
⑨ Shorthand-writer
⑩ Jury box
⑪ Witness box

16 Court Room No.2 at the Old Bailey

of those summoned), who swear to give a true verdict. The leading counsel for the Crown then explains to the jury the case for the prosecution and calls his witnesses one by one to give evidence. Up to this point witnesses are not allowed to be in court. Each witness goes into "the box" and swears or affirms that he will speak the truth, the whole truth, and nothing but the truth. He is then subjected to the "examination-in-chief" by counsel for the prosecution, who gets the required information by asking appropriate questions.

Witnesses do not simply tell their own story of what happened, or they might waste the time of the court and confuse the jury by giving irrelevant facts, or opinions, or evidence, such as "hearsay", which is not allowed. So they have to be led through their evidence by experienced barristers.

Counsel, however, must not put "leading questions", i.e. questions which suggest the answers wanted. For example he must not say "Did you not see the prisoner at eight o'clock on Monday night in Bell Lane with a knife in his hand?" but rather "Did you see the prisoner on Monday, May 10th?" (Answer, "Yes.") "Where?" (A. "In Bell Lane.") "At what time?" (A. "About 8 o'clock at night.") "Was he carrying anything?"

After the examination-in-chief of each witness counsel for the defence may cross-examine him (or her) to show perhaps that he could not be at all certain about what he had seen, or to lead him to contradict his previous evidence. Leading questions are allowed in cross-examination. Q. "Wasn't it very dark at 8 o'clock?" A. "Yes." Q. "Then how can you be sure that it was the prisoner that you saw?"

The prosecuting counsel may "re-examine" the witness if any point was raised in cross-examination which was not dealt with in the examination-in-chief.

When all witnesses for the prosecution have been examined the counsel for the defence explains his case to the jury and calls his witnesses, who are examined, cross-examined, and perhaps re-examined. He then addresses the jury again in order to sum up the defence and emphasize the significance of the evidence given by his witnesses. Counsel for the prosecution makes the last speech, indicating how in his opinion the defence has failed to meet the charges made.

The judge then sums up. He explains to the jury the essential nature of the crime of which the prisoner is accused, e.g. how manslaughter differs from murder, for they must be sure of this before they can properly give their verdict. He gives a critical, but fair, review of the evidence, warning them that this statement is important, that one not so important, or perhaps not quite relevant, or that A. B.'s evidence was not very reliable, and so on. He explains to them that if they are not convinced that the

Crown has made out a clear case against the prisoner he must be given the benefit of any reasonable doubt that remains in their minds.

The jury retire to a separate room to consider their verdict, which must be unanimous. On their return into court their foreman delivers the verdict. If it is "not guilty" the judge acquits the prisoner, and he cannot be tried again for the same crime. If it is "guilty" the judge considers and delivers his sentence.°

In assessing his sentence the judge may consider any previous convictions of the prisoner on criminal charges; but these are not revealed to the jury before their verdict is given, so that their decision between the prisoner's guilt or innocence of this particular crime may not be affected.

The judge is expected to preside impartially, suppressing "hearsay" and other inadmissible evidence, "leading questions" (in the examination-in-chief), or intimidation of witnesses. By judicial impartiality we mean that he will be fair to both sides, approaching the case with an open mind, and not starting with prepossessions in favour of one side or the other; for when the evidence has been unfolded he can hardly be impartial in another sense. He may put questions to witnesses, not however as an advocate, but to make sure that the jury understands the implications of the evidence, and is not puzzled by any ambiguities.

Since 1898 the prisoner has had the option (on his counsel's advice) of going into the witness box to give evidence on his own behalf; but if he does so he may be cross-questioned by prosecuting counsel and led into making some damaging statement. Defence counsel, therefore, are often reluctant to take this risk.

To help in ensuring scrupulous fairness in the treatment of suspected felons by the police, certain "Judges' Rules" were in 1912 drawn up at the request of the Home Secretary. One of the most important was that before any statement was taken from a suspected person he should be cautioned that it might be used in evidence in judicial proceedings; and a judge might reject any evidence unfairly obtained. No "third degree" methods are used and no one may be terrified or tricked into incriminating himself.

Egerton Smith, "A Guide to English Traditions and Public Life", [2]*1955*

The Education System in England and Wales

Children in England begin school at the age of 5 and must stay at school until they are 15. There are two systems of education existing side by side and coming into contact at certain points; State education, to which all children are entitled, free of charge, and education at Independent or Private Schools, where pupils pay fees.

State education is financed and organised partly by the Department of Education and Science, and partly by local authorities. Between the ages of 5 and 11 children attend State Primary Schools, and all children leave Primary School at the age of 11. In many areas there is at this stage a selection process (the 11-plus), which consists of written tests or interviews, or teachers' recommendations, or a combination of these. On the strength of the results each child is sent to one of three kinds of Secondary School; Grammar School, Secondary Modern School (created in 1944 in place of the old Senior Elementary School) or Secondary Technical School.

The Grammar Schools give a formal education to more academically-minded and intelligent children. They receive a very general education for about three years, then the number of subjects is reduced, usually in favour of either the arts or the sciences. At 16 pupils take the General Certificate of Education, Ordinary Level (G.C.E. O-level)—an examination conducted by various university boards—in up to about nine subjects. Depending on the results, pupils may go on into the 6th Form. Here they specialize further in about three main subjects, combined with more or less of a general education, for two years, at the end of which they take the G.C.E. Advanced Level (A-level). Admission to universities and colleges is based on the results of this examination.

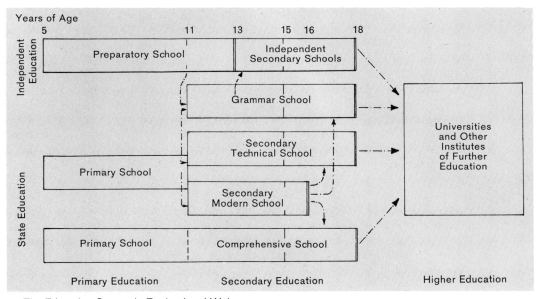

17 The Education System in England and Wales

Most English children over the age of 11 attend Secondary Modern School. They may leave school at 15 or stay on until 16. Some follow a quasi-Grammar School course leading to the G.C.E. O-level. The others receive a less academic education with a greater emphasis on more practical subjects, e.g. Domestic Science, Woodwork, Typing, and on Music and Art. The Secondary Modern Schools now have their own school-leaving certificate, but they are still much less syllabus-bound than the Grammar Schools.

The Secondary Technical Schools are very few in number. At these schools there is a strong emphasis on practical scientific subjects such as Chemistry, Metalwork, Autoengineering, etc., and on vocational training, e.g. Agriculture, Pharmacy, etc. Many pupils stay at these schools until they are 18 and take the G.C.E. at both levels.

An important post-war development in State education is the Comprehensive School System, now firmly established in many areas. At the age of 11 all Primary School pupils, instead of being graded, are sent to the same Comprehensive School. Within this large school there is intricate "streaming" according to pupils' ability and choice of subjects. Some of the courses offered are similar to those at the separate Secondary Schools already described. But more combinations of subjects are possible, and it is easier for a pupil to be transferred to another stream. Further advantages claimed for Comprehensive Schools are largely of a psychological and sociological nature.

The alternative to State education is education at Independent or Private Schools. (In order to avoid a common misconception it must be remembered that all Public Schools are, in spite of their name, Private or Independent Schools, but not all Independent Schools can be described as Public Schools.) Some of these schools are acknowledged by the Department of Education as conforming to its standards, but not all. Like the State system, the Independent Schools provide education for children between the ages of 5 and 18 and enter pupils for the G.C.E.

To come now to the different kinds of Independent Schools; Preparatory Schools educate children between 5 and 13. Thanks to their independent financial support (from fees and endowments) these schools can offer smaller classes and more individual tuition, and the education they provide is often geared to entrance to Public Schools, since the latter require prospective pupils to pass their entrance examination.

The Public Schools are a particularly distinguished and often very old group of Independent Schools which provide education for selected pupils aged 13 to 18. Like most other Independent Schools they too offer small classes and individual attention, and the characteristic way of life so often extolled or condemned. The Public Schools used to supply the majority of Oxbridge students and "senior" civil servants, but their traditional monopoly in these fields is dwindling.

For pupils over the age of 13 who do not succeed in obtaining a place at a Public School (or who do not wish to do so) but nevertheless do not want to go to a State Secondary School, there are numerous Independent Secondary Schools, most of which do not set an entrance examination. Many of these Independent Schools specialize in particular (often non-academic) spheres such as Sport, Domestic Science, Music, etc.

Thus these two systems of education, State Schools and Independent Schools, exist quite separately, but there are two opportunities for transition; Preparatory School pupils often enter State Secondary Schools at the age of 11, after taking the 11-plus, and children at State Secondary Schools can take the Public Schools' entrance examination at the age of 13.

Elizabeth Daymond, Special Contribution for "Britain and America"

Secondary Education

The education of three-quarters of British children, as every parent knows, begins with one decisive selection at the age of eleven—the sorting machine of Britain's élite. Until recently, this was the standard European pattern: after eleven, the clever boys went off to grammar schools in Britain, to *lycées* in France and Italy, to *gymnasien* in Germany and Sweden. Only America could afford to avoid this segregation, and to keep all their children together, without a special élite, until sixteen or eighteen.°

The present educational structure in Britain was the result° of a "curious amalgam of educational aspiration, administrative expedients and end-products of extraneous pressures". It began in 1944, when the great Education Act which provided secondary education for all children to the age of fourteen (with specific provision that it should be raised to fifteen, then sixteen, when possible) transformed 3,000 senior elementary schools into secondary schools at the stroke of a pen. These, renamed Secondary Moderns, were to educate the great bulk of English children (the word "modern", both here and in the French colleges "modernes", was a curious euphemism for "less clever"). They were to provide a "good all-round secondary education, not focused primarily on the traditional subjects of the school curriculum, but arising out of the interests of the children". °Clever children, as before, would go to the grammar schools, and children "good with their hands" should go to technical schools. This was the tripartite system: three kinds of schools for three kinds of children. In most areas it was bipartite: the proportion of technical schools remained tiny.°

The Comprehensives

The ruthless division of all but a privileged stream of rich children into two castes at the age of eleven has come under heavy attack. The eleven-plus was inefficient.° People began to realise, that segregation of "eggheads and serfs" was also dangerous on social and economic grounds.

Abandoning the eleven-plus requires an entirely new kind of school organisation. "Once it is agreed," wrote Crowther in his report, "as more and more people are coming to believe, that it is wrong to label children for all time at eleven, the attempt to give mutually exclusive labels to the schools to which they go at their age will have to be abandoned." It was to avoid these labels, and to mix the streams, that the most spectacular of the post-war experiments were invented—the comprehensive schools. The comprehensives were designed after the war to contain all kinds of children under one roof. But they were *not*, as in America, to be all in one stream: the comprehensives have their own "grammar school" classes, leading on to university, and their own technical and modern classes. The importance of comprehensives is that they allow all children to change streams after eleven, and also to mix out of class with other children cleverer or stupider than themselves.

The comprehensive schools, together with other variations, are growing rapidly. In 1963/64 seven per cent of children were at some kind of comprehensive school, as opposed to only two per cent in 1956. Two thirds of the local authorities were investigating ways of avoiding the eleven-plus in 1964: some had already abandoned it. But there was strong opposition from the middle classes and the grammar schools: comprehensives run against the whole Jamesian grammar school idea of segregating an élite.

The first and one of the most famous of comprehensive schools, founded in 1954, is Kidbrooke, a school for 2,200 girls at Blackheath. °The school timetable, showing the criss-crossing of fifty different classes, looks like a Continental railway timetable. But it shows the freedom, as well as the intimidation, of bigness: it is clear at Kidbrooke, as is far from clear at most British schools, that you can do almost anything, and find any kind of girl. And the school is split up into smaller units: there are eight houses°, which cut across classes and ages, and a huge range of unacademic activities, like an orchestra, an Old Vic Club, rounders or fashion shows.

But while the comprehensives are at odds with the grammar schools, they have much more friendly relations with the public schools—partly because they are not
5 in serious competition; and partly because the public schools are themselves a bit like comprehensives, with stupid and clever boys.

The comprehensives seem to be achieving their object, although it is still too early to judge their final effects. °The comprehensives got 14 per cent "good" O-level results, compared with the average of 10 per cent. And it is clear, that in their main
10 purpose—allowing children to switch streams after eleven—the schools are succeeding.

Anthony Sampson, "Anatomy of Britain today", 1965

What's new in British Universities?

The new University of Stirling will take its first students this October. It is the first new university to be built in Scotland for nearly four hundred years, and is the ninth
15 to be built in Britain since the war. Eight of the new universities have been built in the sixties.

By their tenth year, most of them will have 3,000 students, and they have already established very varied characters. The University of Sussex, at Brighton, is probably the best known. It is the strident, brash, "Mod" university, housed in striking pink
20 brick buildings designed by Sir Basil Spence. The University of York, in contrast, is conservative and has adopted many of the traditions of older universities.

The new universities have given education in this country a great boost. They have publicised the advantages of university education and stimulated demand for it. Among professional educationists, they have provided an opportunity for wide ex-

18 Sussex University, University Campus

periment in teaching methods, and an outlet for the energies and enthusiasms of young and revolutionary teachers. Sussex, East Anglia, and Essex have all experimented with multi-subject "schools of studies" instead of the traditional single-subject departments. At Sussex, for example, all arts students take a preliminary course in philosophy and history as well as their major subject. York, on the other hand, believes that most students will still want single-subject courses, but it has introduced a completely new way of studying music at university. They have also experimented with the social side of university life. At Sussex for instance, dons queue for meals and share a common-room with the students. At most of the new universities, the students are themselves largely responsible for discipline. Altogether, there is a sense of adventure and pioneering which makes them very exciting places.

No more new universities are to be built in Britain for ten years at least. In future, more places will be provided by expanding the older universities and making colleges of technology into universities. An old university can take 3,000 more students by adding staff and laboratories, whereas a completely new university for 3,000 costs up to £ 15 million. Even at Stirling where the Government already owns the site, the buildings alone will cost about £ 8 million, not including halls of residence which are not covered by the Government grant. Even in the first year, when there will be only 150 students, there will be thirteen subject departments to be staffed, not to mention the cost of building up libraries and buying other equipment.

However, some educationists see the halt in building new universities as a good thing. They argue that it is wasteful to duplicate teaching departments covered by other universities and that resources are better spent on enlarging the older civic universities.

Inevitably, the new universities have their difficulties, but whether more are built in the future or not, each is evolving its own traditions, experimenting with a new way of university life which does not exist anywhere else. It is too soon to compare their results, but all of them are exciting.

Margaret Likierman in "London Calling, European Ed.", 1967

The English Press

Any consideration of British journalism must begin with a fundamental statistic—no country buys as many papers per capita as Britain. A UNESCO survey published in 1964 found that an average of 50.6 copies of daily newspapers were sold for every hundred persons in Britain. Sweden followed with 46.2, then came Luxembourg. America, with all its college graduates, buys only about half as many dailies per person as the United Kingdom.

The usual explanation offered for the vast circulation of the London papers is that the British Isles are so compact a morning daily can easily circulate from Land's End to John O'Groat's, giving the capital press access to an audience of 54,000,000. True enough. But nearly as many people live in the Northeast quadrant of the United States, and no New York paper remotely approaches the 5,000,000 sales of the London *Daily Mirror*.°

19 The British Love of Writing Letters to the Editor

The influence and quality of British journalism is an old story, variously attested to by the eminent from Milton and Macaulay (who named it the Fourth Estate), from Oscar Wilde to the Royal Commission on the Press in 1949. ("Newspapers have degenerated", was Wilde's contribution in 1889. "They may now be absolutely relied
5 upon.") What is insufficiently remarked is the extent to which the British press has resisted the homogenizing formulas of mass culture. Diversity is its most conspicuous trait. Fleet street emits, day in and day out, a beguiling dissonance—the sounding brass of the tabloids, the chamber music of *The Times* and *The Guardian*, the bossa nova of the color supplements, the smooth woodwind of the principal weeklies, and
10 even the impudent piccolo of *Private Eye*.

In America, precisely because the press is consolidated into semi-monopolies, editors feel they cater simultaneously to all tastes. The result, too often, is journalism with the texture of processed cheese and about as distinctive a flavor. Significantly, there is no true British counterpart to *The New York Times Sunday Magazine*, the *Saturday*
15 *Review, Time, Look, The Reporter* and *Reader's Digest*. Even *Playboy* is only feebly imitated. Nevertheless, when journalists gather at El Vino's on Fleet Street, the fashionable lament is that the great days have gone and that the giants have perished. I'm not so sure. On the contrary, it can be sensibly argued that the London press today is as robust and readable as at any time in the past. Possibly even more so.
20 The Sixties brought fruitful changes. The *Manchester Guardian* bobtailed its name and became a national daily with a London edition and identity. The *Sunday Telegraph* was also launched. The result has been to give London four quality dailies and three excellent Sunday papers. °In sum, the British have produced unexpected evidence that literacy pays. Why and how?
25 I would venture seven reasons—not exhaustive, mind you, but as a suggestive and provisional prolegomenon. The London press excels because 1) precocity is welcome; 2) nonconformity is indulged; 3) the editor is sovereign; 4) the reader is exploited; 5) trivia is cherished; 6) the critical scalpel is lethally sharp; and 7) the Sabbath is observed.

30 Let us begin again with:

1) *Precocity is welcome*. There is surely no other Western capital in which the brash and young can rise so fast in journalism. It is by now almost a settled pattern. They come down from Oxford or Cambridge, make their reputation as writers in their twenties, and in their thirties become editors and elder statesmen.°

2) *Nonconformity is indulged.* The case of Richard Gott makes the point. Gott is twenty-seven and emerged from Oxford possessed of a mangy red beard and a desire to become a journalist. He got a job writing editorials for *The Guardian* but last January took a leave of absence to embark on a splendidly quixotic campaign that had an outside chance of bringing down a British government. The occasion was a critical by-election in the seaport town of Hull, where the Labour government needed a victory to maintain a precarious three-seat majority in Parliament. To the immense annoyance of the Labour Party, Gott entered the campaign as a candidate of the very left-wing Radical Alliance. For three weeks, he trudged the streets of Hull, speaking earnestly about the misdeeds of America in Vietnam. There was a chill of apprehension among Labour supporters that he might draw off just enough leftist votes to defeat the government candidate in a marginal constituency.

In the event, Labour won decisively and Gott received a mere 253 votes. The dejected Gott suffered no martyrdom; he rejoined *The Guardian*, contributing a dolorous initial article about his experience.°

3) *The editor is sovereign.* The papers on Fleet Street resemble jealous, independent duchies. The throne of power is usually the editor's chair. The business office sticks to business. Far more than in New York, the papers are identified with the personality of an editor. (Who, offhand, can name the editor of even *The New York Times*?)°

4) *The reader is exploited.* Even classified advertisements have a certain flair. *The Times* each Christmas publishes scores of ads, announcing that so-and-so is not sending cards this year. Every now and then one finds a plum in the cake, like: "Mr. Pitt Roche of 21 Devonshire Place, W.C. 1, wishes both his friends a happy Christmas."°

Letters-to-the-editor are as finely turned as antique silver, notably in *The Times*. The favored tone is punctilious; the style elaborate understatement. The more obscure the issue, the more cultivated the sarcasm—as, for example, a recent exchange stretching over weeks in *The Times* concerning the merits of Beowulf and Old English as a compulsory subject in the English curriculum at Oxford.°

As good as the letters are the weekly competitions, the best of which are in the *New Statesman*. On one famous occasion, readers were asked to compose a passage from the biography of Sir Hugh Greene as written by Graham Greene. The competition was won by the brother of the novelist, Sir Hugh, who is the director general of the B.B.C., using a pseudonym. The second prize was won, of course, by Graham Greene himself, using another pen name.

5) *Trivia is cherished.* The traditional roots of the gossip columns and diaries that abound are clearly suggested by the pen names under which some are written: William Hickey (*Daily Express*), Albany (*Sunday Telegraph*), Charles Greville (*Daily Mail*)—all names suggestive of the eighteenth century and Regency England. A primary function is not unlike the old coffeehouse newsletter: to carry gossip of the capital to the provinces.°

The love of trivia is also evidenced in the crossword puzzles, which are the best and most exasperating in the English-speaking world. The most exacting appears in *The Times* and is simply known as "the crossword". Since 1930, readers have been tortured by such audacious definitions as "How to make jaunty (8 letters)" or "He makes children's cakes (7,7)". (The answers: "popinjay" and "Charles Dickens.")°

6) *The critical scalpel is sharp.* In no other city surely is there an equal to *The Times Literary Supplement* in terms of breadth and depth of criticism. Current books in Russian, French, Italian and German are reviewed as if they had been published locally, and the caliber of the unsigned reviews is the more remarkable when one learns that a front-page article, running perhaps to three thousand words, will net the author a fee of as little as twenty-five guineas (which is less than $75).°

7) *The Sabbath is observed.* The great Czech writer, Karel Capek, once marveled: "I do not know for what unspeakable sin the Lord has sentenced the English to the weekly punishment of their Sunday." Perennial efforts are made to relax the blue laws that make the Sabbath synonymous with bleak and desperate restlessness. But the efforts fail, in good part because of the lobbying ability of the Lord's Day Observance Society.°

Still, the desolate Sunday has been a palpable blessing to journalism. Britain is a country where custom enforces ample time for reading newspapers—and it takes pretty nearly a full day to read through the better Sunday papers.°

It happens to be Sunday as I am writing this. The papers are piled high on the breakfast table, and I found myself musing about the apt word to describe the essential quality of the admirable London press. The word, most surely, is "conversational". The best papers rarely screech, grimace, grunt—and never on Sunday. A certain restraint is the beginning of press civility. Only in London could a paper (inescapably *The Times*) have a contest among copy editors to see who could write the *dullest* headline. The winner was: "Small Earthquake in Chile. Not many hurt." In the same salutary spirit of antihyperbole, one could say of newspapers in London, "Quite decadent, really. But they can be read."

Karl E. Meyer in "Esquire", 1966

The National Health Service

The National Health Service provides medical treatment both in hospital and outside. It covers sickness of mind as well as ordinary sickness, and it includes the treatment of teeth and the provision of aids to sight and hearing, as well as wheelchairs, artificial limbs and some other expensive items. It was based at first on Acts of Parliament, one for England and Wales passed in 1946 and one for Scotland passed in 1947, but it is possible to talk of a health service covering the whole of Britain, and this discussion covers Scotland as well as England. People are not obliged to use the service; they may still go to doctors as private patients if they wish to do so, and in big towns there are some private and financially independent hospitals (called "nursing homes") which people may use rather than the hospitals which are within the health service.°

The idea of the family doctor has always been strong in Britain, and remains so. In order to obtain the benefits of the National Health Service a person must be registered on a general practitioner's list, and if he needs medical attention he must first go to his general practitioner or have the general practitioner come to see him. The family doctor gives treatment or prescribes medicine, or, if necessary, arranges for the patient to go to hospital or to be seen at home by a specialist. If the doctor prescribes medicine or pills, his written prescription must be taken to a chemist's shop, where the chemist prepares what is necessary. At first, from 1948, the patient had nothing to pay for medicine, but in 1951 a small payment became necessary. Following an increase in this payment in 1961 the patient paid the chemist two shillings for each item prescribed; the health service funds paid the whole cost of the medicine above two shillings. If a person was poor enough to be receiving national assistance payments he could get his two shillings back later. But the Labour Government abolished all charges for prescriptions in 1964.

Each person is free to choose a general practitioner in the area where he lives, and be registered on his list. He must normally go only to the doctor with whom he is actually registered, or to one of the doctor's partners. It is possible to arrange to be transferred to another doctor's list. A person away from home may go to any doctor. Every general practitioner receives a fixed "capitation" payment from the health service funds of about one pound per year for each patient on his list. The exact calculation of these payments is a little complicated by some statistical "weighting" according to total numbers, though all types of patients, young and old, are paid for at the same rate.°

If a patient under the health service needs specialist or hospital treatment his general practitioner will send him to a hospital. In the hospital all treatment is entirely free, both for out-patients and for patients who remain inside.°

Dental treatment is provided under the health service. At first it was all paid for out of the health service funds, but now each patient must pay £ 1 towards the cost of each series of visits to his dentist, and must also pay up to £ 4 5 s. towards the cost of any false teeth which may be supplied to him. Nursing and expectant mothers and people under twenty-one years old do not have to pay anything for dental treatment, however. The introduction of the health service seems to have done much to improve the condition of people's teeth in general, and also to improve the status of dentists. The service also extends to aids to vision. Any person may have his eyes tested free of charge by an optician or eye specialist, but must pay part of the cost of any glasses that may be provided.

The working of the health service inevitably produces some adverse comment, and in particular it produces a good deal of form-filling and paper-work for all concerned in its operation. On the other side there are some who regret that the main objective of the service has been thwarted—though very slightly—by the fact that individual patients must pay a little towards the cost of medicine from the chemist, of glasses and some appliances, and of dental treatment. But on the whole most British people would agree that the service is achieving its main objectives with outstanding success, though it may be a little damaged by excessive governmental economy. The cost is really not very high; expenditure on the treatment of sickness is much less per head of population, even as a percentage of national income, than in the United States. And whatever some people may say about the cost of the welfare state, it remains true that real expenditure on welfare services in general is not remarkably high in comparison with other European countries.

Peter Bromhead, "Life in Modern Britain", ⁶*1968*

Sport as a Social and an Individual Phenomenon

Man, since Adam, must work. But man also, since society began, has played. His play may show itself in any product of his imagination, in any art or craft pursued for recreation rather than for purposes of technology, or, simply, in sport. And in so far as any of these activities is distinct from what a man regards as his work, a society which has the prospect of considerably increased leisure needs to look at this aspect of its corporate life more closely. Especially, an industrialised society, in which repetitive processes have largely taken the place of individual creation, needs to examine the contribution which play can make to full living, for the individual and for the society. As more and more people live urban lives, play takes its place—for one man as affording an opportunity for social activities with other town-dwellers, for another as affording an opportunity for introducing into his own life a balancing element of the countryside and the open air.°

Certainly it can be said that in Britain there is an ingrained respect for certain attitudes which have their roots in sport. The word *sportsmanship* means something important and valuable; and the notion which underlies it is perhaps still one of the traits on which we customarily pride ourselves most. It is easy to ridicule the *That's not cricket, old boy* attitude. But in its deeper (and usually inarticulate) significance it still provides something like the foundations of an ethical standard, which may not be highly intellectual but which does have a considerable influence on the day-to-day behaviour of millions of people. It has by now been generalised to cover conduct far removed from any actual sports field; but it retains the notions of not simply keeping just within the letter of the law and of avoiding action which however difficult it is to define is yet of a kind which would infringe the rights and spoil the proper enjoyment of other people. This may seem a rudimentary form of ethical theory; but in hard practice it is no bad elementary guide to decent living together in society. To define it too closely would be to spoil it, for that would reduce to the letter of a law what is fundamentally an attitude; and as a national characteristic, arising from the traditional British love of sport, it is one in which we can legitimately take some pride.

"*Sport and the Community*", 1960

Sport is War minus the Shooting

Nearly all the sports practised nowadays are competitive. You play to win, and the game has little meaning unless you do your utmost to win. On the village green, where you pick up sides and no feeling of local patriotism is involved, it is possible to play simply for the fun and exercise: but as soon as the question of prestige arises, as soon as you feel that you and some larger unit will be disgraced if you lose, the most savage combative instincts are aroused. Anyone who has played even in a school football match knows this. At the international level sport is frankly mimic warfare. But the significant thing is not the behaviour of the players but the attitude of the spectators; and, behind the spectators, of the nations who work themselves into furies over these absurd contests, and seriously believe—at any rate for short periods—that running, jumping and kicking a ball are tests of national virtue.°

20 A Rugby Match

As soon as strong feelings of rivalry are aroused, the notion of playing the game according to the rules always vanishes. People want to see one side on top and the other side humiliated and they forget that victory gained through cheating or through the intervention of the crowd is meaningless. Even when the spectators don't intervene physically they try to influence the game by cheering their own side and "rattling" opposing players with boos and insults. Serious sport has nothing to do with fair play. It is bound up with hatred, jealousy, boastfulness, disregard of all rules and sadistic pleasure in witnessing violence: in other words it is war minus the shooting.

Instead of blah-blahing about the clean, healthy rivalry of the football field and the great part played by the Olympic Games in bringing the nations together, it is more useful to inquire how and why this modern cult of sport arose. Most of the games we now play are of ancient origin, but sport does not seem to have been taken very seriously between Roman times and the nineteenth century. Even in the English public schools the games cult did not start till the later part of the last century. Dr. Arnold, generally regarded as the founder of the modern public school, looked on games as simply a waste of time. Then, chiefly in England and the United States, games were built up into a heavily financed activity, capable of attracting vast crowds and rousing savage passions, and the infection spread from country to country. It is the most violently combative sports, football and boxing, that have spread the widest. There cannot be much doubt that the whole thing is bound up with the rise of nationalism— that is, with the lunatic modern habit of identifying oneself with large power units and seeing everything in terms of competitive prestige.

George Orwell, "The Sporting Spirit", 1945

A View of Young People in Britain today

Recently a student of the new university at Canterbury tried to explain the lack of interest in politics on the part of his contemporaries. "The trouble with young people in Britain," he said, "is this. On the one hand they see the crying needs of a world full of problems—fear of war, hunger, political unrest and racial discrimination; on the other, they feel that there is nothing whatever they can do about it. Their background of material security and the comfort of their lives make it just possible to bear what is going on elsewhere and to try to ignore it."

Generalisations are dangerous. Should we, in any case, always be isolating the "problem of youth"? Perhaps not, but we are all inclined to think and speak of young people as a special section of society, if only because they are more noticeable than they were in the days when children were seen but not heard. Gone is the time when parents could exact unquestioning obedience. Instead, they have to watch their headstrong offspring making mistakes and try not to interfere. Older people have felt threatened by the Rockers of some years ago and in a different way by the mini-skirted products of the Quant boutiques. Innumerable articles have been written in newspapers, and many television programmes have been devoted to hooligans who break up the amenities of seaside resorts or disturb football matches, to youngsters who scream and shout at the approach of the Beatles or the Rolling Stones, to long-haired youths and short-cropped girls in coffee bars and to Hippies with ideas emanating from San Francisco. Carnaby Street has influenced clothes and has given us colourful waistcoats of Edwardian style and gaudy traditional uniforms to be worn by the up-and-coming in the streets of London. Young girls welcome the greater interest young men take in smart clothes, in contrast to their fathers, who stick to the more conventional outfits of the older generation.

But can we leave our picture of young people in Britain there? By no means, for this is only part of the portrait. Though most teenagers are more or less influenced by the fashions of their age-group, the much-discussed hooligan element does not account

21 The Easter March 1968

for the vast majority. It is true that young people are more independent and have far more money than they used to have. Parents help them willingly and sometimes unwisely; shop assistants, factory workers and even apprentices have more money than formerly. Students are generously supported by the state, which provides university education for a higher proportion of working-class children than in almost any other country in the world. These young people often live away from home and do not like restrictions, but there are advantages too. More of them than ever before have a higher education; they hear about and see more of the world they live in; they study languages and travel—often adventurously in old cars or land-rovers and survive on a shoe-string. There is widespread interest in the overseas aid programmes organised by V.S.O. (Voluntary Service Overseas) and similar bodies. Hundreds of dedicated, unsentimental young Britons take aid and know-how to developing countries each year. We can think of the ex-schoolgirl of 19 helping to teach illiterate Africans, of the young man digging wells in India, of others devoting two years to work in hospitals after training as doctors, and of others again who are sweating alongside Ghanaians in the building of dams and irrigation of the desert.

The Duke of Edinburgh has helped to channel the enthusiasm and energy of the younger generation. His own "Duke of Edinburgh Award" is a much-coveted reward for tests of endurance and skill, undertaken by older Scouts and Girl Guides. The Outward Bound schools have shown teenagers—often from bad homes or from depressing environments in large cities—what it means to be faced by the challenge of mountains and sea. Older schoolchildren often help to look after old people in their spare time. They dig their gardens or paint their houses.

In the fifties many thousands of young people took part in the Aldermaston Marches, and there are many now who demonstrate against the war in Vietnam.

As they sing of the Family of Man, they are trying to make their more complacent elders realise that the world is changing fast and that war in the future is unthinkable. They may be disillusioned by party politics, but their songs of protest show that they care about world problems.

Perhaps the biggest single asset of the new generation is that they are trying to be honest—both about themselves and the world around them. They are tired of hypocrisy, of empire-building, prejudice and the conventions of today's society. Certainly they have their own conventions, they are often intolerant of their elders, but they are trying to find a way of living in the framework of a much freer society. Mistakes are inevitable, but ultimately they want to use their new freedom wisely.

Rosalind Priestman, Special Contribution for "Britain and America"

The Position of Women in Britain

Some weeks ago I was travelling on a crowded bus. In front of me sat two elderly ladies, talking at the tops of their voices.

"I don't know what to do with my hair," said one, "It's such a mess. I can never get it to lie down the way I'd like it to."

"Why don't you have one of those smart, short styles? It would suit you," said her friend.

"I couldn't do that," was the reply, "My better half doesn't like me with short hair. He'd be ever so annoyed if I thought of having it cut."

Did she mean her "better half"? Was she secretly proud and pleased that her husband was still interested enough to notice her hair? Was she making a mockery of men being lords and masters? I could not tell, but it made me wonder again where women really stood today.

At the dawn of the 19th century aristocratic Whig ladies could, in practice, do much as they pleased. The working-class women earned their bread alongside their menfolk and children, but with the growth of the middle classes there came special problems for the women. While their husbands were forging careers in industry and trade, not all wives and daughters were content to sit at home with fine embroidery and idle gossip. Some great names stand out. Elizabeth Fry went to visit the prisoners of Newgate Prison and did much to change the public attitude towards them. Florence Nightingale was well known for her remarkable nursing record in the Crimean War. Some of the greatest 19th century novelists were women: Jane Austen, Charlotte and Emily Brontë, George Eliot and Mrs Gaskell. They were able to reflect the life of their time from their own special point of view.

There was, however, another side to the picture. Governesses were underpaid and under-privileged, little more than servants "below stairs", and teaching was the only possible career for well-bred impecunious ladies. Women who tried to break away from their accepted, conventional backgrounds had neither right nor sympathy on their side. Only the most determined were able to face the stumbling-blocks involved. Once married, women lost all claim to property or wealth of their own, they could not claim custody of their children, politically they had no rights, nor could they hope to have a good education. The professions and universities were barred to them. For most women this state of affairs seemed natural enough. Was it not true that "the hand that rocks the cradle rules the world?" Was Britain not fortunate to have a majestic and venerated Queen on the throne—a model of virtuous womanhood?

In 1792 Mary Wollstonecraft had written *Vindication of the Rights of Women,* and perhaps the real battle for equality began there. By 1882 women were given ownership of their own property and women like Elizabeth Blackwell and Elizabeth Garrett were fighting for their right to qualify as doctors—quite a shocking idea to the Victorian gentlemen that belonged to that profession.

By the turn of the century Mrs Pankhurst and her faithful followers were organizing their semi-military Suffragette movement. Women felt that they had to fight for equality—their dearest wish being that they should share the privileges so far denied

22 Mrs Pankhurst at her Eleventh Arrest

to the "weaker sex". These ladies were fervent and often masculine in their approach. They were willing to go to prison, to suffer all sorts of indignities—one even to sacrifice her life by throwing herself in front of the horses at the Derby race.

It is just over 50 years since women were first given the vote in Britain, so it is a good time to look back and take stock. Women have certainly won the right to be heard, though too many men still listen to them with condescension. Women are represented in the world of politics, of the professions and in the literary world. Have they achieved what they really want? Have they equal opportunities? Since the militant struggle has faded into the background, women recognize more clearly that most of them are still wives and mothers and they would like to carry out these tasks as intelligently as possible.

Recently there was an interesting debate at the famous Oxford Union. It took place on the occasion of the retirement of the first-ever woman president, and the motion before the house was *Vive la différence*. Both men and women students spoke in favour of equality with a difference—of women developing their special gifts and aptitudes and yet not denying their femininity: of men not discounting women's opinions and listening to them seriously. Would our Suffragette grandmothers with their tweed skirts and independent self-reliance have agreed with this view? They could not and would not deny that women are the mothers of the next generation and that most of them will have to devote some of their active years to child-bearing and home-making. They might, however, regret that there are not more women who can make their voices heard in politics, that the Stock Exchange is still a man's preserve. They would certainly want employers in industry and commerce to abandon the idea that women are cheap labour and are incapable of shouldering responsibility.

One thing is certain: with every year that passes there are more possibilities for the modern young woman. She can look forward to a training in an interesting career, to marriage that is a partnership, to spending some years bringing up her children and then, if she feels able to do it, to returning to satisfying employment. Perhaps we should stop worrying about which is the "better half".

Rosalind Priestman, Special Contribution for "Britain and America"

Britain's Changing Anatomy

The changes seem quite spectacular. In politics, in the boardrooms, the senior common rooms, the Inns of Court and even in the BBC, the familiar chorus of *Old Freddies*—of peers, soldiers or courtiers—has begun to troop off-stage. °The splendours and follies of the Empire, and of the last world war, have faded and the angry debates about Suez, Cyprus or Central Africa seem to belong to a quite separate era.

Reverence and stuffiness are out of fashion, and nearly everyone, from the head of the BBC to the Lord Chancellor, likes to think of himself as being "anti-Establishment". °The old Aunt Sallies like the palace, the House of Lords or the Foreign Office, have become drabber and less important, °while the rest of Britain gets down to the harder problem of Britain's commercial survival.°

Pragmatism is less often talked about, and the phrase "it's odd but it works" is less often heard. The decimal system and Continental road signs are on their way. Re-organisation and rationalisation have become national slogans. °Parliament, the Law, the Church, Oxford, the Foreign Office, have all been investigated. The fighting services have been marshalled into a single vast organogram and the First Lord of the Admiralty has ceased to exist. °Management consultants, led by McKinsey's, have invaded the big corporations, to redraw the lines of responsibility, and strengthen the profit motive. Even Buckingham Palace has called in efficiency experts. The Bank of England no longer insists on being protected by a troop of guardsmen in full dress, marching through the traffic, but allows them to arrive in battle dress, in a truck, like Shakespearean actors in modern dress.

Introspection has become a national hobby, and everywhere the sociologists and Prodnose people, armed with statistics and surveys, have entered their unfriendly kingdom. No profession is now complete without its figures to show how few of them went to university, and how many want to emigrate.°

In Whitehall, in industry or even in the city, a new post-war generation of men has emerged near the top, with a much more thrusting and self-aware attitude than their pre-war elders; and this split between generations, accentuated by the post-war birthrate, can be seen running through every British institution.°

On the one hand are the outstanding men in their fifties, who started their careers in the slump years of the thirties, and who are now permanent secretaries, directors or ambassadors. They joined their government department or corporation often with a mixture of a genuine sense of service, and thankfulness for a safe job in bad times. They were loyal to their institution as they were loyal to their college, and however unsettled the world and the rest of Britain might be, the colleges, clubs or departments remained—looking with hindsight—extraordinarily *there*. The Indian army, the hierarchies of the Indian and colonial services and the huge protocol of the pre-war navy, gave a military backbone to the middle-classes. However impoverished, they could and did lead whole lives with no thought of commercial competitiveness, either for themselves or for their country. Of course many of this generation did make fortunes, and remain to this day acquisitive and crafty. But even in the city, if you set out to make a fortune, it was helpful to do so behind a military moustache, and with a handle to your name.

The last war, when so many men proved themselves, encouraged the feeling that companies should be run like armies: and after the war, however much the English liked to think of themselves as a civilian nation, the colonels and generals moved confidently and briskly into the city, industry, British Railways, or the BBC, inspired by thoughts of patriotism and loyalty, rather than commercial or technical efficiency. Looking back now on the Britain of the fifties, where generals and brigadiers ran everything, it is hard to remember how little analytical thought, or commercial drive, went into British institutions.

But now a generation of administrators has come up who were at school during or after the war, who have been brought up alongside a crumbling Empire, a dwindling army, and recurring balance of payments crises. They do not have the same loyalty (as their elders sadly assured me) to their institutions. At university, the ablest realised that they would be much in demand, and if they felt they were not properly valued by one employer, they could move elsewhere. "Officer-like qualities" were far less required, and a drunken poet who could write silly ditties for commercials might earn twice as much as a long service manager. And, as an extra training ground for the ambitious, America loomed closer: ten times as many people crossed the Atlantic in 1960 as did in 1930: and many of them brought back new techniques of salesmanship, efficiency and commercial vigour.

And the new generation were much more aware of themselves—their value, their reputation and their power. °Talking to civil servants or industrial managers in both age-groups, you cannot fail to notice the difference. The younger men are reluctant to accept the old tradition of reticence and anonymity, or to feel calmly detached from their work as if it were an extension of Greek verse or mediaeval history. They feel themselves in the midst of a shifting scene, and part of the scenery, with cold winds blowing, and arc lights glaring. The public service is no longer so cut off from private industry; permanent secretaries troop out to profitable jobs in industry, and some industrialists, even, stride into the Treasury building.

Any British outfit, given half a chance, will settle down into behaving like an Oxford college, or a country estate. But in the last few years that illusion has been harder to maintain. In industry, the competition from America and Europe, and the end of the fat years of a seller's market, has at last produced a new competitiveness, in which the word "profits" is mentioned without shame. In ICI, Unilever, Bowaters, AEI, English Electric or General Electric, new chairmen have generated a new ruthlessness, and (as John Tyzack put it) "We are at last coming back to accepting that the job of management is to manage. We are trying to jump over a generation, and to put into senior management young men who have been conditioned since the war to the new world." The word *entrepreneur*, which for so long had a stigma, has come back into fashion.°

And playing all round this changing, competitive scene, with glitter and fantasies, is the glaring light of publicity. It opens up secret places, makes heroes overnight, and quickens the pace of envy and self-awareness. It is hard to recall what Britain was like eight years ago, before that first television toothpaste advertisement, and the whole noisy invasion of jingles and ephemeral fame which followed it. Television broke through the high walls which separate British institutions from each other, and dragged almost everyone into its studios; but most of all it knocked down its own wall, between private and public enterprise, and turned the BBC, the most influential of the nationalised industries, inside out. The young "apparatchiks" there became the central figures in the New Boy Net, who hold the keys to promotion, salesmanship and fame. They demolished much of the stateliness of the existing Old Boy Networkers, and have built up their own jolly show-biz parade, with teenagers and David Frost as their pacemakers—a parade which any strong, silent man joins at his peril. They have unleashed "the power of laughter" (in Sir Hugh Greene's phrase), which makes stuffiness and squareness the deadliest sins.

Anthony Sampson, "Anatomy of Britain today", 1965

23 Road Signs—a highly Unreliable Guide for Motorists in Britain

Ban half of the bombs | Natives are hostile | One in six make it | Betting shop ahead | Military tattoo ahead | You are clear to take off | Beware of escaping convicts | Drunken drivers only

III The U.S.A.—The Land

Climate in Britain and America

Britain's climate is a poor thing, but her own, and she is touchy about it. She's like a family which reserves the right to tear each other limb from limb, but let an outsider presume to criticize one member, and the whole family bristles with indignation. The
5 British talk about the weather continuously and grumble no little. Some comment on the state of the day almost invariably follows a greeting: "Good morning. It's better to-day," or, "It's wet this afternoon." I remember once in making a tour of small shops where I was doing the family marketing, I got so bored talking about the weather that I resolved to say "Yes, isn't it?" no matter what form the comment took. The results
10 were so amusing that I found myself going into more shops than necessary in order to play my game. Not a single shopkeeper disappointed me!

Every well-ordered British household has a barometer—an instrument which I had never seen until I came to England. Tapping the barometer to get some clue to the day's weather is a morning ritual which is just about as regular as winding the clock.
15 Each member of the family pauses to add his tap and take his squint at the barometer on his way down to breakfast.

But Americans in England would be well advised to soft-pedal complaints about the weather even though it does give them a big headache. The British are used to it, and on the whole they prefer their temperature, which is neither very hot nor very cold,
20 to the extremes of sunshine and frost which prevail over most of the American continent. Any Englishman who has worked through a summer in Washington could say plenty about the American climate. One such wrote home: "After six weeks in this... steaming Turkish bath, no one will ever make me believe that the English climate isn't the finest in the world." Washington is hot and moist, and has just about
25 as unpleasant a climate as can be found in the whole country. It is not typical of America, nor, indeed, can any section be said to represent the whole, since almost any weather conditions prevailing in any part of the world can be found somewhere within the American borders.

Americans, who are used to extremes of weather and a generous supply of sunshine,
30 really do feel considerable discomfort in the dull damp days which so often follow each other in grey succession in England. But the time they find most trying is the English winter, during which they seldom ever feel warm, though the actual temperature may be considerably higher than they're used to. Americans cannot understand why the English like their houses so cold in winter and their drinks so warm in summer!
35 They don't realize that the extremes of temperature (if any) are likely to be of such short duration that the average Englishman doesn't think it worth while making any special preparations to cope with them. The British rely on wool—and plenty of layers—the year round to ward off the cold, and they rightly have so little confidence in their fickle climate that they cling to their woollies even on a hot day. After quite a
40 spell of hot weather they begin to realize why they feel so uncomfortable, and shed a

few garments. But on the most brilliant day in England you will see women wearing coats or furs. I've never known an Englishman to abandon his coat. Sometimes, walking through a slum district on a sultry day, I have longed to snatch off the heavy woollen jerseys (pullovers to the English) which most of the children continue to wear. But I imagine the youngsters would feel uncomfortably naked without them.°

The outstanding thing about the American climate is the dry, sparkling, invigorating quality of the air (which accounts in some measure for the tireless energy of the Americans), and the sudden swing from winter days of snow and ice to summer days so hot that the pavements (sidewalks to an American), often made of tar composite, grow soft under one's feet.°

Spring in England, with its tentative sunshine and its long-drawn-out promise of flower and fruit, is far more lovely than the same season in America. Indeed, there is hardly any spring in America—it is icy winter to-day, and suddenly summer to-morrow. But the American autumn with its extravagant colouring and its lingering "Indian summer" cannot be surpassed.

Lella S. Florence in "America and Britain", 1946

Sweet Land of Liberty

The map of America goes on and on. The map of America is a map of endlessness, of opening out, of forever and ever. No man's face would make you think of it but his hope might, his courage might. But it isn't only in length and breadth that the map of America is big. It is big in time, too. In the small countries the clocks strike all together— all one hour. With us it is still deep night at San Francisco, and dark still on the High Plains, and only barely gray on Lake Michigan, when the sun comes up at Marblehead. The same thing is true of the seasons. In the small countries the weather is all one weather more or less, but with us there are a thousand weathers and a choice of seasons. Beans will be out of the ground in Alabama when the snow is four feet deep in Minnesota and the gardens around Charleston will be blooming when the oil-burners at Kennebunkport are still blasting away. Some of us avoid the changes, cruising up and down the continent with the seasons, living in a wandering summer. But most of us stay put: we wouldn't quit the American changes if we could. Change and diversity are the meaning of our world: the American dimension. It is because the season changes, the weather changes, the country changes, that the map goes on and on. What can change will never have an ending.

America is a country of extremes. Those who think she should be all of a piece, all of a kind, every farm like every other farm, every house like its neighbor and all minds alike, have never traveled on this continent. American wholeness, American singleness, American strength, is the wholeness, the singleness, the strength of many opposites made one.°

If you could read a country the way you read the palm of a hand, the American lines of heart and head and life would be the three great branching rivers of the Mississippi Valley, but the American line of fortune would take a different course: it would follow the flow of steel and oil. It is the combination of steel and oil which has begotten American industry and it is American industry which has built the American cities.

24 Tulsa, Oklahoma

When a foreigner thinks of the United States he does not think of Frost and Faulkner, or of Harvard and Columbia and Yale, or of the Shenandoah and the Yellowstone; he thinks of New York and San Francisco and Chicago, and the steel that built them and the oil by which they live. It is the fabulous sky line which shapes itself in the
5 imagination of the world when the name, America, is spoken. And the thought that goes with that sky line in the world's mind is the thought "materialism". To our neighbors, East and West, the symbols of the United States are enormous chimneys leaking their pink smoke into the clean, blue sky, or huge derricks wading into the sea itself for oil, or deserted mining towns where gold and silver were once dug. But we our-
10 selves—what do we think of the world's talk? Consider that sky line. Do steel and oil alone explain it? Is it only metal that speaks here and an ooze pumped out of muck? Or have the minds of men imagined these tall towers?

   Ours was a new continent. What have we done with it? What have we left behind us—as the sea leaves driftwood on the rocks? Much ugliness, much devastation—
15 gullied fields, eroded prairies, burnt forests, filthy slums, imitative and pretentious buildings, litter, trash. Yes, all that: but like the driftwood, beauty too. Unintended beauty perhaps—unsuspected beauty: an enormous oil tank rounded by the shadow of its stair; a great bridge strung like a harp across sea water; the pure, remembering profiles of a country graveyard. And how did this beauty come here? By accident?
20 By chance? Or did men make it? Are these perhaps the monuments of a particular temper of the human spirit—an American sensibility which expresses itself as well in the shuttered front of a city warehouse as in the trim competence of a valley farm or the weathered patience of a railroad station on a one-track line?

Because the movement of the discoverers and conquerors and colonists was a movement from east to west across the Atlantic, and because the frontiersmen and the settlers moved across the continent from east to west, west has always been the direction of the future in American history. The American dream has been a dream of the west, of the world farther on. But now that the great journey across the ocean and the continent has come to the coast of the Pacific, there are those who say we have come to the end of the dream also. We must look backward now, they say, not forward; we must fear, not hope; we must hate, not love; we must conform, not imagine. It is strange doctrine to hear from Americans. No man can come to the Pacific coast of this continent, no man can watch the fog move in from that immeasurable ocean, and feel he has come to the end of anything. The land still faces westward and still dreams as the hills do here, the mist along their flanks, the sea before them. California, it is quite true, has filled up with people: her valleys are richly farmed, her cities are among the greatest in the world, her industries are fabulous. But even so the American journey has not ended. America is never accomplished, America is always still to build; for men, as long as they are truly men, will dream of man's fulfillment. West is a country in the mind, and so eternal.

Archibald MacLeish in "Collier's", 1955

New York

All but a few years of my life have been spent in and around New York City, but I cannot claim an intense feeling of identification with the city. In a sense, one is cheated by being born here. The newcomer never entirely recovers from his stunning first impression, while the native becomes aware of the city gradually and without a thrill of wonder. Very early, those of us raised in the outlying areas fall into the habit of saying we are "going to the city" when, in fact, we are already within its boundaries. By the city we mean, of course, Manhattan, as does everyone who speaks of New York. Yet there is another New York, unstoried and rather drab, consisting of provincial Brooklyn, Queens, and the Bronx.

The people who sleep in Manhattan are mainly the rich and the poor. Eight out of ten of the middle and upper middle income families in the New York metropolitan area live in the outlying parts of the city and the suburbs. These millions of people are the unnoticed New Yorkers, the blurred walk-ons who provide the human backdrop for Manhattan's vivid extremes of glamor and squalor. They come from places like Richmond Hill, a neighborhood in south Queens where three generations of my family have lived in tree-shaded frame houses on 40-foot lots. The people in Richmond Hill, and all the neighborhoods like it, do not live splendidly or squalidly; they merely try to live decently. The purpose of this essay is to explore some of the obstacles to achieving this modest objective in the world's greatest city.

I am not immune to the drama of the city, nor do I undervalue the city's unique advantages; but I know that most of the ones that matter—I am not thinking of the Museum of Natural History—are available only to those who can afford them. New York is too often judged by its exceptional features, and excused for the mean quality (or total absence) of ordinary amenities. It is destroying itself under the impact of

forces that are being felt in every city. New York represents the fullest expression—for
good or ill—of our urban culture. It is the macrocosm of every city's problems and
aspirations. It matters everywhere what New York is—and what it is not.

New York is, of course, a miracle. Through an infinitely complex mechanism,
millions of people are fed, housed, clothed, transported, and organized for work that
organizes the work of millions of others throughout the world. On Manhattan Island
is found the greatest concentration of human skill and energy in the world. Here is
the economic, cultural and intellectual capital of the Western world. But how fares
the human spirit in this great metropolis?

New York's failure is in human arrangements, a failure with many sources. It can
be traced to the apathy and venality of the city's politicians; to the cold unconcern
of the city's builders, among whom a kind of Gresham's Law of architecture prevails;
to the remoteness and indifference of the city's business and financial leaders; to the
selfishness of competing groups and interests whose actions and demands take little
account of the general welfare.°

New York is an economic entity; it exists primarily to perform work; to permit
the ease of human contact that facilitates exchange of goods and services. But the
city functions today only with growing difficulty and inefficiency. The economic costs
of its malfunctioning have become staggering.°

However, it is not the economic disorder of New York that throws a shadow across
an urban civilization. The truly terrible costs of New York are social and spiritual.

As Lewis Mumford has observed in *The Culture of Cities*, "the so-called blighted
areas of the metropolis are essentially *do without* areas". In this sense, much of New
York outside the slums is "blighted," and the people living there, as Mumford has
written, are "people who do without pure air, who do without sound sleep, who do
without a cheerful garden or playing space, who do without the very sight of the sky
and the sunlight, who do without free motion, spontaneous play . . . .". And among those
imprisoned within such an environment, he writes, "chronic starvation produces lack
of appetite. Eventually, you may live and die without even recognizing the loss."

New York shows alarming signs of spiritual malnutrition and death-by-inches. It
is frowning, tight-lipped, short-tempered, the most nervous city in America. It is a city
without grace.

Richard J. Whalen in "Life", 1965

Chicago

Chicago, sprawling in boisterous disorder along the southwestern shore of Lake
Michigan, is the central terminal of the United States. It is the greatest railroad hub
in the world, and its stockyards are the world's largest. Surrounded by the broad, fertile
farmlands and vast mineral deposits of the Midwest, it is the manufacturing center
and market place of 36 per cent of the nation's population.

Chicago's pre-eminence in the Midwest, and in the nation, is the result both of
location and of a vigorous, gusty, proud initiative. Chicago was not raised—it grew.
It emerged from a wild territory bought from the Indians in 1833. It amassed great
fortunes from corn and hogs, and cattle, dairy products, iron ore, lumber and real

estate—all near at hand. Bitter labor wars, race riots, boom times and depressions forged into it a bold hardiness. From native sons and daughters like detective Allan Pinkerton, reaper inventor Cyrus McCormick, meat packer P. D. Armour, railroad magnate George Mortimer Pullman, merchant Marshall Field and social worker Jane Addams it gained a strident, vital confidence.

Tempered by these qualities, Chicago survived the great fire of 1871, the gang wars of Al Capone's day, the political machinations of mayors like Big Bill Thompson and the speculations of Samuel Insull. It fascinated a world already dulled by fascinations with the Columbian Exposition in 1893 and the World's Fair of 1933–34. And in raucous, hard-drinking political conventions it helped nominate Abraham Lincoln, Grover Cleveland, Theodore Roosevelt, Warren G. Harding—and Franklin Delano Roosevelt twice.

Old-timers maintain that Chicago has never changed—despite the fact that in a little over a century it has skyrocketed from an unincorporated village of 50 people to one of the largest cities in the world, with a population of over four and one half million. It has somehow retained the high-spirited friendliness of the frontier town. Its people are still enthusiastic about the future, still willing to take a chance, still like to have a roaring good time. It lives by no set pattern or rules, has little of the worldly polish or formality of New York. In its own relaxed, uninhibited way Chicago resembles a small boy who knows he can catch more fish with a bent pin and a worm than can his well-dressed cousins with all their fancy flies and bait.

But Chicago is no unblemished gem in the heart of the prairie. In many ways it is a beautiful city, but in just as many others it is not. Packed into 23 of its 212 square miles are some of the worst slums in the nation. The Loop—with its ancient elevated and surface streetcars, its noise and confusion, its heterogeneous architecture and traffic-snarling river bridges—is sometimes as much a test of the visitor's patience as

26 Chicago, Marina City with Marina Towers

27 Chicago, The Union Stock Yards

are the stockyards and oil refineries and steel mills a test of olfactory endurance. In summer, dry winds off the western plains can turn Chicago into a brazier of baking heat. In winter, roaring blizzards sweep down the lake to harry shoppers and office workers pushing their way along the city's narrow streets.

In its bustling growth, the city spread back from the lake without plan or design. The Loop, around which wind the north and south branches of the Chicago River, became the financial, shopping and amusement center. Below the black belt and the stockyards, mile upon mile of middle-class residential flats filled up the South Side. The West Side was adopted as the home of a large majority of Chicago's half million foreign-born Poles, Germans, Russians, Italians, Swedes, Czechs, Austrians, English, Hungarians, Norwegians and Yugoslavs. Along the North Shore's Gold Coast congregated most of Chicago's very rich. And around the fringes, and within the "sections" themselves, sprang up the thousands of factories that have made Chicago's industrial output second only to that of New York.

"*Look at America*", by the editors of "*Look*" in collaboration with Louis Bromfield, 1947

Los Angeles

Los Angeles is probably the fastest-growing city in the history of the world. No European laid eyes on it until 1769, when an expedition of Spanish explorers came upon an Indian village called Yang-na and renamed the site "Nuestra Señora la Reina de los Angeles—Our Lady Queen of the Angels". Twelve years later, the area was settled by 44 low-caste peons (including ten Negroes) from Mexico. The pueblo came under American occupation in 1846, was incorporated (pop. 1,610) in 1850—the same year that California received statehood.°

28 Los Angeles, Pasadena Freeways during Rush-hour Traffic

    Though Los Angeles proper ranks third in population among U.S. cities (after New York and Chicago), Greater Los Angeles is already the second-most-populous metropolis in the U.S., is almost sure to surpass New York by 1975.° By 1990, such growth will make the city the hub of an uninterrupted urbanized stretch of almost 19 million inhabitants occupying the 175 mile-long, coastal area that runs from Santa Barbara in the north to San Diego in the south. Already sociologists are calling this Southern California megalopolis the prototype of the city of the future.°
    Having grown outward, Los Angeles is now in the process of growing upward, a shift reflected in the thrusting towers near the city hall and the modern, luxury high-rise apartment houses that now line the west end of Wilshire Boulevard in Beverly Hills and Westwood. Still, for all the city's growth, there remain many areas of country living deep inside the city limits, where hills and valleys, treed lawns and wild animals abound. Patios, swimming pools—preferably in odd shapes—and private tennis courts are numerous enough to be taken for granted.
    To move around in this eye-popping urbanized sprawl, Angelenos depend almost completely on the auto. Fifty-five percent of downtown Los Angeles is given over to cars—in space occupied by freeways, offstreet parking and streets—and nearly 500 miles of freeways snake their way through the city's environs.°
    Along with its amazing physical growth, Los Angeles has also grown mightily in other ways. As the golden city in a golden state, it has become the symbol of vitality, youth, growth and opportunity—a municipal magnet in the West. Once overly dependent on the movie industry, it is now the hub of a huge industrial complex of top firms in aircraft, electronics and research, all attracted by the year-round sunshine. Long considered as a sort of cultural desert, the city now boasts some of the nation's top universities, a huge number of intellectual enterprises, and a music center and museum that rival any in the U.S. Of course, it also has its seamy side and the problems that come with growth—and one of the difficulties of solving them is that the average Angeleno seems too busy living and building in the sun to worry much about them.

No longer can the visitor scowl at the architecture as California gaudy or Hollywood vulgar or Spanish phony. While Los Angeles, like many big cities, has mile after mile of uninspired, tractlike homes, more and more of its buildings and residences are the work of some of the world's best architects: Richard J. Neutra, John Lautner, Lloyd Wright, William Pereira, Victor Gruen, Welton Becket. Tasteful homes have sprouted everywhere—along the streets and boulevards, in the glens and canyons, around the foothills, up the sides of the hills along the beaches, out into the Mojave Desert.°

The vast majority of Los Angeles' citizens° have easy access to what Los Angeles offers: natural beauty, climate, the comfort and pleasant living of a city filled with color, palms and tropical breezes. Hurdling space in its voracious lust for land, defying time in its blinding bursts of change, Los Angeles nonetheless maintains an easy, vacation-like atmosphere that is foreign to the East.°

Los Angeles is the holy temple of the American cult of youth°, it is a city that seeks ceaselessly after youth. Sports cars and motorcycles are everywhere—but so, too, are the symptoms of another Los Angeles fixation: death. In the city that made interment a high art, and to which oldsters gravitate to spend their final years, busstop benches double as advertisements for funeral homes and cemeteries.°

The growth and excitement of Los Angeles are far more than its boulevards, its opulent living and its gaudy entertainments. The city's job-sprouting economy (average family income: $ 9,000) also ripples with new muscle—and diversity. The sociology and economy of the whole area have been molded by the aerospace industry, by research into pure science, and by such think factories as RAND Corp. California Institute of Technology's satellite-tracking Jet Propulsion Laboratory in Pasadena has become all but synonymous with the race to the moon and deep space probes. Along "science strip", a 130-mile coastal stretch encompassing dozens of laboratories, test ranges and research companies, scientists have become leaders of such communities as Redondo Beach and Santa Monica.

"Time", 1966

Niagara Falls

The Falls. He who sees them instantly forgets humanity. They are not very high, but they are overpowering. They are divided by an island into two parts, the Canadian and the American.

Half a mile or so above the Falls, on either side, the water of the great stream begins to run more swiftly and in confusion. It descends with ever-growing speed. It begins chattering and leaping, breaking into a thousand ripples, throwing up joyful fingers of spray. Sometimes it is divided by islands and rocks, sometimes the eye can see nothing but a waste of laughing, springing, foamy waves, turning, crossing, even seeming to stand for an instant erect, but always borne impetuously forward like a crowd of triumphant feasters. Sit down close by it, and you see a fragment of the torrent against the sky, mottled, steely, and foaming, leaping onward in far-flung criss-cross strands of water. Perpetually the eye is on the point of descrying a pattern in this weaving, and perpetually it is cheated by change. In one place part of the flood plunges over a ledge a few feet high and a quarter of a mile or so long, in a uniform and stable curve. It gives an impression of almost military concerted movement, grown suddenly out of confusion. But it is swiftly lost again in the multitudinous tossing merriment. Here and there a rock close to the surface is marked by a white wave that faces backwards and seems to be rushing madly upstream, but is really stationary in the headlong charge. But for these signs of reluctance, the waters seem to fling themselves on with some foreknowledge of their fate, in an ever wilder frenzy. But it is no Maeterlinckian prescience. They prove, rather, that Greek belief that the great crashes are preceded by a louder merriment and a wilder gaiety. Leaping in the sunlight, careless, entwining, clamorously joyful, the waves riot on towards the verge.

But there they change. As they turn to the sheer descent, the white and blue and slate-colour, in the heart of the Canadian Falls at least, blend and deepen to a rich, wonderful, luminous green. On the edge of disaster the river seems to gather herself, to pause, to lift a head noble in ruin, and then, with a slow grandeur, to plunge into the eternal thunder and white chaos below. Where the stream runs shallower it is a kind of violet colour, but both violet and green fray and frill to white as they fall. The mass of water, striking some ever-hidden base of rocks, leaps up the whole two hundred feet again in pinnacles and domes of spray. The spray falls back into the lower river once more; all but a little that fines to foam and white mist, which drifts in layers along the air, graining it, and wanders out on the wind over the trees and gardens and houses, and so vanishes.°

The American Falls do not inspire this feeling in the same way as the Canadian. It is because they are less in volume, and because the water does not fall so much into one place. By comparison their beauty is almost delicate and fragile. They are extra-

29 Niagara Falls, The Canadian Falls

ordinarily level, one long curtain of lacework and woven foam. Seen from opposite, when the sun is on them, they are blindingly white, and the clouds of spray show dark against them. With both Falls the colour of the water is the ever-altering wonder. Greens and blues, purples and whites, melt into one another, fade, and come again, and change with the changing sun. Sometimes they are as richly diaphanous as a precious stone, and glow from within with a deep, inexplicable light. Sometimes the white intricacies of dropping foam become opaque and creamy. And always there are the rainbows. If you come suddenly upon the Falls from above, a great double rainbow, very vivid, spanning the extent of spray from top to bottom, is the first thing you see. If you wander along the cliff opposite, a bow springs into being in the American Falls, accompanies you courteously on your walk, dwindles and dies as the mist ends, and awakens again as you reach the Canadian tumult. And the bold traveller who attempts the trip under the American Falls sees, when he dare open his eyes to anything, tiny baby rainbows, some four or five yards in span, leaping from rock to rock among the foam, and gambolling beside him, barely out of hand's reach, as he goes. One I saw in that place was a complete circle, such as I have never seen before, and so near that I could put my foot on it. It is a terrifying journey, beneath and behind the Falls. The senses are battered and bewildered by the thunder of the water and the assault of wind and spray; or rather, the sound is not of falling water, but merely of falling; a noise of unspecified ruin. So, if you are close behind the endless clamour, the sight cannot recognize liquid in the masses that hurl past. You are dimly and pitifully aware that sheets of light and darkness are falling in great curves in front of you. Dull omnipresent foam washes the face. Farther away, in the roar and hissing, clouds of spray seem literally to slide down some invisible plane of air.

Rupert Brooke, "Letters from America", 1916

The New Conservation

In 1961, President Kennedy redefined the policy for national resources and gave direction to many new programs. As part of these programs the conservation of single resources gave way to the preservation and development of the entire American environment, using fully the tools of modern science but using them to enhance rather than destroy the surroundings.

Today Americans are working out the basic tenets of the new conservation. They are developing a new approach to growth by adding a new sense of proportion, by developing guidelines for a new, satisfactory relation between the people and the land.

Americans today are working out this new concept of conservation in their backyards, on neighborhood councils, in letters-to-the-editor columns, through service organizations, in city halls, in state and national legislatures. Major industries have made room in their organizations for pollution-control executives. Individuals and groups of citizens, businesses and governments, all are working, often in unusual combinations, to create beauty and set a high standard of quality in the areas where their responsibilities lie. Americans are at last launched on building a country that is not just big and prosperous but clean and beautiful as well.

5 Britain Oberstufe

The new conservation is the beginning of the realization that the worth of a nation—its inner greatness—lies in the quality of its products rather than the quantity of its goods. A nation's sense of history, the hospitality it offers the spirit of man, the appeal of its environment, an intellectual climate that is stimulating to man—these are the things, Americans now see, that characterize a great society. The new conservation brings balance into America's environment. Before, there was power but no grace, rich cities but few handsome cities. Americans excelled as developers but not as conservers.

Although action to implement the new conservation has been taking place everywhere in the country, the remarkable record of landmark legislation in the United States Congress is perhaps the most dramatic sign. In the past five years it has added five national seashores; established a great new national park at Canyonlands in Utah; authorized for the first time a new type of park, the Ozarks National Scenic Riverways in Missouri; and created a new category, the national recreation area, designed to serve the increasing number of city dwellers who most need such areas. Previously, Americans had taken the easy way, establishing nine tenths of the nation's 283 million acres of public parkland in Alaska and the Far West, whereas the Northeast—with 25 percent of the U.S. population—struggled along with only 4 percent of the park and forest acreage. The Delaware Water Gap National Recreation Area, signed into law in September 1965, has 30 million people living within 100 miles of its borders.

The Land and Water Conservation Fund, passed in 1965, may well provide one of the most powerful conservation instruments yet devised, drawing together the park and recreation aims of all levels of government and concentrating them in the Department of the Interior's Bureau of Outdoor Recreation. In 1966 more than $ 60 million was made available from the fund for acquisition and development of public outdoor recreation areas. The federal government retains 40 percent of the fund's revenues from motorboat-fuel taxes, sale of surplus government property, and federal recreation permits. The remainder is allocated on a matching grant basis to states and their political subdivisions.

There are controversies raging in almost every area of the country today. In nearly every instance the antagonists are fighting for "the public good". Everyone has deemed it wise to get into the conservation act, and everyone claims to be conserving the right thing. The acceptance of the basic idea of conservation is a sign of the success of the movement.

Stewart L. Udall in "Collier's Yearbook", 1967

IV The American People and their Institutions

Analysis of the American Character

The American is optimistic, takes for granted that his is the best of all countries, the happiest and most virtuous of all societies, and that the best is yet to be. He lives, therefore, much in the future, makes ambitious plans, thinks nothing beyond his powers, has boundless faith in each new generation. It is commonly said that America is a young country. That is only partially true, but it is certainly true that it is, above all others, a country made for young people, a paradise for children—at least for children who have the good fortune to be Nordic.°

This optimism, and what we must call innocence, has its drawbacks. The corollary of the feeling that America is superior is the assumption that other nations and peoples are inferior. This assumption goes back to the early days of the Republic, when it was almost an article of faith among Jeffersonians. In our own time it has found support in the high standard of material prosperity which Americans enjoy and in our fortunate freedom from what we call "power politics". We tend to ascribe to our own genius much that is in fact ascribable to the bounty of nature and the accident of geography. Lowell's famous complaint that the nineteenth-century English displayed a "certain condescension toward foreigners" might be echoed now by most European people when thinking of Americans. It cannot be denied that there is a tendency among Americans to equate plumbing and kitchen fixtures with civilization.

This is natural enough, for American culture is predominantly material, its thinking quantitative, its genius inventive, experimental and practical. The American tends to compute almost everything in numbers—even qualitative things. He takes pride in statistics of population growth, of college enrollment, of magazine circulation. He wants the highest office buildings, the largest number of telephones, the most books in his libraries.

This faith in numbers is often looked upon as naïve, sometimes as vulgar, by Europeans. It has its advantages. For the American wants the highest standard of living; he rejoices when another million children are at school. He can fight when outnumbered—as the history of the Confederacy testifies—but prefers to fight with the largest numbers and the best equipment.°

The American is ingenious and experimental. This is in part an inheritance from the frontier, in part a consequence of democracy. He likes to do old things in a new way, and the fact that something has never been done before seems to him a challenge rather than an obstacle. Wonderfully inventive in all merely mechanical matters, he is almost equally inventive in the realm of politics, social relationships, and war. There were antecedents, of course, but he largely invented the federal system, the written constitution, the constitutional convention, and the modern colonial system, and there are some who would insist that he took out the original patent on democracy. His willingness to experiment augurs well for international relations. No one person or people can claim authorship of international organization, but none will deny that Woodrow Wilson was chiefly responsible for the League of Nations and Franklin Roosevelt for the United Nations.

The American is, too, intensely practical. He is the born enemy of all abstractions, all theories and doctrines. Benjamin Franklin is his favorite philosopher and, after him, William James, who asserted that it was only minds debauched by learning that ever suspected common sense of not being true. He requires that everything serve a practical purpose—religion, education, culture, science, philosophy.°

This trait, also, is regarded by many Europeans as deplorable, but it has its points. It means that philosophy has been used for practical purposes. Pragmatism, the most characteristic of American philosophies, is the obvious example. Even more interesting, however, is the Americanization of Idealism or Transcendentalism. That philosophy, which in Germany, and even in England, lent itself to the cultivation of individual salvation and to conservatism and even reaction, became in America a powerful instrument for social reform. It means that education has broken away from its classical mold and been required to serve the needs of society. It means that religious leaders have abandoned theology for humanitarianism. It means that in the realm of politics the American will not waste his vote on third parties; will not follow the will-o'-the-wisp of speculative theories.

Every foreigner laments that there are no discernible differences between the Democratic and the Republican Parties, but Americans know instinctively that parties are organizations to run the government, not to advance theoretical principles, and the American party system is, along with the British, the most efficient in the world. American practicality extends into the fields of international relations. Americans want an international organization that can function efficiently, regardless of abstract questions of sovereignty. They are interested in its practical activities—in relief, in science and education, in the suppression of civil war and disorder—and they judge any organization by its immediate effectiveness.

Yet the American record here is not wholly encouraging, and some of the difficulties of present-day international relations—to say nothing of the fiasco of the League of Nations—are traceable to qualities in the American character. The American is accustomed not only to success, but to speedy success. He is something of a perfectionist, and he is not patient. As he has solved his own problems of Federal relation, he is inclined to think that the problems of international relations are equally simple, and to ascribe the failure of international organizations, whether imperial or world, to a natural depravity in foreigners.°

Americans who were, in the past, fierce nonconformists, are coming increasingly to demand conformity. In a hundred ways—in speech, dress, manners, food, furnishing—America is becoming more and more uniform and standardized. The demand for conformity is extending even to things of the mind—witness the interest in loyalty oaths, in patriotic clichés, in agreement on political and even economic fundamentals. All this is in part the result of recent pressures, which always tend to squeeze out the eccentric, and in part, the result of growing stability in society and economy.

Along with individualism, and related to it, goes carelessness and lawlessness. The American is careless about speech, dress and manners, about tradition, precedent and law, about the rights of others. He is careless, too, about larger things—about natural resources, for example, or about honesty in politics or in business. This carelessness is, doubtless, a trait of youth; it may be doubted whether a United States that has achieved world leadership can continue to indulge itself in it.°

There is an undeniable strain of vulgarity in the American character—vulgarity which can be seen at its worst in advertisements, in the movies, and on the radio and television. There is a strain of lawlessness which can be traced in the statistics of police courts or can be noted by anyone who cares to check on traffic violations.° There has been a gradual decline in the standards of sportsmanship; there has been a gradual growth in class-consciousness and snobbery; there has been an alarming increase in intolerance.

What does all this add up to, so far as the role of America in world affairs is concerned? What emerges most impressively are the positive traits. The American is optimistic, experimental, practical, intelligent, mature, generous, democratic and individualistic. He has heretofore fulfilled his responsibilities and can be expected to do so in the future. He has, in the last analysis, little confidence in other countries—except Britain—little confidence in their ability, their intelligence, or their good will. He is therefore inclined to think that the rest of the world will have to follow American leadership—not primarily because America is so rich and powerful, but because the American way is the sensible, practical and right way.

Henry St. Commager in "American Colloquy", 1963

Blending Many Strains into a Single Nationality

Oscar Handlin has said, "Once I thought to write a history of the immigrants in America. Then I discovered that the immigrants were American history." In the same sense, we cannot really speak of a particular "immigrant contribution" to America because all Americans have been immigrants or the descendants of immigrants; even the Indians as mentioned before migrated to the American continent. We can only speak of people whose roots in America are older or newer. Yet each wave of immigration left its own imprint on American society; each made its distinctive "contribution" to the building of the nation and the evolution of American life. Indeed, if, as

Cowboy   31 American Indian   32 Negro Worker   33 Albert Einstein   34 Minoru Yamasaki

some of the older immigrants like to do, we were to restrict the definition of immigrants to the 42 million people who came to the United States *after* the Declaration of Independence, we would have to conclude that our history and our society would have been vastly different if they all had stayed at home.

As we have seen, people migrated to the United States for a variety of reasons. But nearly all shared two great hopes: the hope for personal freedom and the hope for economic opportunity. In consequence, the impact of immigration has been broadly to confirm the impulses in American life demanding more political liberty and more economic growth.

So, of the fifty-six signers of the Declaration of Independence, eighteen were of non-English stock and eight were first-generation immigrants. Two immigrants—the West Indian Alexander Hamilton, who was Washington's Secretary of the Treasury, and the Swiss Albert Gallatin, who held the same office under Jefferson—established the financial policies of the young republic.° Every ethnic minority, in seeking its own freedom, helped strengthen the fabric of liberty in American life.

Similarly, every aspect of the American economy has profited from the contributions of immigrants. We all know, of course, about the spectacular immigrant successes: the men who came from foreign lands, sought their fortunes in the United States and made striking contributions, industrial and scientific, not only to their chosen country but to the entire world. In 1953 the President's Commission on Immigration and Naturalization mentioned the following:

Industrialists: Andrew Carnegie (Scot), in the steel industry; John Jacob Astor (German), in the fur trade; Michael Cudahy (Irish), of the meat-packing industry; the Du Ponts (French), of the munitions and chemical industry; Charles L. Fleischmann (Hungarian), of the yeast business; David Sarnoff (Russian), of the radio industry; and William S. Knudsen (Danish), of the automobile industry.

Scientists and inventors: Among those whose genius has benefited the United States are Albert Einstein (German), in physics; Michael Pupin (Serbian), in electricity; Enrico Fermi (Italian), in atomic research; John Ericsson (Swedish), who invented the iron-clad ship and the screw propeller; Giuseppe Bellanca (Italian) and Igor Sikorsky (Russian), who made outstanding contributions to airplane development; John A. Udden (Swedish), who was responsible for opening the Texas oil fields; Lucas P. Kyrides (Greek), industrial chemistry; David Thomas (Welsh), who invented the hot blast furnace; Alexander Graham Bell (Scot), who invented the telephone; Conrad Hubert (Russian), who invented the flashlight; and Ottmar Mergenthaler (German), who invented the linotype machine.

But the anonymous immigrant played his indispensable role too. Between 1880 and 1920 America became the industrial and agricultural giant of the world as well as the world's leading creditor nation. This could not have been done without the hard labor, the technical skills and the entrepreneurial ability of the 23.5 million people who came to America in this period.

Significant as the immigrant role was in politics and in the economy, the immigrant contribution to the professions and the arts was perhaps even greater. Charles O. Paulin's analysis of the *Dictionary of American Biography* shows that, of the eighteenth- and nineteenth-century figures, 20 percent of the businessmen, 20 percent of the scholars and scientists, 23 percent of the painters, 24 percent of the engineers, 28 percent of the architects, 29 percent of the clergymen, 46 percent of the musicians and 61 percent of the actors were of foreign birth—a remarkable measure of the impact of immigration on American culture. And not only have many American writers and artists themselves been immigrants or the children of immigrants, but immigration has provided American literature with one of its major themes.

Perhaps the most pervasive influence of immigration is to be found in the innumerable details of life and the customs and habits brought by millions of people who never became famous. This impact was felt from the bottom up, and these contributions to American institutions may be the ones which most intimately affect the lives of all Americans.

In the area of religion, all the major American faiths were brought to this country from abroad. The multiplicity of sects established the American tradition of religious pluralism and assured to all the freedom of worship and separation of church and state pledged in the Bill of Rights.

So, too, in the very way we speak, immigration has altered American life. In greatly enriching the American vocabulary, it has been a major force in establishing "the American language," which, as H. L. Mencken demonstrated thirty years ago, had diverged materially from the mother tongue as spoken in Britain.

Even the American dinner table has felt the impact. One writer has suggested that "typical American menus" might include some of the following dishes: Irish stew, chop suey, goulash, chile con carne, ravioli, knackwurst mit sauerkraut, Yorkshire pudding, Welsh rarebit, borsch, gefilte fish, Spanish omelet, caviar, mayonnaise, antipasto, baumkuchen, English muffins, Gruyère cheese, Danish pastry, Canadian bacon, hot tamales, wiener schnitzel, petits fours, spumone, bouillabaisse, maté, scones, Turkish coffee, minestrone, filet mignon.

Immigration plainly was not always a happy experience. It was hard on the newcomers, and hard as well on the communities to which they came. When poor, ill-educated and frightened people disembarked in a strange land, they often fell prey to native racketeers, unscrupulous businessmen and cynical politicians. Boss Tweed said, characteristically, in defense of his own depredations in New York in the 1870s, "This population is too hopelessly split into races and factions to govern it under universal suffrage, except by bribery of patronage, or corruption."

But the very problems of adjustment and assimilation presented a challenge to the American idea—a challenge which subjected that idea to stern testing and eventually brought out the best qualities in American society. Thus the public school became a powerful means of preparing the newcomers for American life. The ideal of the "melting pot" symbolized the process of blending many strains into a single nationality, and we have come to realize in modern times that the "melting pot" need not mean the end of particular ethnic identities or traditions. Only in the case of the Negro has the melting pot failed to bring a minority into the full stream of American life. Today we are belatedly, but resolutely, engaged in ending this condition of national exclusion and shame and abolishing forever the concept of second-class citizenship in the United States.

John F. Kennedy, "A Nation of Immigrants", 1964

Condition and Fate of the American Indian

From time to time over the years, since long before the frigid Plains winter of 1890 when United States forces armed with Hotchkiss machine guns mowed down men, women, children and some of their own soldiers in the final slaughter at Wounded Knee, the Congress of the United States has become guiltily concerned about the condition and fate of the native American Indian. The most recent manifestation of that concern is the House of Representatives Bill 10560, also known as the Indian Resources Development Act of 1967.°

If enacted, the bill would allow the Indians greater freedom in selling, mortgaging, and developing what lands they still possess, encourage them through Government loans to bring industry to the reservations, and enable them with the approval of the Interior Department's Bureau of Indian Affairs to obtain loans from private sources. Indians in general, after years of bitter experience with Congressional maneuvers and of watching the depletion of their lands despite Federal largesse, are wary of the bill's benevolence, but most of their tribal councils have chosen to go along with it, chiefly because they hope that this time around the economic provisions will really work and because they figure that this is as good a bill as they can get at this time.°

The ever-diminishing land is almost the sole source of subsistence for the inhabitants of the Pine Ridge Reservation—or, more colorfully, the Land of Red Cloud—which is the seventh largest of the 300-odd reservations in the United States. It stretches for 90 miles east from the Black Hills and about 50 miles from the northern Badlands south to the Nebraska line.

In the eastern part some of the land is fertile enough to bear wheat, oats, safflower and the like, but 99 per cent of this farm land is now and forever in the hands of the white man. The rest of the reservation consists of rolling short-grass prairie land, an enormous landscape divided into four parts: endless green grass, tall blue sky, low ridges of ponderosa pine, and a constant rustling, sighing wind. Through these great plains wander cottonwood-shaded creeks such as Bear in the Lodge, Potato, Wounded Knee, and the twisted White and Cheyenne Rivers. In the summer, thunderclouds build up towers on the far horizons and the uninhibited sun may produce temperatures of 120 degrees; in the winter, the creeks become ice and blizzard winds such as those that froze the bodies at the massacre of Wounded Knee into such baroque and unusual shapes can bring the thermometer down to 40 below.°

There are miles and miles of good black-top roads kept in repair by Indians working for the Interior Department road service; and there are miles and miles of roads that are no good at all. There are modern boarding schools exclusively for Indian children as well as local public schools and a Catholic mission school, outlying clinics and a good free hospital with doctors, surgeons, dentists and a psychiatrist. There are churches of all kinds (40 per cent of the Indians profess to be Catholics and more to be Protestants, but the old beliefs still lie heavily in their souls).° Nearly all of the Sioux (or Dakotas, their own pre-reservation name for themselves) speak English as well as their native Lakota dialect, and there are still a few medicine men around.° The center of nearly everything—government, society, law and order, education—is Pine Ridge, a town of 1,256 people close enough to the state line to have a "suburb" in Nebraska, Whiteclay, center of shopping (three supermarkets) and entertainment (bars and dance halls).

On this reservation live, in one fashion or another, nearly 10.000 Teton Sioux of the Oglala tribe. They are not the poorest nor the richest of the country's Indians. The Hopis and some of the Apaches of the Southwest are poorer, and the inhabitants of the Aguacaliente reservation in Southern California, who more or less own Palm Springs, are richer, to say nothing of those few tribes that have oil wells. But the Oglalas range from a state of imminent starvation to fair affluence.°
  "Sioux" is short for "Nadowessioux", which is French for "Nadowessi", which is Chippewa meaning "little snakes" or, in other words, treacherous enemies. The Sioux fought everybody—the Chippewa, the Crow, the Cheyenne, the Kiowa and the white man after he came pushing onto the plains, stealing, pushing, lying, slaughtering the buffalo, always pushing.°
  After all that misery, bravery, and bloodshed, the Sioux, romanticized by the white man, became the Ideal Indian, the Mounted Warrior in War Bonnet, the End of the Trail, the Indian at the Medicine Show, the All-American Buffalo-Nickel Indian.
  The last treaty the Sioux made with the United States Government (1868—69) set aside nearly half of South Dakota, including the Sacred Black Hills, and part of North Dakota as the "Great Sioux Reserve". But white men discovered gold in the Black Hills,° so an Act of Congress in 1877 removed the Black Hills from the Indians' reserve. Later, another act divided what was left of the "Great Sioux Reserve" into five reservations with still more loss of land, settling the Oglalas at Pine Ridge. It is no wonder, indeed, that the Indian leaders look twice and twice again at Acts of Congress.°
  The chief complaints they have against the Government were that the Government treated them like digits instead of human beings, that it didn't understand the Indians' attachment to their people and their land, and that the Indians themselves didn't yet understand the white man's notion of business and money and private property. "We're not ready to be let out on our own", Johnson Holy Rock had told them, "but treat us like people instead of numbers".
  I remarked that all of us, not just the Indians, were victims of the official digital computer, that we were all cards full of little holes. "We've given up", I said, but this time he didn't understand, because he means to go right on trying to keep his people what they are, more so than any other Americans I know—human beings.
  Calvin Kentfield in "The New York Times Magazine", 1967

The First Vote against Slavery

This is to the monthly meeting held at Richard Worrell's:
  These are the reasons why we are against the traffic of men-body, as followeth: Is there any that would be done or handled at this manner? viz., to be sold or made a slave for all the time of his life? How fearful and faint-hearted are many at sea, when they see a strange vessel, being afraid it should be a Turk, and they should be taken, and sold for slaves into Turkey. Now, what is *this* better done, than Turks do? Yea, rather it is worse for them, which say they are Christians; for we hear that the most part of such negers are brought hither against their will and consent, and that many of them are stolen. Now, though they are black, we cannot conceive there is more liberty

to have them slaves, as [than] it is to have other white ones. There is a saying, that we should do to all men like as we will be done ourselves; making no difference of what generation, descent, or colour they are. And those who steal or rob men, and those who buy or purchase them, are they not all alike? Here is liberty of conscience, which is right and reasonable; here ought to be likewise liberty of the body, except of evil-doers, which is another case. But to bring men hither, or to rob and sell them against their will, we stand against. In Europe, there are many oppressed for conscience-sake; and here there are those oppressed which are of a black colour. And we who know that men must not commit adultery—some do commit adultery *in* others, separating wives from their husbands, and giving them to others: and some sell the children of these poor creatures to other men. Ah! do consider well this thing, you who do it, if you would be done at this manner—and if it is done according to Christianity! You surpass Holland and Germany in this thing. This makes an ill report in all those countries of Europe, where they hear of [it], that the Quakers do here handel men as they handel there the cattle. And for that reason some have no mind or inclination to come hither. And who shall maintain this your cause, or plead for it? Truly, we cannot do so, except you shall inform us better hereof, viz.: that Christians have liberty to practise these things. Pray, what thing in the world can be done worse towards us, than if men should rob or steal us away, and sell us for slaves to strange countries; separating husbands from their wives and children. Being now this is not done in the manner we would be done at; therefore, we contradict, and are against this traffic of men-body. And we who profess that it is not lawful to steal, must, likewise, avoid to purchase such things as are stolen, but rather help to stop this robbing and stealing, if possible. And such men ought to be delivered out of the hands of the robbers, and set free as in Europe. Then is Pennsylvania to have a good report, instead, it hath now a bad one, for this sake, in other countries; Especially whereas the Europeans are desirous to know in what manner *the Quakers* do rule in *their* province; and most of them do look upon us with an envious eye. But if this is done well, what shall we say is done evil?

If once these slaves (which they say are so wicked and stubborn men,) should join themselves—fight for their freedom, and handel their masters and mistresses, as they did handel them before; will these masters and mistresses take the sword at hand and war against these poor slaves, like, as we are able to believe, some will not refuse to do? Or, have these poor negers not as much right to fight for their freedom, as you have to keep them slaves?

Now consider well this thing, if it is good or bad. And in case you find it to be good to handel these blacks in that manner, we desire and require you hereby lovingly, that you may inform us herein, which at this time never was done, viz., that Christians have such a liberty to do so. To the end we shall be satisfied on this point, and satisfy likewise our good friends and acquaintances in our native country, to whom it is a terror, or fearful thing, that men should be handelled so in Pennsylvania.

This is from our meeting at Germantown, held y^e 18th of the 2d month, 1688, to be delivered to the monthly meeting at Richard Worrell's.

Garret Henderich, Derick op de Graeff,
Francis Daniel Pastorius, Abram op de Graeff.
"*American History told by Contemporaries*", II, [6]1950

35 The Funeral Procession
of Martin Luther King

For Freedom and Equality

The last half century has seen crucial changes in the life of the American Negro. The social upheavals of the two world wars, the great depression, and the spread of the automobile have made it both possible and necessary for the Negro to move away from his former isolation on the rural plantation. The decline of agriculture and the parallel growth of industry have drawn large numbers of Negroes to urban centers and brought about a gradual improvement in their economic status. New contacts have led to a broadened outlook and new possibilities for educational advance. All of these factors have conjoined to cause the Negro to take a fresh look at himself. His expanding life experiences have created within him a consciousness that he is an equal element in a larger social compound and accordingly should be given rights and privileges commensurate with his new responsibilities. Once plagued with a tragic sense of inferiority resulting from the crippling effects of slavery and segregation, the Negro has now been driven to reëvaluate himself. He has come to feel that he is somebody. His religion reveals to him that God loves all His children and that the important thing about a man is not "his specificity but his fundamentum"—not the texture of his hair or the color of his skin but his eternal worth to God.

This growing self-respect has inspired the Negro with a new determination to struggle and sacrifice until first-class citizenship becomes a reality.°

Along with the Negro's changing image of himself has come an awakening moral consciousness on the part of millions of white Americans concerning segregation. Ever since the signing of the Declaration of Independence, America has manifested a schizophrenic personality on the question of race. She has been torn between selves— a self in which she has proudly professed democracy and a self in which she has sadly practiced the antithesis of democracy. The reality of segregation, like slavery, has always had to confront the ideals of democracy and Christianity. Indeed, segregation and discrimination are strange paradoxes in a nation founded on the principle that all men are created equal. This contradiction has disturbed the consciences of whites both North and South, and has caused many of them to see that segregation is basically evil.

Climaxing this process was the Supreme Court's decision outlawing segregation in the public schools. For all men of good will May 17, 1954, marked a joyous end to the long night of enforced segregation. In unequivocal language the Court affirmed that "separate but equal" facilities are inherently unequal, and that to segregate a child on the basis of his race is to deny that child equal protection of the law. This decision brought hope to millions of disinherited Negroes who had formerly dared only to dream of freedom. It further enhanced the Negro's sense of dignity and gave him even greater determination to achieve justice.°

But it is still not too late to act. Every crisis has both its dangers and opportunities. It can spell either salvation or doom. In the present crisis America can achieve either racial justice or the ultimate social psychosis that can only lead to domestic suicide. The democratic ideal of freedom and equality will be fulfilled for all—or all human beings will share in the resulting social and spiritual doom. In short, this crisis has the potential for democracy's fulfillment or fascism's triumph; for social progress or retrogression. We can choose either to walk the high road of human brotherhood or to tread the low road of man's inhumanity to man.

History has thrust upon our generation an indescribably important destiny—to complete a process of democratization which our nation has too long developed too slowly, but which is our most powerful weapon for world respect and emulation. How we deal with this crucial situation will determine our moral health as individuals, our cultural health as a region, our political health as a nation, and our prestige as a leader of the free world. The future of America is bound up with the solution of the present crisis. The shape of the world today does not permit us the luxury of a faltering democracy. The United States cannot hope to attain the respect of the vital and growing colored nations of the world unless it remedies its racial problems at home. If America is to remain a first-class nation, it cannot have a second-class citizenship.

A solution of the present crisis will not take place unless men and women work for it. Human progress is neither automatic nor inevitable. Even a superficial look at history reveals that no social advance rolls in on the wheels of inevitability. Every step toward the goal of justice requires sacrifice, suffering, and struggle; the tireless exertions and passionate concern of dedicated individuals. Without persistent effort, time itself becomes an ally of the insurgent and primitive forces of irrational emotionalism and social destruction. This is no time for apathy or complacency. This is a time for vigorous and positive action.

Martin Luther King, "Stride toward Freedom", 1958

Black Power

I first met Stokely Carmichael in the deep South when he was just another non-violent kid, marching and talking and getting his head whipped. This time now seems as far behind us as the Flood, and if those suffering, gallant, betrayed boys and girls who were then using their bodies in an attempt to save a heedless nation have since concluded that the nation is not worth saving, no American alive has the right to be surprised—to put the matter as mildly as it can possibly be put. Actually, Americans are not at all surprised; they exhibit all the vindictiveness of the guilty; what happened to those boys and girls, and what happened to the Civil Rights movement, is an indictment of America and Americans, and an enduring monument which we will not outlive, to the breath-taking cowardice of this sovereign people.

Naturally, the current in which we all were struggling threw Stokely and me together from time to time—it threw many people together including, finally, Martin Luther King and Malcolm X. America sometimes resembles, at least from the point of view of the black man, an exceedingly monotonous minstrel show; the same dances, same music, same jokes. One has done (or been) the show so long that one can do it in one's sleep. So it was not in the least surprising for me to encounter (one more time) the American surprise when Stokely—as Americans allow themselves the luxury of supposing—coined the phrase "Black Power". He didn't coin it. He simply dug it up again from where it's been lying since the first slaves hit the gang-plank.

36 Harlem

I have never known a Negro in all my life who was not obsessed with Black Power. Those representatives of White Power who are not too hopelessly brain-washed or eviscerated will understand that the only way for a black man in America not to be obsessed with the problem of how to control his destiny and protect his house, his women and his children, is for that black man to become in his own mind the something less than a man which this republic, alas, has always considered him to be. And when a black man, whose destiny and identity have always been controlled by others, decides and states that he will control his own destiny and rejects the identity given to him by others, he is talking revolution.

In point of sober fact, he cannot possibly be talking anything else, and nothing is more revelatory of the American hypocrisy than their swift perception of this fact. The "white backlash" is meaningless twentieth-century jargon designed at once to hide and to justify the fact that most white Americans are still unable to believe that the black man is a man—in the same way that we speak of a "credibility gap" because we are too cowardly to face the fact that our leaders have been lying to us for years. Perhaps we suspect that we deserve the contempt with which we allow ourselves to be treated.°

Now, I may not always agree with Stokely's views, or the ways in which he expresses them. My agreement, or disagreement, is absolutely irrelevant. I get his message. Stokely Carmichael, a black man under 30, is saying to me, a black man over 40, that he will not live the life I've lived, or be corralled into some of the awful choices I have been forced to make, and he is perfectly right. The Government and the people who have made his life, and mine, and the lives of all our forefathers, and the lives of all our brothers and sisters and women and children an indescribable hell has no right now, to penalise the black man, this so-despised stranger here for so long, for attempting to discover if the world is as small as the Americans have told him it is. And the political implications involve nothing more and nothing less than what the Western world takes to be its material self-interest.

I need scarcely state to what extent the Western self-interest and the black self-interest find themselves at war, but it is precisely this message which the Western nations, and this one above all, will have to accept if they expect to survive. Nothing is more unlikely than that the Western nations, and this one above all, will be able to welcome so vital a metamorphosis. We have constructed a history which is a total lie, and have persuaded ourselves that it is true. I seriously doubt that anything worse can happen to any people.

One doesn't need a Stokely gloating in Havana about the hoped-for fall of the United States, and to attempt to punish him for saying what so many millions of people feel is simply to bring closer, and make yet more deadly, the terrible day. One should listen to what's being said, and reflect on it, for many, many millions of people long for our downfall, and it is not because they are Communists. It is because ignorance is in the saddle here, and we ride mankind. Let us attempt to face the fact that we are a racist society, racist to the very marrow, and we are fighting a racist war. No black man in chains in his own country, and watching the many deaths occurring around him every day, believes for a moment that America cares anything at all about the freedom of Asia. My own condition, as a black man in America, tells me what Americans really feel and really want, and tells me who they really are. And, therefore, every bombed village is my home town.

That, in a way, is what Stokely is saying, and that's why this youth can so terrify a nation. He's saying the bill is in, the party's over, are we going to live here like men or not? Bombs won't pay this bill, and bombs won't wipe it out. And Stokely did not begin his career with dreams of terror but with dreams of love. Now he's saying, and he's not alone, and he's not the first, if I can't live here, well then, neither will you. You couldn't have built it without me; this land is also mine, we'll share it, or we'll perish, and I don't care.

I do care—about Stokely's life, my country's life. One's seen too much already of gratuitous destruction; one hopes, always, that something will happen in the human heart which will change our common history. But if it doesn't happen, this something, if this country cannot hear and cannot change, then we, the blacks, the most despised children of the great Western house, are simply forced, with both pride and despair, to remember that we come from a long line of runaway slaves who managed to survive without passports.

James Baldwin in "Manchester Guardian Weekly", 1968

Excerpts from the National Advisory Commission's Report on Civil Disorders

On July 28, 1967, the President of the United States established this commission and directed us to answer three basic questions: What happened? Why did it happen? What can be done to prevent it from happening again?

To respond to these questions, we have undertaken a broad range of studies and investigations. We have visited the riot cities; we have heard many witnesses; we have sought the counsel of experts across the country.

This is our basic conclusion: our nation is moving toward two societies, one black, one white—separate and unequal.

Reaction to last summer's disorders has quickened the movement and deepened the division. Discrimination and segregation have long permeated much of American life; they now threaten the future of every American.

This deepening racial division is not inevitable. The movement apart can be reversed. Choice is still possible. Our principal task is to define that choice and to press for a national resolution.

To pursue our present course will involve the continuing polarization of the American community and, ultimately, the destruction of basic democratic values.

The alternative is not blind repression or capitulation to lawlessness. It is the realization of common opportunities for all within a single society.

This alternative will require a commitment to national action—compassionate, massive and sustained, backed by the resources of the most powerful and the richest nation on this earth. From every American it will require new attitudes, new understanding, and, above all, new will.

The vital needs of the nation must be met; hard choices must be made, and, if necessary, new taxes enacted.

Violence cannot build a better society, disruption and disorder nourish repression, not justice. They strike at the freedom of every citizen. The community cannot—it will not—tolerate coercion and mob rule.

Violence and destruction must be ended—in the streets of the ghetto and the lives of people.

Segregation and poverty have created in the racial ghetto a destructive environment totally unknown to most white Americans.

What white Americans have never fully understood—but what the negro can never forget—is that white society is deeply implicated in the ghetto. White institutions created it, white institutions maintain it, and white society condones it.

It is time now to turn with all the purpose at our command to the major unfinished business of this nation. It is time to adopt strategies for action that will produce quick and visible progress. It is time to make good the promises of American democracy to all citizens—urban and rural, white and black, Spanish-surname, American Indian, and every minority group.

Our recommendations embrace three basic principles:

5 To mount programs on a scale equal to the dimension of the problems.

To aim these programs for high impact in the immediate future in order to close the gap between promise and performance.

To undertake new initiatives and experiments that can change the system of failure and frustration that now dominates the ghetto and weakens our society.

10 These programs will require unprecedented levels of funding and performance, but they neither probe deeper nor demand more than the problems which called them forth. There can be no higher priority for national action and no higher claim on the nation's conscience.

"Wireless Bulletin from Washington", 1968

Principles of American Higher Education

15 Under the American democratic political system each individual plays a part in determining social policies and through his vote each tells the government what actions to take. Hence it is important that all receive as broad a general education as possible so that their decisions on public affairs will be illuminated by reliable knowledge. Throughout American higher education, therefore, there is a component of general
20 studies to supplement the specialised knowledge and skills cultivated in professional courses of study. Instruction in science and technology is accompanied by courses in the humanistic subjects and in the social sciences. Instruction in philosophy, history, literature, and the arts provide the student with the understanding of himself required in a society in which each person determines his own destiny as a human being, in
25 contrast to a social order in which the state makes the major decisions. Studies in sociology, political science, and economics provide an understanding of the social forces which shape a culture, and give the student the essential knowledge on the basis of which he can influence the development and improvement of the society in which he lives. They also introduce the student to other cultures and other political
30 systems than his own in other parts of the world and thus prepare him to understand the international scene in an objective manner.

Later, this approach to higher education was rationalised in an all-embracing philosophy of education by John Dewey, the dominant American philosopher at the turn of the century. The result of the spread of his doctrines has been a closer adaptation
35 of higher education to the emerging social and economic needs of society and a shift in emphasis away from the ancient and classical towards the modern and scientific. This philosophy of education has been responsible for the rapid growth of science and technology in America. But it has not impoverished the departments of philosophy and belles-lettres even in the universities where engineering and agriculture have
40 been most prominent. Many a state university has on its faculty the world's most learned scholars in literature and the other humanistic studies.

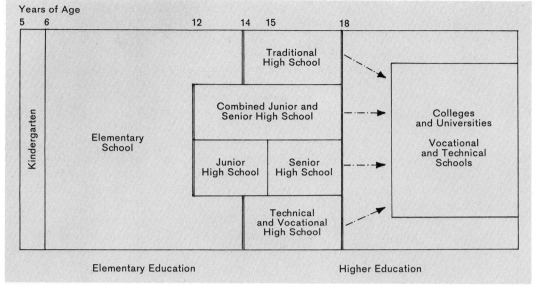

37 The Education System in the U.S.A.

John Dewey has had another basic influence on American higher education through his emphasis on *learning by doing*. He observed that students learned more and faster and retained their intellectual accomplishments longer if abstract learning was immediately reinforced by practical applications of the principles of the subject. This view led not only to the introduction of the activity movement in the lower schools, but also to the use of real life situations in the universities. In law, moot courts have been introduced. In sociology students have visited slum districts, courts, and welfare agencies. All branches of learning have been affected by this philosophy.

Earl J. McGrath in "*Higher Education in the United States*", 1964

American Colleges and Universities

American colleges are sometimes separate entities and sometimes the undergraduate units of the universities. Colleges and universities are largely residential and in recent decades more urban than rural. The colleges are basically concerned with humanistics, liberal education though inevitably involved in the careers of their students. They offer a four year curriculum drawn from the humanities and the natural and social sciences, and maintain a distinctive collegiate way of life. Universities which have several colleges and schools offer graduate and undergraduate programs.°

Students in these colleges normally take a series of courses combining concentration in one discipline and distribution over a wide field. The concentration may represent a career focus or an intellectual interest; the distribution is intended to make sure that the student has an introduction to the diverse areas of the humanities and the natural and social sciences. This planned dispersion of college students' academic interests sometimes seems to be superficial, but at the same time it may establish the broad foundation of interests which is requisite to an effective "liberal education in a free society".

Few students can go through college without some insight into the major areas of the civilised tradition and the predominant characteristics of contemporary society. Professional education, as in law or medicine, and scholarly concentration in any of the academic fields comes at the postgraduate level in the university. Graduate and undergraduate students are together on university campuses and share many common interests and facilities, but the life of the undergraduate in the liberal arts college is more distinctive to America.

American student life, although occupied with many extra-curricular activities, is also made up of a series of deadlines for assignments, tests, papers, examinations and research projects in contrast to the demands on students in most other countries who, typically, must face only final exams.

One evidence of this characteristic collegiate life lies in the dormitories and Student Unions which are to be found on almost every American college campus. About a third of the students live in dormitories, generally with one or several room-mates; additional students live in residential clubs or fraternities; others live at home or in lodgings away from the campus.

The dormitories and houses are important assets to the college. They have not only sleeping quarters and dining halls, but often they own libraries, television and radio installations, and recreational facilities. They are closely related to the Student Unions—bodies which provide offices for student organisations, additional dining facilities and recreational resources. Student Unions or Centres are living rooms for the campus, where students and professors meet in a wide variety of informal, but

38 Blackburn College, Carlinville, Ill., Campus

educative, sessions. Student Unions, managed by committees composed of students and faculty members, arrange art exhibitions, stage debates, hold conferences and concerts, schedule lectures by outside visitors. Many have a theatre, a swimming pool, and bedrooms for guests.

On most American campuses there will be more students attending events in the Student Unions each year than will be attending all the competitive athletic events of the college. Student Unions are a sort of informal "cultural and social department" of college life and they have great influence in the general education of the students. In a large number of colleges and universities there are many fraternities and sororities, which are really independent private clubs.°

The student learns history through academic classes but also through students' "history clubs", through campus lectures, through his individual reading, through participation in projects and clubs which are a part of the social process. But he is also continually faced with the problems of economies, even though these problems may be temporarily solved by scholarship grants. He has a considerable responsibility for his own living arrangements and for the scheduling of his life, even when surrounded by classes to attend and examinations to take.

His college and university years are an experience, not only in the pursuit of learning but also in responsible living, in the procedures of group action, in the debates and discussions of the democratic process. He faces the problems of participating in politics, of sharing in the infinite varieties of group living, of learning about matters dear to the world of scholars, of planning a career, of building friendships.

Howard E. Wilson in "Higher Education in the United States", 1964

Television in the U.S.A.

Some people may think that American television is one long series of commercials occasionally interrupted by a program. That is a bit unkind and slightly untrue. Television in the U.S.A. is much more like Caesar's Gaul. It is divided into three parts: commercial, instructional, and public. The 95 % of the population who own a TV set (20 % have two sets), have a wide programing choice in both color and black-and-white for anywhere from 10 to 20 hours a day.

Right now there are 787 stations on the air. They range across 3,000 miles from the Atlantic to the Pacific, and are allotted on the basis of population. Therefore, New York and Los Angeles have the largest number.

The group which grants these licenses is a Federal government agency called the Federal Communications Commission. It consists of seven commissioners appointed by the President, and they have the final say about who can operate a station and who cannot. Once a channel is assigned, it comes up for renewal every three years. If the owner follows the FCC rules, such as refraining from what is considered bad taste in program content, he generally has no trouble in keeping his license. Two other rules he must follow are letting both sides of a controversial question be heard, and giving equal time to political candidates for the same office during an election campaign.°

Since the FCC charges no fee—except a small filing fee—to the licensee, critics of the system have asked, "Isn't a TV license just a license to make money?" That is largely true when it comes to the 637 stations which are in the commercial domain. As in industry, they represent big business, they use big capital and they like to show a big profit. The only way they can make money is through selling time on their various programs to companies that want to advertise products to the viewers. The larger the audience, the more the stations can charge the sponsor. In fact, checking the size of the audience for a given program is so important that the stations engage rating services for just this purpose.

The toughest problem that commercial television has then is attracting viewers on a large scale. The men who run these stations have to figure out what captivates a mass audience. Catering to the majority means catering to people's desire to relax and be entertained. Programs and performers come and go depending not upon their intrinsic merit but upon what makes the majority tune in. Occasionally, quality and quantity go together. But it's the latter that counts.

What programs are most popular these days? The following in descending order: Movies—no matter what vintage. Sports events like professional football and baseball; wrestling has lost some of its appeal. Westerns—in series form on a once-week basis. Situation comedy series. Variety shows with plenty of popular singing and dancing into which an occasional bit of ballet and opera are slipped. Whodunits which feature violence and foul play. Quiz games played for big money prizes. Dramas as long as they don't last more than one hour.

The commercial stations also provide excellent public affairs programs such as panel discussions, interviews and documentaries. These are seldom shown in prime time (7 until 11 in the evening) because they usually receive a low rating—and that's no way to make a sponsor happy. Straight news programs which last from five to fifteen minutes are popular, however, as are live coverage of on-the-spot events like election returns, the Kennedy tragedy, launching of the first astronaut, and meetings at the United Nations during a particularly worrisome crisis.

The law does not permit any person or group to control more than 7 television stations for commercial use. Out of these, no more than 5 can be in the VHF (very high frequency) broadcasting band; the other two would have to be in the UHF (ultra high frequency) band.°

In spite of the 7-station limit, three commercial networks dominate national television. They are NBC—National Broadcasting Company; CBS—Columbia Broadcasting System; and ABC—American Broadcasting Company. They achieve their control through a system of affiliates. These are independently owned stations which ally themselves with one of the three networks during certain broadcasting hours so that they can be fed some of the major programs which they could not afford to produce on their own. Each network has a large block of these affiliated stations, creating a tremendous coast-to-coast sales medium for clients.

As a result, television is the leading outlet for advertising messages, surpassing newspapers and magazines by far. A show at a prime evening hour can attract as many as 70 million viewers. What other form of communication can offer that?

Not only has commercial television preempted the areas of advertising and mass entertainment, but it has taken over national and international news coverage as well.

It has more money to do this than the other media, although its handling of the news is often criticized as too limited and too shallow. People who like to be more fully informed get their bulletin-type news from television and radio, and their depth news from newspapers.

The press and television keep pointing this out in their disclaimers of rivalry. They insist that they supplement each other. But the fact remains—whether due to several recent prolonged newspaper strikes which may have gotten some people out of the habit of reading or whether due to people's preference for capsulated news as given on television—the number of newspapers in the United States is shrinking. In New York City alone, 4 out of 7 dailies have gone out of business in the past three years.

Since commercial television takes up so much room as a business-in-the-billions, what place is there for the other two types of television—the instructional and the public? Both fall into the category of non-profit television, and for this the FCC has made 623 allocations. Due to lack of funds, however, non-commercial video can only claim 150 stations, divided equally between UHF and VHF. As the total FCC reservations are for 116 VHF and 507 UHF, the future of non-profit TV lies in the path of UHF, reception of which is fortunately becoming increasingly available.

To define instructional television, a just published report on the subject says it is "programing which is directed at students in the classroom or otherwise within the general context of formal education". It not only uses the familiar VHF and UHF channels, but has access to closed-circuit receivers as well as a new frequency band of 2500-megacycles opened by the FCC in 1963. It reaches about 10 million students most of whom are in elementary schools. Its programing is not intended to replace standard methods of teaching—merely to supplement it. Should a teacher shortage become acute, however, who knows how far instructional TV would go?°

The area of television which is of deepest concern to thoughtful community leaders, however, is public television. Although under the umbrella of educational TV, it is much broader in concept. It has been defined as including "all that is of human interest and importance which is not at the moment appropriate or available for support by advertisers and which is not arranged for formal instruction". Among its features are documentaries on current political events, discussions of the arts, classical and serious modern dramas, concerts and operas, lectures on science, and lessons in such subjects as foreign languages, fine cooking and photography.

Not that many of these programs would fail to attract a mass audience as do the programs on commercial television. But sponsors are afraid to take a chance on what might be culture with a capital "C". The improvement of public opinion and the elevation of public taste are not their worry. Unless commercial TV takes a radical turn, only public TV will do this job.°

Perhaps as forthright a statement as any on the subject of television in the U.S.A. is this one from Thomas Hoving, Director of the Metropolitan Museum of Art and Chairman of the National Citizens Committee for Public Television. In urging greater cooperation between public and commercial broadcasters, he said, "Public broadcasting and commercial broadcasting are not meant to be enemies. If we want an enemy, we can share a common one: the shoddy, over-popular, banal, mediocre, rinky-dink, hand-me-down, Mickey Mouse pap of no quality, whether it exists on commercial, non-commercial, educational, public, cultural or any other kind of television".

Whether this sort of "pap" is a national characteristic of American television is a value judgment I wouldn't care to make since I happen to be a TV-Radio broadcaster myself. Naturally, I wouldn't want to think it was true.

As far as the viewers are concerned, they are not a captive audience. They can be guided by an astute critic like Jack Gould, TV-Radio Editor of the *New York Times*—a man who is referred to as "the conscience of broadcasting". Or they can switch their sets off altogether and take a walk, read a book or have a drink. But if they want to be reasonable, they will have to concede that television is a miraculous instrument about which they—according to their response—have the ultimate say.

Lee Graham, 1968, here first published in English

America—A Sports-loving Nation

Even the "winning of the West" was not all serious business. From the hard-driving cattle trade developed the rodeo, with its riding and roping for competition and relaxation.

Early in our history, man's tools against the wilderness were often only his hands and his rod and gun. In his rare leisure time he used his hands for wrestling, sometimes Indian style, more often in the classic forms indulged in by such confirmed heroes as Sam Houston and Abe Lincoln. With his rod and gun he turned the utilitarian business of getting food on the table into the sports that made a name for Annie Oakley and brought us the modern pleasure-time pursuits of trap, skeet and target shooting, hunting and fishing.

The utilitarian peach baskets of the growing fruit industry, when nailed high on gymnasium walls, became essential props for James Naismith's invention of basketball in 1891.

Nearly every development in the transportation industry brought a counterpart sport. The invention of the steamboat led to the great Mississippi River paddle-wheel boat races, ancestors of today's race for the blue ribbon that represents the fastest transoceanic passenger ship time to Europe. Railroad locomotives and entire trains vied for the best time to a specified finish line. With the invention of the internal

39 American Professional Football

combustion engine another score of sports activities got their start: auto races, transcontinental dashes, endurance contests, rallies; then races for airplane and auto speed records of distances as short as a measured mile or as long as around the world. Competitive Americans continue to seek challenges, and even now, (though probably only for a while) our goal is to be first on the moon.

The story of America at play is also the story of American creativity. New games have been created; games that are totally American, although sometimes deriving from other sports. Baseball finds its origins in English rounders; football in British rugby. The American games are now completely stylized, however, and no self-respecting rounders or rugby fan would see the faintest resemblance in these off-shoot sports.

Although baseball is called "the national pastime", the average amateur player is hard put to get together seventeen others and locate a regulation-size baseball field. Hence the development of softball. The softer ball used provides a margin of safety; the smaller playing field makes the real estate search simpler. Another growing offspring of standard baseball is Little League baseball, which even has its own hard-fought world series each year in Williamsport, Pennsylvania. Teams of young boys from all over the United States, and from as far as Japan, compete in the scaled-down sport.°

The relationship of television and professional athletics was strengthened with the purchase, in 1966, of the New York Yankees baseball team by the Columbia Broadcasting System.

So successful has professional football been in this country that a star college athlete can set himself up for life by playing football. In 1965, the New York Jets of the American Football League paid star University of Alabama quarterback Joe Namath a reported $ 400,000 for signing.

The football season culminates with the traditional Thanksgiving Day games between longtime rivals; the Yale-Harvard game; the Army-Navy game, which draws in excess of 100,000 fans to Philadelphia; and the bowl games, held about usually on New Year's Day. The most famous is the Rose Bowl game, which follows a civic parade of floral-decorated floats and draws 100,000 people to Pasadena's Rose Bowl, to see the top Pacific coast team tangle with the leading Midwestern eleven.

It was the enormous crowds drawn by college football that set the athletic department cash registers tinkling—and which today serve the important purpose of paying for most of the rest of the schools athletic program—usually subsidizing baseball, swimming, track und field, gymnastics, rowing, tennis, skiing, golf, boxing and wrestling.

In most cases, basketball pays its own way. In a number of small colleges noted for their basketball teams (and their acumen in acquiring student bodies with sufficient men over seven-feet tall), the game pays the way of the other sports. Basketball—college, professional, semi-professional and amateur—is America's most widely-attended indoor sport.

Of all the games that Americans play and watch, none is thought more typical of the country than baseball. The first game of baseball in history was played in 1839 at Cooperstown, New York. Abner Doubleday laid out the first baseball diamond for the cadets of the military school where he taught. The dimensions of the field set by Doubleday have remained the same to this day. In 1919, Cooperstown leased the ground where this first game was played and built the National Museum of Baseball and Hall of Fame, which contains names and memorabilia of the sport's past.°

Although Yankee Stadium epitomized the baseball park of the Ruth-Lou Gehrig era, one of the new wonders of the national pastime is the vast Astrodome, home of the Houston Astros baseball team. Being completely enclosed, it is the only stadium in which games can be played, conventions held and special entertainment provided in any weather and at any season of the year. Its mammoth air conditioning plant, plastic roof and synthetic grass amaze even the most blasé visitor.°

Amateur golf also enjoys a fantastic popularity in the United States. The golf course, at the country club level, remains one of the greatest excuses for doing business, exercising and keeping physically fit.°

A new sport, sky-diving—jumping out of an airplane with a parachute, executing certain maneuvers, delaying opening of the "chute" as long as possible and then hitting a target with a bull's-eye in the center—is becoming increasingly popular.

Bowling is one of our most popular and readily available amateur sports. Originally called nine-pins, it came under severe criticism as a game for ruffians and was restricted or banned by law in certain communities, especially on Sundays. Ingeniously, a pin was added, thus making ten pins which evaded the law and created the modern game.

Ivan T. Sanderson, "This Treasured Land", 1966

American Women

The American woman is often written about almost as though she belonged to a separate species. Both domestic and foreign observers seem to find her, among all the world's women, uniquely easy to characterize. Admirers as well as critics tend to agree that she can readily be identified anywhere, in a distinctive combination of most if not all of certain qualities, as: good-looking, youthful, energetic, capable, independent, restless, confused, frustrated, spoiled—lucky.

Whatever the truth of the image, the American woman is more vulnerable to this kind of cataloguing than other women if only because she has been in the vanguard of changes in human ideas and institutions which are so profound that men and women everywhere in the world are being shaken and stirred by them. American women have simply been conspicuous in a historical process in which their similarities to the other millions caught up in it are actually more important than their differences.

The right to self-determination, the dignity of the individual, the essential equality of all human beings: these are not just slogans or theories in the modern world but matters of passionate conviction. °All the old hierarchies are challenged by humanistic ideas, and modern science and technology seem to offer the means of making those ideas a reality. Women were bound to respond to this dynamic current, bound to take a fresh look at the roles which history and tradition, as well as biology, assigned to them.°

The women who first ventured into the American wilderness early in the 17th century and in the next 300 years took part in making it habitable had a clear idea of what was expected of them. It was an idea perhaps as old as the human race, and there is still ample evidence of its durability in many parts of the world. Both principle and practice seemed to make it plain that women were wholly subordinate to men, if not actually inferior in most respects, and that marriage and motherhood were the sum of their destiny and proper function. Rights and privileges were masculine concerns.°

The survival of such a view was challenged from the first by facts of existence which were sharply in conflict with it. As soon as the first settlers followed the explorers and adventurers, women were desperately wanted and needed in America. A group of the earliest Virginia colonists headed a list of "necessities" sent back to England with the category "wives", and as the frontier moved steadily westward, the supply of women never seemed to keep up with the demand. But it was far more than scarcity that enhanced women's value. The work they performed was at least as hard as a man's—and often included almost the same tasks.°

In a country where from the first there was obviously so much productive work to be done, respect for work—hard work of every kind—early became an American tradition which despite conventional ideas of propriety encouraged women to turn their hands to new kinds of jobs. At the same time, the country was long enriched by floods of immigrants coming to create new lives in "the land of opportunity". Women as well as men expected to work as hard as they were able to make the opportunity a reality. In their hope and faith that they would live better than their parents and that their children would live much more fully than they had, they helped set in motion the vital current of aspiration in American life.

But the feelings about women underlying the conventional ideas of the 19th century continued to be a powerful influence. They determined that most working women should enter only certain occupations, and particularly those—such as textile and garment manufacturing and teaching—with some ostensible relationship to their traditional tasks. They determined that most married women would still devote themselves exclusively to family life. For all the strength of the countervailing forces, the conventional ideas also persisted with remarkable vigor, and by a relatively small group of women in the 19th century were felt as an intolerable burden. These were the women who sought a place for themselves in higher education and professional careers and who fought for civil and political equality with men. In their own time they had to contend with ridicule, hostility, and their own doubts and dismay, but they are honored today for their part in opening to other women so many new doors.°

In the years leading up to the Civil War, women were among the most active and outspoken advocates of the abolition of slavery, and many of them linked the emancipation of the slave to their own cause. Their disappointment was bitter when the franchise was extended after the war only to all males of 21 and over.

It is a fact, however, that American women in one part of the country were apparently the first in the world to win equal voting rights with men. Thanks largely to the efforts of one determined woman, a large, plain-spoken, warmly witty storekeeper's wife named Esther Morris, they were granted the franchise in the territory of Wyoming in 1869, voted in 1870, and even began to serve on juries.°

The process completed in 1920 with her enfranchisement opened up to the American woman a vast new range of basic choices. The changes that have occurred since have given her, in sum, far more time, more strength, more money, and more incentives of various other kinds to see what those choices mean to her.°

On the educational scene, girls have continued to outstrip boys as high school diploma-winners, although as completion rates for both sexes have soared, the boys

have almost closed the gap. Men have made proportionally greater advances in higher education, but women have chosen higher education, too, in growing numbers. Since 1920, enrollment of women in colleges and universities has quadrupled, and they now earn more than a third of all the bachelor's degrees, almost a third of the master's de-
5 grees, and about a tenth of the doctorates. Several colleges and universities have recently begun programs designed particularly for women whose education or creative work was interrupted by family responsibilities.°

Anyone riding a rush-hour bus in America today will be struck by the utterly accustomed look of all the women going to or from their jobs. They have gone on choosing
10 to work for pay in increasing proportions. Some 24,000,000 of them, more than a third of the women of working age, are job-holders, and they make up a third of the labor force. Most striking has been the choice made by more and more wives and mothers to combine jobs with family life. More than half the women working today are married. No other alternative to work would even occur to an able-bodied single woman, and
15 girls just out of school think nothing of going off alone to distant cities—distant countries—to take promising jobs. The more education a woman has, the more likely she is to be at work, and more than half the women college graduates are employed.°

Goodlooking, youthful, energetic, capable, independent, restless, confused, frustrated, spoiled, lucky. This was the inventory we considered at the beginning of this
20 glance at the record. American women (and men) would cheerfully accept the complimentary half of it, with the thought that as a sweeping generalization it is probably more accurate than not. Most of them would be inclined to agree that, in the relative ease, comfort and freedom of their lives, they are indeed lucky to be women in America. Spoiled? While the circumstances of their lives obviously no longer call for the heroism
25 of their pioneer great-grandmothers, a fair judgment must find that the overwhelming majority are no less anxious to make responsible, useful lives as best they know how.

Restless, confused, frustrated? Sometimes, no doubt, they seem so. As millions of other women in the world are discovering, the new choices that change means are not always easy to make, and uncertainty is a price to be paid—willingly—for new freedom
30 to discover one's best und truest self.

Malissa Redfield in "American Women"

The Macbeth Murder Mystery

"It was a stupid mistake to make," said the American woman I had met at my hotel in the English lake country, "but it was on the counter with the other Penguin books—the little sixpenny ones, you know, with the paper covers—and I supposed of course it was
35 a detective story. All the others were detective stories. I'd read all the others, so I bought this one without really looking at it carefully. You can imagine how mad I was when I found it was Shakespeare." I murmured something sympathetically. "I don't see why the Penguin-books people had to get out Shakespeare plays in the same size and everything as the detective stories," went on my companion. "I think they have different-
40 colored jackets," I said. "Well, I didn't notice that," she said. "Anyway, I got real comfy in bed that night and all ready to read a good mystery story and here I had *The Tragedy of Macbeth*—a book for high-school students. Like *Ivanhoe*," "Or *Lorna Doone*," I said.

40 J. Thurber, Lady Macbeth

"Exactly," said the American lady. "And I was just crazy for a good Agatha Christie, or something. Hercule Poirot is my favorite detective." "Is he the rabbity one?" I asked. "Oh, no," said my crime-fiction expert. "He's the Belgian one. You're thinking of Mr. Pinkerton, the one that helps Inspector Bull. He's good, too."

Over her second cup of tea my companion began to tell the plot of a detective story that had fooled her completely—it seems it was the old family doctor all the time. But I cut in on her. "Tell me," I said. "Did you read *Macbeth?*" "I *had* to read it," she said. "There wasn't a scrap of anything else to read in the whole room." "Did you like it?" I asked. "No, I did not," she said, decisively. "In the first place, I don't think for a moment that Macbeth did it." I looked at her blankly. "Did what?" I asked. "I don't think for a moment that he killed the King," she said. "I don't think the Macbeth woman was mixed up in it, either. You suspect them the most, of course, but those are the ones that are never guilty—or shouldn't be, anyway." "I'm afraid," I began, "that I—" "But don't you see?" said the American lady. "It would spoil everything if you could figure out right away who did it. Shakespeare was too smart for that. I've read that people never *have* figured out *Hamlet,* so it isn't likely Shakespeare would have made *Macbeth* as simple as it seems." I thought this over while I filled my pipe. "Who do you suspect?" I asked, suddenly. "Macduff," she said, promptly. "Good God!" I whispered, softly.

"Oh, Macduff did it, all right," said the murder specialist. "Hercule Poirot would have got him easily." "How did you figure it out?" I demanded. "Well," she said, "I didn't right away. At first I suspected Banquo. And then, of course, he was the second person killed. That was good right in there, that part. The person you suspect of the first murder should always be the second victim." "Is that so?" I murmured. "Oh, yes," said my informant. "They have to keep surprising you. Well, after the second murder I didn't know *who* the killer was for a while." "How about Malcolm and Donalbain, the King's sons?" I asked. "As I remember it, they fled right after the first murder. That looks suspicious." "Too suspicious," said the American lady. "Much too suspicious. When they flee, they're never guilty. You can count on that." "I believe," I said, "I'll have a brandy," and I summoned the waiter. My companion leaned toward me, her eyes bright, her teacup quivering. "Do you know who discovered Duncan's body?" she demanded. I said I was sorry, but I had forgotten. "Macduff discovers it," she said, slipping into the historical present. "Then he comes running downstairs and shouts, 'Confusion has broke open the Lord's anointed temple' and 'Sacrilegious murder has made his masterpiece' and on and on like that." The good lady tapped me on the knee. "All that stuff was rehearsed," she said. "You wouldn't say a lot of stuff like that, offhand, would you—if you had found a body?" She fixed me with a glittering eye. "I—" I began. "You're right!" she said. "You wouldn't! Unless you had practiced it in advance. 'My God, there's a body in here!' is what an innocent man would say." She sat back with a confident glare.

I thought for a while. "But what do you make of the Third Murderer?" I asked. "You know, the Third Murderer has puzzled Macbeth' scholars for three hundred years." "That's because they never thought of Macduff," said the American lady. "It was Macduff, I'm certain. You couldn't have one of the victims murdered by two ordinary thugs—the murderer always has to be somebody important." "But what about the banquet scene?" I asked, after a moment. "How do you account for Macbeth's guilty actions there, when Banquo's ghost came in and sat in his chair?" The lady leaned forward and tapped me on the knee again. "There wasn't any ghost," she said. "A big, strong man like that doesn't go around seeing ghosts—especially in a brightly lighted banquet hall with dozens of people around. Macbeth was *shielding somebody!*" "Who was he shielding?" I asked. "Mrs. Macbeth, of course," she said. "He thought she did it and he was going to take the rap himself. The husband always does that when the wife is suspected." "But what," I demanded, "about the sleepwalking scene, then?" "The same thing, only the other way around," said my companion. "That time *she* was shielding *him*. She wasn't asleep at all. Do you remember where it says, 'Enter Lady Macbeth with a taper'?" "Yes," I said. "Well, people who walk in their sleep *never carry lights!*" said my fellow-traveler. "They have a second sight. Did you ever hear of a sleepwalker carrying a light?" "No," I said, "I never did." "Well, then, she wasn't asleep. She was acting guilty to shield Macbeth." "I think," I said, "I'll have another brandy," and I called the waiter. When he brought it, I drank it rapidly and rose to go. "I believe," I said, "that you have got hold of something. Would you lend me that *Macbeth?* I'd like to look it over tonight. I don't feel, somehow, as if I'd ever really read it." "I'll get it for you," she said. "But you'll find that I am right."

I read the play over carefully that night, and the next morning, after breakfast, I sought out the American woman. She was on the putting green, and I came up behind her silently and took her arm. She gave an exclamation. "Could I see you alone?" I asked, in a low voice. She nodded cautiously und followed me to a secluded spot. "You've found out something?" she breathed. "I've found out," I said, triumphantly, "the name of the murderer!" "You mean it wasn't Macduff?" she said. "Macduff is as innocent of those murders," I said, "as Macbeth and the Macbeth woman." I opened the copy of the play, which I had with me, and turned to Act II, Scene 2. "Here," I said, "you will see where Lady Macbeth says, 'I laid their daggers ready. He could not miss 'em. Had he not resembled my father as he slept, I had done it.' Do you see?" "No," said the American woman, bluntly, "I don't." "But it's simple!" I exclaimed. "I wonder I didn't see it years ago. The reason Duncan resembled Lady Macbeth's father as he slept is that *it actually was her father!*" "Good God!" breathed my companion, softly. "Lady Macbeth's father killed the King," I said, "and, hearing someone coming, thrust the body under the bed and crawled into the bed himself." "But," said the lady, "you can't have a murderer who only appears in the story once. You can't have that." "I know that," I said, and I turned to Act II, Scene 4. "It says here, 'Enter Ross with an old Man.' Now, that old man is never identified and it is my contention he was old Mr. Macbeth, whose ambition it was to make his daughter Queen. There you have your motive." "But even then," cried the American lady, "he's still a minor character!" "Not," I said, gleefully, "when you realize that he was also *one of the weird sisters in disguise!*" "You mean one of the three witches?" "Precisely," I said. "Listen to this speech of the old man's. 'On Tuesday last, a falcon towering in her pride of place, was by a mousing owl hawk'd at and kill'd.' Who does that sound like?" "It sounds like the way the three witches talk," said my companion, reluctantly. "Precisely!" I said again. "Well," said the American woman, "maybe you're right, but—" "I'm sure I am," I said. "And do you know what I'm going to do now?" "No," she said. "What?" "Buy a copy of *Hamlet*," I said, "and solve *that!*" My companion's eye brightened. "Then," she said, "you don't think Hamlet did it?" "I am," I said, "absolutely positive he didn't." "But who," she demanded, "do you suspect?" I looked at her cryptically. "Everybody," I said, and disappeared into a small grove of trees as silently as I had come.

James Thurber in "*Vintage Thurber*", 1963

Living in 2000

Let's open the door and peek at a typical home in the year 2000.

It's in the countryside, because we've succeeded in dispersing jobs widely over rural America, bringing the factories to where the people want to live, rather than stacking up most of the people in crowded urban complexes, where most of the jobs are to be found today.

The home—part of a cluster surrounded by an open park—is in one of the thousands of "new towns" which now dot rural America, each containing its own shopping center and factories within easy walking or driving distance.

Inside, the home is divided by movable partitions, rather than by rigid walls, to increase or diminish the number of rooms as the size of the family changes.

In the kitchen, one wall contains the refrigerator, a built-in unit with pull-out drawers, each with a different temperature for different foods, each with its automatic defrosting unit. There's still a dishwasher, for, although disposable dishware is used for everyday occasions, most housewives still prefer china when company drops in.

The contents of the refrigerator may startle us:° square tomatoes bred by plant geneticists for less damage in shipping,° frozen lettuce and salad mix—preserved by cryogenic advances—with all the flavor and characteristics of today's fresh lettuce,° instant sandwich mixes.

Contents of the cupboard are even more exotic:° sheets of freeze-dried catsup, barbecue sauce, gravy, pickle relish, and syrup, ready to be reconstituted at the housewife's convenience, good indefinitely without refrigeration.

Some of the products look familiar, but are radically different from today's food: High-protein corn products and cereals, bred by plant geneticists,° meat, tailor-produced for the exact fat content desired,° milk with whatever butterfat content the family desires for its own dietary requirements.

We'll still like the old foods, but we'll also be trying new flavors. Breakthroughs in the molecular chemistry of flavor are not far away now, and will be an accomplished fact in another three decades, allowing us to intensify the flavor of bland foods; remove objectionable flavors from otherwise nutritious commodities; or even to make an inexpensive food—soybeans, for instance—taste like steak.

On the wall, above the laser-beam slicer, is a hook, but no flyswatter hangs on it. The flyswatter has joined the buggy-whip in oblivion, for the common housefly will have been eliminated by new techniques in black light, infrared or magnetic waves, or perhaps bred out of existence by sterilization of the population, much as the screwworm was eliminated by Department scientists back in the sixties.

Harmful insects will be just as rare in the fields where this food is produced, and the fields themselves will be programmed to produce exactly the produce needed, when it's needed, and in the form wanted. Whole fields of vegetables will mature at the same hour, in standardized sizes, to allow machine harvesting, the only kind of harvesting we'll know in another 33 years.°

But some things will be still the same: Expenditures will still rise to meet available income in the average family; the cry of the harassed husband "Where does all the money go?" will still be heard in the land.

"*Agriculture/2000*", ed. by the U.S. Department of Agriculture, 1967

V British Politics

Excerpts from Magna Carta, 1215

XII. Scutages and Aids
No scutage or aid shall be imposed in our kingdom, unless by the common council of our kingdom; except for ransoming our person, making our eldest son a knight, and for once marrying our eldest daughter; and for these there shall be paid no more than a reasonable aid. In like manner it shall be done concerning the aids of the City of London.

XIII. City Liberties
And the City of London shall have all its ancient liberties and free customs, as well by land as by water: furthermore, we will and grant that all other cities, boroughs, towns, and ports, shall have all their liberties and free customs.

XIV. The Council
And for holding the common council of the kingdom concerning the assessment of an aid, except in the three cases aforesaid and the assessing of a scutage, we will cause to be summoned the archbishops, bishops, abbots, earls, and greater barons of the realm, singly by our letters.

XV. Aids from Sub-Tenants
We will not for the future grant to anyone that he may take aid of his own free tenants, unless to ransom his body, and to make his eldest son a knight, and once to marry his eldest daughter; and for this there shall be paid a reasonable aid only.

XX. Amercements
A freeman shall not be amerced for a small offence, except according to the degree of the offence; and for a great crime according to the heinousness of it, saving to him his contenementum; and after the same manner a merchant, saving to him his merchandise. And a villain shall be amerced after the same manner, saving to him his means of livelihood, if he falls into our mercy; and none of the aforesaid amercements shall be imposed but by the oath of honest men in the neighbourhood.

XL. Justice and Right
To no man will we sell, to no man will we deny or delay, right or justice.

Historical Association, Constitutional Documents II

Excerpts from the Habeas Corpus Act, 1679

I. Preamble
Whereas great delays have been used by sheriffs, gaolers, and other officers, to whose custody any of the king's subjects have been committed for criminal or supposed criminal matters, in making returns of writs of Habeas Corpus to them directed° whereby

41 Extract from the Habeas Corpus Act, 1679

many of the king's subjects have been and hereafter may be long detained in prison, in such cases where by law they are bailable, to their great charges and vexation.

II. Body and Cause to be Produced

For the prevention whereof, and the more speedy relief of all persons imprisoned for any such criminal or supposed criminal matters: be it enacted° that whensoever any person or persons shall bring any Habeas Corpus directed unto any sheriff or sheriffs, gaoler, minister, or other person whatsoever, for any person in his or their custody° the said officer or officers° shall within three days after the service thereof as aforesaid —unless the commitment aforesaid were for treason or felony—° make return of such writ, and bring or cause to be brought the body of the party so committed or restrained, unto or before the Lord Chancellor, or Lord Keeper of the Great Seal of England for the time being, or the judges or barons of the said court from whence the said writ shall issue.° The said writ° shall° certify the true causes of his detainer or imprisonment.

V. Penalties for Disobedience

If any officer or officers° shall neglect or refuse to make the returns aforesaid, or to bring the body or bodies of the prisoner or prisoners according to the command of the said writ, within the respective times aforesaid,° the head gaolers and keepers of such prisoners, and such other person in whose custody the prisoner shall be detained, shall for the first offence forfeit to the prisoner or party grieved the sum of £ 100, and for the second offence the sum of £ 200, and shall and is hereby made incapable to hold or execute his said office.°

VI. Recommitment Forbidden

No person or persons which shall be delivered or set at large upon any Habeas Corpus shall at any time hereafter be again imprisoned or committed for the same offence by any person or persons whatsoever, other than by° legal order.

Historical Association, *Constitutional Documents IV*

Excerpts from the Bill of Rights, 1689

The said Lords Spiritual and Temporal, and Commons° do declare:

1. That the pretended power of suspending of laws, or the execution of laws, by regal authority, without consent of Parliament, is illegal.

4. That levying money for or to the use of the Crown by pretence of prerogative, without grant of Parliament, for longer time or in other manner than the same is or shall be granted, is illegal.
5. That it is the right of the subject to petition the King, and all commitments and prosecutions for such petitioning are illegal.
6. That the raising or keeping a standing army within the kingdom in time of peace, unless it be with the consent of Parliament, is against law.
8. That elections of members of Parliament ought to be free.
9. That the freedom of speech, and debates and proceedings in Parliament, ought not to be impeached or questioned in any court or place out of Parliament.
10. That excessive bail ought not to be required nor excessive fines imposed; nor cruel and unusual punishment inflicted.
13. And that for redress of all grievances, and for the amending, strengthening, and preserving of the laws, Parliament ought to be held frequently.

Historical Association, Constitutional Documents V

Of the Beginning of Political Societies

95. Men being, as has been said, by nature all free, equal, and independent, no one can be put out of this estate and subjected to the political power of another without his own consent. The only way whereby any one divests himself of his natural liberty and puts on the bonds of civil society is by agreeing with other men to join and unite into a community for their comfortable, safe, and peaceable living one amongst another, in a secure enjoyment of their properties and a greater security against any that are not of it. This any number of men may do, because it injures not the freedom of the rest; they are left as they were in the liberty of the state of nature. When any number of men have so consented to make one community or government, they are thereby presently incorporated and make one body politic wherein the majority have a right to act and conclude the rest.

96. For when any number of men have, by the consent of every individual, made a community, they have thereby made that community one body, with a power to act as one body, which is only by the will and determination of the majority; for that which acts any community being only the consent of the individuals of it, and it being necessary to that which is one body to move one way, it is necessary the body should move that way whither the greater force carries it, which is the consent of the majority; or else it is impossible it should act or continue one body, one community, which the consent of every individual that united into it agreed that it should; and so every one is bound by that consent to be concluded by the majority. And therefore we see that in assemblies impowered to act by positive laws, where no number is set by that positive law which impowers them, the act of the majority passes for the act of the whole and, of course, determines, as having by the law of nature and reason the power of the whole.

97. And thus every man, by consenting with others to make one body politic under one government, puts himself under an obligation to every one of that society to submit to the determination of the majority and to be concluded by it; or else this

original compact, whereby he with others incorporates into one society, would signify nothing, and be no compact, if he be left free and under no other ties than he was in before in the state of nature. For what appearance would there be of any compact? What new engagement if he were no further tied by any decrees of the society than he himself thought fit and did actually consent to? This would be still as great a liberty as he himself had before his compact, or any one else in the state of nature has who may submit himself and consent to any acts of it if he thinks fit.

98. For if the consent of the majority shall not in reason be received as the act of the whole and conclude every individual, nothing but the consent of every individual can make anything to be the act of the whole; but such a consent is next to impossible ever to be had if we consider the infirmities of health and avocations of business which in a number, though much less than that of a commonwealth, will necessarily keep many away from the public assembly. To which, if we add the variety of opinions and contrariety of interests which unavoidably happen in all collections of men, the coming into society upon such terms would be only like Cato's coming into the theatre only to go out again. Such a constitution as this would make the mighty leviathan of a shorter duration than the feeblest creatures, and not let it outlast the day it was born in; which cannot be supposed till we can think that rational creatures should desire and constitute societies only to be dissolved; for where the majority cannot conclude the rest, there they cannot act as one body, and consequently will be immediately dissolved again.

99. Whosoever, therefore, out of a state of nature unite into a community must be understood to give up all the power necessary to the ends for which they unite into society to the majority of the community, unless they expressly agreed in any number greater than the majority. And this is done by barely agreeing to unite into one political society, which is all the compact that is, or needs be, between the individuals that enter into or make up a commonwealth. And thus that which begins and actually constitutes any political society is nothing but the consent of any number of freemen capable of a majority to unite and incorporate into such a society. And this is that, and that only, which did or could give beginning to any lawful government in the world.

John Locke, "The Second Treatise of Government", 1690

Conciliation with the Colonies

My hold of the colonies is in the close affection which grows from common names, from kindred blood, from similar privileges, and equal protection. These are ties which, though light as air, are as strong as links of iron. Let the colonies always keep the idea of their civil rights associated with your government; they will cling and grapple to you, and no force under heaven will be of power to tear them from their allegiance. But let it be once understood that your government may be one thing and their privileges another, that these two things may exist without any mutual relation; the cement is gone, the cohesion is loosened, and everything hastens to decay and dissolution. As long as you have the wisdom to keep the sovereign authority of this country as the sanctuary of liberty, the sacred temple consecrated to our common faith, wherever the chosen race and sons of England worship freedom, they will turn

their faces towards you. The more they multiply, the more friends you will have;
the more ardently they love liberty, the more perfect will be their obedience. Slavery
they can have anywhere. It is a weed that grows in every soil. They may have it from
Spain, they may have it from Prussia. But until you become lost to all feeling of your
true interest and your natural dignity, freedom they can have from none but you.
This is the commodity of price of which you have the monopoly. This is the true act
of navigation which binds to you the commerce of the colonies, and through them
secures to you the wealth of the world. Deny them this participation of freedom and
you break that sole bond which originally made and must still preserve the unity of
the empire. Do not entertain so weak an imagination as that your registers and your
bonds, your affidavits and your sufferances, your cockets and your clearances are
what form the great securities of your commerce. Do not dream that your letters of
office, and your instructions, and your suspending clauses are the things that hold
together the great contexture of the mysterious whole. These things do not make your
government. Dead instruments, passive tools as they are, it is the spirit of the English
communion that gives all their life and efficacy to them. It is the spirit of the English
constitution which, infused through the mighty mass, pervades, feeds, unites, invigorates, vivifies every part of the empire, even down to the minutest member.

Is it not the same virtue which does everything for us here in England? Do you
imagine that it is the Land Tax Act which raises your revenue, that it is the annual
vote in the committee of supply which gives you your army? or that it is the Mutiny
Bill which inspires it with bravery and discipline? No! surely no! It is the love of the
people, it is their attachment to their Government, from the sense of the deep stake
they have in such a glorious institution, which gives you your army and your navy,
and infuses into both that liberal obedience, without which your army would be a base
rabble, and your navy nothing but rotten timber.

All this, I know well enough, will sound wild and chimerical to the profane herd
of those vulgar and mechanical politicians, who have no place among us; a sort of
people who think that nothing exists but what is gross and material; and who, therefore,
far from being qualified to be directors of the great movement of empire, are not fit
to turn a wheel in the machine. But to men truly initiated and rightly taught, these
ruling and master principles which, in the opinion of such men as I have mentioned,
have no substantial existence, are in truth everything and all in all. Magnanimity in
politics is not seldom the truest wisdom; and a great empire and little minds go ill
together.

Edmund Burke, "On Conciliation with the Colonies", 1775

The Victorian Age in Retrospect

The period of reaction against the nineteenth century is over; the era of dispassionate
historical valuation of it has begun. We can by this time examine without prejudice
what we have inherited from the Victorians, what we have improved away, and what
we have lost; how like we are to them and how unlike. The period to be covered cannot
be strictly confined to the reign of Victoria (1837—1901). To see the origin of Victorian
ideas and the conditions in which the early Victorians were brought up, we must

42 A Victorian Interior

look back to 1815, the end of the Napoleonic wars, the age of Cobbett and Lord Eldon, of Shelley, Byron and Scott. The close of the century, the age of Gladstone, Salisbury and the Fabian Society, of Hardy and Meredith, of the Savoy Opera, and the grand old Victorian Bernard Shaw, presents a very different scene. For the main characteristic of the Victorian era was constant change, variety and self-criticism.

Between these two points in time lies an age of many achievements and many famous men. Economic historians call it the railway age. That name marks it off from the eighteenth century and the Regency, the world of stage coaches and canals; and distinguishes it no less from the twentieth century, the age of the internal combustion engine—motor traction, submarines and aeroplanes. Yes, it was the railway age, though the steam-engine did not put the horse out of action as motors have done. It was George Stephenson of Tyneside who began the railway age. The mine-owners wanted him to shift their coal, but his locomotive steam-engine shifted everything else as well. The railway was as native to Britain as parliamentary government, franchise reform, free trade, freedom of the press, slavery-abolition, factory inspection, grants in aid, trade unions, "public schools", and income tax. All these British policies, though many of them had their roots in earlier English history, came to their strength in the nineteenth century.

The railway age in Britain was also an age of peace and security. We enjoyed internal peace, though it was seriously threatened by the economic and social maladjustments that came in the train of the Industrial Revolution. But we managed, by a gradual process, to mitigate these evils enough to preserve civil peace, and by a series of Reform Bills we democratised the system of parliamentary government which we had inherited in an aristocratic form from the eighteenth century. Britain alone of the great European countries saw no barricades in 1848, and was proud of it. And the Chartists in the end got their way without fighting. The British Labour movement remained law-abiding and parliamentary. External peace and security were also ours. For a hundred years after Waterloo, Britain and her trade and her colonies were peacefully protected by the sheathed sword of naval power, by the mere existence of a navy which held the surface of the sea, and in those days feared no attack either from below its surface, or from the sky overhead. So long as the navy was there, Britain could not be invaded—

or bombed. "Our right little, tight little island" we boasted with truth was our "inviolate isle". After the fall of Napoleon, no Great Power dominated Europe or threatened our security. Our only wars were small affairs in the Crimea, in Africa, in India.

The other governing condition of the period, closely related to that of peace and security, was ever-increasing wealth. Until, after 1870, American and German competition began to be acute, we had enjoyed a start over all the world in methods of machine production—in textiles and above all in iron and steel. Our capital and our engineering skill developed foreign lands and drew the tribute of dividends in return. We became the great creditor country. We were called "the workshop of the world". And London was the world's financial centre. In exchange for our money and our machine-made goods we garnered the food and luxuries of all lands, brought by our unrivalled merchant navy.

At the end of the century Britain's wealth, that is her command over goods, was enormous. Its distribution among the classes of the community was shamefully uneven; but that was already less bad than in the days of Peterloo, the Corn Laws and the Chartists. At the time of Queen Victoria's two Jubilees (1887 and 1897) goods were cheap, taxes, both direct and indirect, were very light, and real wages were much higher than half a century before. So all classes joined heartily in celebrating the Queen's long reign, because it had been a period of progress in well-being, since the "hungry forties". There were still appalling slums and slum life, but it had been worse before.

It was in the nineteenth century that Australia, New Zealand, South Africa, and in part Canada, received their English-speaking populations. Taught by the results of George III's folly, the statesmen and parliaments of Victorian England had the wisdom to grant to the white colonies responsible self-government, though our wisdom in that matter stopped short of Ireland. By the loosening of the bonds of empire, the Empire was saved.°

It was a time of active political, philosophical and religious speculation, carried on in an atmosphere of freedom, with the impact of Darwin and Huxley to stimulate it with new conceptions of the universe. It was good, serious stuff that was read. The competition of cheap journalism and literature, aimed at the lowest level of intelligence, only became dangerous at the latter end of the century.

Throughout the whole period, science, thought and literature were ahead of the arts. Owing to the destruction of craftsmanship in the machine age, the fashion in architecture, furniture and many of the arts of life was deplorable at the time of the Great Exhibition of 1851. Mass production had destroyed quality and taste.

George M. Trevelyan, "The Historical Background", 1948

Government by the Party System

Briton: Until the beginning of the twentieth century, it would be true to say that there were really only two parties: first, Whigs and Tories, then, Liberals and Conservatives. Today, the number of parties has grown, but, at the risk of getting into trouble, I think it is true to say that there are only two main parties now: Socialist or Labour, and Conservative. Liberals, Independents, National Liberals, and Communists have a very much smaller following.

American: In the United States we have only two great parties, although their names are different and they are agreed on their support of Capitalism—our Socialists are not strong enough to form a party of their own. We call them the Republican and the Democratic Parties. We have had this two-party system right down through the years, although the names of the political parties have changed from time to time.

Briton: In Great Britain there are parts of the country which tend to remain fairly constant in their party loyalties; for instance, the mining areas vote solidly Labour, as indeed do many of the industrial areas in Yorkshire, Lancashire, and the Midlands. The middle-class residential areas of our big towns, the country areas and seaside resorts, tend to vote Conservative. When one party or the other manages to win seats in these preserves, you can generally say that that party will win an election. I expect in America party loyalty and strength are divided geographically?

American: That is correct. We speak of the "solid south" in America—that means the states that are in the southern part of the country. These states go Democratic regularly, and have done so since the Civil War. New England, up in the north-eastern part of the country, regularly goes Republican. There are areas over the country that are pretty solidly one political party or the other.

You can say in general that the industrial workers of the big industrial cities of the north tend generally to vote for the Democratic ticket. You can say that the business and professional people tend to vote for the Republican ticket to the extent, perhaps, of two-thirds.

Briton: One of our great Prime Ministers, Disraeli, said: "England does not like coalitions." The only time when we have a coalition government is in war, or if the country is facing some particularly grave crisis. But otherwise, we prefer one party to win a sufficiently large majority so that it can get on with the job of governing without worrying too much about whether it will have enough votes in Parliament to achieve its objects. Would you say coalition—several parties working together—was as rare in America as in Britain?

American: Coalition is almost impossible. In a very deeply critical situation such as the Second World War the President may be able to bring enough prominent figures from the opposition party into his organization to establish what might in a general sort of way be called a coalition, but that is about as close as we come to it.

Briton: Now in this country we attach great importance to the existence of a strong and effective opposition; indeed, we pay the Leader of the Opposition £ 4,500 a year to oppose the Government.

American: In the United States opposition may come from almost any quarter: it may come from leaders of the opposition political party, but it may also come from the President's own political party, as does happen rather frequently.

Briton: Just a word or two about the way the parties do their job of educating public opinion. There are many people, as I have already suggested, who think that party politics is a dirty business; that they play upon people's ignorance; appeal to passion rather than reason by their propaganda; distort and falsify. I think there is something in this charge, and the best way to prevent it, of course, is to have a politically educated body of electors. Much is being done to educate people in the nature of the problems they have to solve, and I think voters realize that there is no quick way to heaven.

"London Calling, European Ed."

What is British Socialism?

I stress the word *British* because it owes very little to Continental socialism, and has its roots in distinctively British ideas and British institutions. Its ideas are the modern expression of that great tradition of British radicalism which, ever since Cromwell's soldiers talked at Putney, has striven to transform the privileges of the few into the rights of the citizen, and to subject irresponsible power to duly constituted public control. And the soil in which those ideas took root was that uniquely British institution, the voluntary association—the trade union, the friendly society, the co-operative society and, not least, the church and the chapel.°

British socialism is essentially democratic and evolutionary. Throughout its history it has rejected the revolutionary use of armed force, or of industrial action for the attainment of political ends. The cult of violence inspired by the French and Russian Revolutions has made no appeal to the British Labour Movement, which has been concerned not to destroy but to construct, not to level down but to level up. Both in national and local government, it has built up its power by patient organization, by persistent education, and by the victories of the ballot box.°

How does the Labour Party define its socialist creed? Since I am concerned in this article not with the past but with the present and the future, I can best summarize it by quoting in full the declaration adopted by the party in 1960.°
It runs as follows:

The British Labour Party is a democratic socialist party. Its central idea is the brotherhood of man. Its purpose is to make this ideal a reality everywhere. Accordingly—

1) It rejects discrimination on grounds of race, colour, or creed and holds that man should accord to one another equal consideration and status in recognition of the fundamental dignity of man.
2) Believing that no nation, whatever its size or power, is justified in dictating to or ruling over other countries against their will, it stands for the right of all peoples to freedom, independence and self-government.
3) Recognizing that international anarchy and the struggle for power between nations must lead to universal destruction, it seeks to build a world order within which all will live in peace. To this end it is pledged to respect the United Nations Charter, to renounce the use of armed force except in self-defence and to work unceasingly for world disarmament, the abolition of all nuclear weapons and the peaceful settlement of international disputes.
4) Rejecting the economic exploitation of one country by another it affirms the duty of richer nations to assist poorer nations and to do all in their power to abolish poverty throughout the world.
5) It stands for social justice, for a society in which the claims of those in hardship or distress come first; where the wealth produced by all is fairly shared among all; where differences in rewards depend not upon birth or inheritance but on the effort, skill and creative energy contributed to the common good; and where equal opportunities exist for all to live a full and varied life.
6) Regarding the pursuit of material wealth by and for itself as empty and barren, it rejects the selfish, acquisitive doctrines of capitalism, and strives to create instead

a socialist community based on fellowship, co-operation and service in which all can share fully in our cultural heritage.

7) Its aim is a classless society from which all class barriers and false social barriers have been eliminated.

8) It holds that to ensure full employment, rising production, stable prices and steadily advancing living standards the nation's economy should be planned and all concentrations of power subordinated to the interests of the community as a whole.

9) It stands for democracy in industry, and for the right of the workers both in the public and private sectors to full consultation in all the vital decisions of management, especially those affecting conditions of work.

10) It is convinced that these social and economic objectives can be achieved only through an expansion of common ownership substantial enough to give the community power over the commanding heights of the economy. Common ownership takes varying forms, including state-owned industries and firms, producer and consumer co-operation, municipal ownership and public participation in private concerns. Recognizing that both public and private enterprise have a place in the economy it believes that further extension of common ownership should be decided from time to time in the light of these objectives, and according to circumstances with due regard for the views of the workers and consumers concerned.

11) It stands for the happiness and freedom of the individual against the glorification of the state—for the protection of workers, consumers and all citizens against an exercise of arbitrary power, whether by the state, by private or by public authorities, and it will resist all forms of collective prejudice and intolerance.

12) As a democratic Party believing that there is no true Socialism without political freedom, it seeks to obtain and to hold power only through free democratic institutions whose existence it has resolved always to strengthen and defend against all threats from any quarter.

Harold Wilson, "The Relevance of British Socialism", 1964

Principles of Liberal Policy

Liberalism is more than a political movement; it is an attitude of mind, a way of life, a faith. As such, it is to be found in every age and generation and in all classes of society. There are times when it flourishes and times when it is despised and persecuted; but it never perishes. It is indestructible.

The word *liberal* is derived from the Latin *liber* and has a two-fold meaning: 1) free, and 2) generous. From the first springs the demand for individual liberty; from the second comes the attributes of fairmindedness and tolerance and of generosity towards those who are oppressed or economically less fortunate than their fellows. These are some of the outstanding characteristics of the liberal attitude of mind.

In striving for a liberal society it is important to recognise that there are these two basic ideas—freedom and generosity. Although many pay lip service to the liberal ideal, the effort to achieve a liberal society is a continuous struggle. There can be no once for all victory. Those who believe in the liberal way of life must always be prepared to face new challenges and be ready to apply liberal concepts to new and changing conditions. This inevitably involves political action.°

The Liberal view about defence is closely linked with the Liberal attitude to nationalism. In the nineteenth century British Liberals were on the side of self-determination, as they are today. They supported the Liberal movements which sprang up throughout Europe to over-throw authoritarian rulers and to pave the way for the creation of independent self-governing nations. In principle, this Liberal point of view has not changed. Liberals supported the unification of Italy and they now support the unification of Europe. Liberals stood for self-determination through parliamentary democracy and still do so. But their attitude to nationalism has been modified. Self-determination for each separate nation has indirectly contributed to the outbreak of two disastrous world wars and we have learned from experience that extreme nationalism is the enemy of personal liberty. It is for this reason that Liberals are now looking beyond national boundaries. Ever since the last war Liberals have whole-heartedly supported the movement for European unity to ensure that there should never again be a war between one European nation and another. Liberals will support other movements for greater unity in other parts of the world. As to Europe, it is a tragedy that Britain did not take the lead in this movement when offered the opportunity.°

Every political party must have some view about ownership. The Liberal view is based on the belief that the possession of private property enlarges personal freedom. Liberals are determined to see that every person shall enjoy this advantage. Their policy has been appropriately summed up in the phrase "Ownership for All". There is, of course, no one single way of achieving this. The policy of "ownership for all" means the introduction of a wide range of measures deliberately designed to bring about this spread of ownership. It has a two-fold aim:
a) to halt the accumulation of property by the few, and
b) to provide a widespread opportunity for the acquisition of property by the many.

Transferring ownership to the State is no solution. It merely creates a greater concentration of power. It is for that reason that Liberals have opposed the concept of nationalisation as a solution to our economic and political ills. It is an outmoded panacea and can prove to be an expensive one for the community.°

Liberals laid the foundations of the Welfare Society and they have no intention of seeing it destroyed. But a Liberal society, as we have seen, will not be static but ever-changing and progressive. The form and extent of the social services, therefore, cannot be frozen. Liberals do not accept the view that people should be dependent upon the State for all the necessities of life or that the same range of services must be made available by the State to everyone for all time. Nor, on the other hand, do they accept the view that the social services as a whole should be gradually whittled away as the community becomes more affluent.°

Expenditure on education is bound to increase. It is also an essential investment. There is need for more schools, more universities, more and better paid teachers. With this expansion the aim must always be equality of opportunity—irrespective of the parents' income. Every child matters. But there is no reason why there should not be variety and individuality in schools with more opportunity for heads of schools to use their own initiative in educational development. And there is no reason why all schools should be of the same pattern. Liberals believe in the comprehensive principle but are not in favour of the State trying to impose one form of comprehensive school on everyone regardless of the buildings available. What is needed is a flexible approach to non-selective secondary education, with well-planned schemes suited to local needs. As to the public schools, the aim must be to find ways in which to integrate fee-paying schools into the State system without sacrificing their identity and traditions. A sensible first step would have been to put the public schools into the same category as the direct grant schools, instead of trying to eliminate the direct grant system. Again we must get our priorities right. The most important task is to concentrate on improving standards throughout our educational system, reducing the size of classes and removing the social distinctions that exist today. Some parents will still want to send their children to independent schools; let them.°

We have had financial crises every few years—each one rather more severe than the last—and every time these occur it is the people who are least well organised—the modern under-privileged—who suffer most. Because of so many Government failures, planning has become discredited, but in our complex modern world it is necessary to plan ahead. Liberals see the need to plan but they recognise that planning in a free society can only succeed if the people have confidence a) that when restraints are needed the burden will be borne equitably by all and b) that when productivity and the standard of living rises the benefits will be fairly shared. It is only in this climate that long-term planning can work without a great many bureaucratic controls.°

The Liberal Party has always been a reforming party and at times has been called a party of protest. For this no apology is needed. Liberals have protested against the privileges of a small ruling class; they have protested against harsh social conditions; they have protested against the unjust treatment of minorities. When the people of Ireland were appealing for the right to manage their own affairs, Liberals protested against the suppression of that demand. In the twenties and thirties Liberals protested against the evils of widespread unemployment. On all these occasions Liberals have put forward proposals which have seemed to some people at the time to be revolutionary, but were later admitted to be right.

Much has happened since the great Reform Bill of 1832, but, if a comparison is made between life today and the principles and ideals set out earlier, it is all too clear that a great gulf exists between the world as it is and the world as Liberals would wish it to be. So long as that is so the Liberal Party will continue to be a party of reform— and often a party of protest.

Donald Wade, "Our Aim and Purpose", ⁴*1967*

The Philosophy of the Conservative Party

The Conservative Party is an evolutionary party in its growth and it is evolutionary in its outlook. A basic strand of Conservatism is opposition to revolution and a preference for evolution. The Conservative observes that revolutions sometimes make nations jump very high but they are not advanced very far forward when they come down again. Conservatives do not believe that men can be made better or more free simply by a violent change of institutions. Their philosophy tells them that there can be no single panacea, as left-wing protagonists are apt to imagine, that will by itself release the hitherto chained energies of man and move him forward to Utopia.

The first philosopher of English Conservatism, Edmund Burke, held that society was such a complex organic network that a direct assault on this organism was not a mere "change in the social contract"—it was a blow at the whole basis of human happiness. Conservatism instinctively respects institutions. The left-wing attitude when it finds an anomaly in an institution is inclined to demand the abolition of the institution. Conservatism prefers to remove the anomaly rather than remove the whole institution.

To the Conservative the left-wing outlook seems habitually to exaggerate the sphere of political action. The extent to which man's lot can be improved depends on his capacity to achieve improvement, on the adaptability of social institutions, on the national wealth and on many other such factors. Conservatives believe that man's lot can no more be improved by violent and doctrinaire assaults on existing institutions than man himself can be made good by passing laws.

But State action can provide the framework within which men can evolve to better things, and this is what political Conservatism is about. In the nineteenth century the view was strongly held by the Liberals that the State should never interfere with the market. Sound enough as an economic guide-line, this view led to harsh results in terms of human relations when it became erected into a dogma. The Conservatives of the day, with their strong sense of social obligation, opposed it and showed how the State should be brought in to redress the balance when the individual is wholly at a disadvantage when faced with the untrammelled play of forces.

This remains true. When in office in recent years the Conservatives took action against over-powerful monopolies and passed a wealth of social legislation for the protection of the vulnerable elements of the population. But at the same time the struggle has shifted. Today the forces of the left do not demand the minimum of State interference. On the contrary, they are constantly asserting that State action can solve everything, that inherently wiser decisions will come from the Minister or from the gentleman in Whitehall or from an official than decisions left to the individuals concerned. Conservatives oppose this view that would bring us nearer the all-powerful State or the collective concentration of power, before which the individual no longer counts and the Government's or the official's will is supreme.°

The State is the source of law and the guarantee of ordered society. Traditionally Conservatism supports our monarchical parliamentary constitution. It does not take these things lightly and upholds the virtues of patriotism. Conservatism believes in Britain and has always maintained her interests and worked for the voice of Britain to be respected overseas. But the fundamental basis of an influential Britain is not an all-powerful State machine: it is a sound competitive economy and a set of conditions in which the individual citizens can give of their best. Conservatism holds that the State (or the public authority) is not an aim in itself. The State exists to enable the individual to live the fullest life.

Several things flow from this principle. As noted above, where the balance of society is heavily weighted against the individual the Conservatives will not hesitate to redress this balance in the individual's favour. Historically, Conservatives have never accepted the peculiar Whig view that the greatest happiness of the greatest number will be achieved by the unregulated interplay of economic or social forces. They pioneered factory legislation and public health laws, they laid the foundations of the Welfare State between the wars and greatly strengthened and improved it in the post-war decades. They first established orderly marketing schemes for farm products when the open market had collapsed.

But all things considered, the Conservative view is that the more scope the public authority leaves for individual's choice the better. By lowering the amount it takes from him in taxes the State enables the individual to take more economic decisions himself. The less of the citizen's money the State takes the more he will be able to provide for himself and shape his own life and the less dependent he will be on the State.°

It is significant that most of the legislation that has shaped the modern system of local government was passed by Conservative Parliaments. The administrative counties, the county boroughs, the London boroughs were all given their present form by Conservative Acts; and Conservative legislation gave them most of their powers such as education, health, housing and welfare. Conservative belief in decentralisation accounts for this continuing interest in local government.°

A final example of the Conservative attitude to change is provided by the Commonwealth. Under Conservative government thirteen countries were given independence and arrangements made for the independence of two more. The Empire underwent a dramatic change and was peacefully transformed into a Commonwealth with a radically altered composition and balance.°

The Conservative Party is a party whose basic aim is the protection of the individual. It is a national party, not the party of one class or section. It believes in an ordered society and the diffusion of power within the State. It wants to ensure freedom under the law, protection for the weak, and the opportunity for enterprise to flourish. Its philosophy is empirical, not doctrinaire. It sees the value of sound institutions. It opposes change for change's sake. But it accepts, in Disraeli's phrase, that change is inevitable and in a progressive country change is constant. In a more recent phrase, the Conservative believes that change is our ally.

Geoffrey D. M. Block, "About the Conservative Party", 1965

	1945	1950	1951	1955	1959	1964	1966	1970	1974 (Feb)	1974 (Oct)
Labour	396	315	296	277	258	317	363	288	301	319
Conservative	189	298	320	344	365	303	253	330	296	276
Liberal	25	9	6	6	6	9	12	6	14	13

43 General Election Results, 1945-1974, Seats in the House of Commons

Into Europe, andante

"If the trumpet give an uncertain sound, who shall prepare himself to the battle?" Well, it's a pity that the Fanfare for Europe is not more harmonious, but in politics as in music dissonance has always been inevitable if the Second Fiddles play a different tune. In this case it must be acknowledged that a large part of the country is not ecstatic about the score. The journey into Europe will be bumpy and discordant.

That is sad, but not disastrous. What will be disastrous is if Britain devotes the next two, three, or four years to introspective champing over the issue: "Who went wrong when?" Among the most human and least attractive phrases in the English language is "I told you so." There will be much scope for such a Great Recriminative Debate. The transition period will not be all Beaujolais and boules. Change is always painful, and although the change arising from membership of the European Community will not be as sudden or all-pervasive as either its zealots or its most fiery critics believe, there will be enough change to cause trouble if people are determined.

Surely enough inconclusive balance sheets have now been drawn up, worried over, and discarded. If every change in prices, costs, wages, taxation, growth, and unemployment is to be put under the microscope to separate its European from its non-European elements, the effect on British politics and possibly on Britain's rôle in Europe and the world will be corrosive. Can we remember in the next few years that in the past few years prices have been rising sharply, unemployment has been worse than at any time since the war, and the balance of payments has recently showed signs of dipping into the same old trough from which only Labour's painful post-devaluation squeeze temporarily rescued it? And can we remember that all this happened before we entered Europe?

Can we remember also that it was partly in the hope of rescuing Britain from growing political aimlessness and economic lassitude that governments of the two parties have in turn sought membership of the Community? Labour is entitled, if it regains power, to seek changes, particularly with the benefit of experience. The Community is, and needs to be, an evolving institution. Even the Common Agricultural Policy may not be written on tablets of stone.

One temptation should be avoided, however: to prepare a future Labour Government's negotiating position by seeking, month after month, to prove that membership of the Community has created all Britain's ills. We enter Europe with the reputation of being a nation of shopkeepers; we would be unwise to present ourselves as a nation of second-hand-car dealers. Above all we should avoid creating a new, semi-permanent rift in British society, between pro- and anti-Europeans. Britain has much to contribute to the new Europe's main need—for effective democratic control of a bureaucracy that grows in power all the time. In making that contribution we may even give our own parliamentary institutions a new injection of vigour and some relief from the staleness that long unsolved problems have created at Westminster.

"The Guardian", January 1, 1973

VI Commonwealth Problems

Why Great Britain survived her Rivals

I will conclude this lecture with some remarks on the large causes which, in the struggle of five states, left the final victory in the hands of England. Among these five we have seen that Spain and Portugal had the start by a whole century, and that Holland was
5 in the field before England. Afterwards for about a century France and England contended for the New World on tolerably equal terms. Yet now of all these states England alone remains in possession of a great and commanding colonial power. Why is this?

We may observe that Holland and Portugal laboured under the disadvantage of
10 too small a basis. The decline of Holland had obvious causes, which have often been pointed out. For her sufferings in a war of eighty years with Spain she found the compensations I have described. But when this was followed, first by naval wars with England, and then by a struggle with France which lasted half a century, and she had now England for a rival on the seas, she succumbed. At the beginning of the eighteenth
15 century she shows symptoms of decay, and at the Treaty of Utrecht she lays down her arms, victorious indeed, but fatally disabled.

The Portuguese met with a different misfortune. From the outset they had recognised the insufficiency of their resources, regretting that they had not been content with a less ambitious course of acquisition on the northern coast of Africa. In 1580 they
20 suffered a blow such as has not fallen on any other of the still existing European states. Portugal with all her world-wide dependencies and commercial stations fell under the yoke of Spain, and underwent a sixty years' captivity. In this period her colonial Empire, which by becoming Spanish was laid open to the attacks of the Dutch, suffered greatly.°

25 As to the ill-success of Spain and France, it would no doubt be idle to suppose that any one cause will fully explain it. But perhaps one large cause may be named which in both cases contributed most to produce the result.

Spain lost her colonial Empire only, as it were, the other day. Having founded it a century earlier, she retained it nearly half a century later than England retained her
30 first Empire. Compared to England, she has been inferior only in not having continued to found new colonies. And this was the effect of that strange decay of vitality which overtook Spain in the latter half of the sixteenth century. The decline of population and the ruin of finance dried up in her every power, that of colonisation included.

No similar decline is observable in France. France lost her colonies in a series of
35 unsuccessful wars, and perhaps you may think that it is not necessary to inquire further, and that the fortune of war explains everything. But I think I discern that both States were guilty of the same error of policy, which in the end mainly contributed to their failure. It may be said of both that they "had too many irons in the fire."

There was this fundamental difference between Spain und France on the one side
40 and England on the other, that Spain and France were deeply involved in the struggles of Europe, from which England has always been able to hold herself aloof. In fact,

as an island, England is distinctly nearer for practical purposes to the New World, and almost belongs to it, or at least has the choice of belonging at her pleasure to the New World or to the Old. Spain might perhaps have had the same choice, but for her conquests in Italy and for the fatal marriage which, as it were, wedded her to Germany.°

As to France, it is still more manifest that she lost the New World because she was always divided between a policy of colonial extension and a policy of European conquest. If we compare together those seven great wars between 1688 und 1815, we shall be struck with the fact that most of them are double wars, that they have one aspect as between England and France and another as between France and Germany. It is the double policy of France that causes this, and it is France that suffers by it. England has for the most part a single object and wages a single war, but France wages two wars at once for two distinct objects. When Chatham said he would conquer America in Germany, he indicated that he saw the mistake which France committed by dividing her forces, and that he saw how, by subsidising Frederick, to make France exhaust herself in Germany, while her possessions in America passed defenceless into our hands. Napoleon in like manner is distracted between the New World and the Old. He would humble England; he would repair the colonial and Indian losses of his country. But he finds himself conquering Germany and at last invading Russia. His comfort is that through Germany he can strike at English trade, and through Russia perhaps make his way to India.

England has not been thus distracted between two objects. Connected but slightly with the European system since she evacuated France in the fifteenth century, she has not since then lived in chronic war with her neighbours. She has not hankered after the Imperial Crown or guaranteed the Treaty of Westphalia. When Napoleon by his Continental System shut her out from Europe, she showed that she could do without Europe. Hence her hands have always been free, while trade of itself inevitably drew her thoughts in the direction of the New World. In the long run this advantage has been decisive. She has not had to maintain a European Ascendency, as Spain and France have had; on the other hand she has not had to withstand such an Ascendency by mortal conflict within her own territory, as Holland and Portugal, and Spain also, have been forced to do. Hence nothing has interrupted her or interfered with her, to draw her off from the quiet progress of her colonial settlements. In one word, out of the five states which competed for the New World success has fallen to that one—not which showed at the outset the strongest vocation for colonisation, not which surpassed the others in daring or invention or energy—but to that one which was least hampered by the Old World.

   John R. Seeley, "The Expansion of England in the Eighteenth Century", 1883

The Commonwealth and Britain

The British Commonwealth of Nations, as given legal shape by the Statute of Westminster, 1931, is a free association of sovereign, independent states and their dependencies, if any, each member of which is equal in status and has joined of its own choice. All members recognize the Queen as Head of the Commonwealth whether or not such states are republics or countries of which she is Queen.°

It is not easy to say what binds together these nations with their diversity in race, religion, history, and tradition. All the members other than the United Kingdom were formerly under some form of British rule. Each state started as a parliamentary democracy, though there have been a few variations from the Westminster parliamentary model. Laws are made with the consent of freely elected parliaments, and all have a general pattern of law-making, executive, and judicial institutions. In a high proportion of the states there is the unifying effect of the use of the English language.

Some non-Commonwealth people find it difficult to understand the whole idea, and this is probably due to the fact that there are so many things which the Commonwealth is not. For example, it is without a written constitution: there is no such thing as a Parliament of the Commonwealth. Complete financial freedom is enjoyed by all members, and each is fully responsible for its own security. All are members of the United Nations, but it is very rare that they speak with one voice on a subject that is controversial. One fact often not appreciated is that the United Kingdom is neither more or less independent than any other member state, and therefore cannot and does not attempt to give orders to her fellow-members. No idea exists in Britain today that she is a mother to whom her daughters should come for advice; it is realized that the daughters have grown into independent persons anxious to develop their lives in their own way. As Sir Kenneth Bradley, the Director of the Commonwealth Institute, has stated, "The Commonwealth is an association of peoples and not merely of Governments; and adults rightly resent being treated as children".

Nevertheless it is true that there is much co-operation among members of the Commonwealth, particularly in the fields of finance, education, and economics. Help in various ways is given by one member to another. °Possibly one of Britain's most important functions is to offer London as the venue for the conferences of Commonwealth Prime Ministers. At these, Prime Ministers are able to discuss matters of common interest frankly and freely. Of course, any agreements reached on these occasions are not binding on members; the place for actual decisions is in the Parliament of each state. This free exchange of ideas on problems is also from time to time carried on at ministerial level—for instance, when Finance Ministers meet. In the matter of aid in various forms Britain does not lag behind.°

When one looks at the Commonwealth as a whole it is possible to realize that it is a unique grouping of nations dedicated to peace. Therefore it is not an exaggeration to claim that it is something that presents a valuable picture for the world. In a Commonwealth Institute pamphlet Sir Kenneth Bradley has excellently expressed what the Commonwealth is doing for the world. In his view, it is of considerable value "because it provides a working model for effective international and inter-racial co-operation, and because it forms a natural bridge of mutual understanding between the developed and underdeveloped nations".

To summarize, the members of the Commonwealth have complete independence, yet a broad community of interests and, allowing for some diversities, a similar pattern of institutions—legislative, judicial, and executive. There are no obligations or commitments in this Commonwealth which is able to adapt itself to changing circumstances and needs. No less important is the fact that much voluntary co-operation takes place among its members.

H. W. Howes, *"Presenting Modern Britain"*, 1966

I Oxford, New College Quadrangle

II London, Carnaby Street

III Cornwall, St. Ives

IV New York, Verrazano-Narrows Bridge

V Indian Summer in New Hampshire

VI Scene in the Old Part of New Orleans

VII Montana, Glacier National Park

VIII Loch Linnhe, Argyllshire, Scotland

IX Bag-Piper

X View from Edinburgh Castle

XI India, Rourkela

XII Nairobi, Kenya, Bazaar Street

XIII   Henry Moore in his Studio, 1968

XIV   Henry Moore, "King and Queen", 1952/53

"Reg Butler, who in the war, as a conscientious objector, was allowed to work for a village smith and learned the art of forging, after he had given up his training and career as an architect, may be said to mark the change of direction after Moore and Barbara Hepworth. This is in no slight degree attributable to the fact that in 1954 an international jury awarded his maquette the grand prix in a contest for a 'Monument to the Unknown Political Prisoner'."

(A. M. Hammacher, "Modern English Sculpture", 1967)

XV   Reg Butler, Model No. 2 to "The Unknown Political Prisoner", 1957

XVI Lynn Chadwick, "Elektra", 1968

"In Chadwick's work we are confronted with a creation that has a perfectly individual history. He has not enjoyed, like most artists in England, the training of one of the local or university art schools, or of the Royal College of Art. He worked in architects' offices, and in the war he was a pilot. When he was back in civil society as designer of textiles and an interior decorator, he started constructing mobiles, and later, balanced sculptures ('The Inner Eye' had a moving crystal); then the closed stabiles in series of animal motives, bird motives, human figures, dancers, strangers and watchers. His conception of architecture and interior decoration is still visible in the manner in which he reconstructed his own interior in a neo-Gothic country-house in Lypiatt Park near Stroud with an inventiveness which is a perfect union of his sense of space and his sense of sculpture, from which emerges furniture (tables, seats) deviating from every convention and perfectly embodied in the given space."

(A. M. Hammacher, "Modern English Sculpture", 1967)

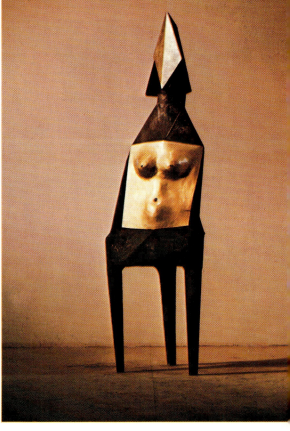

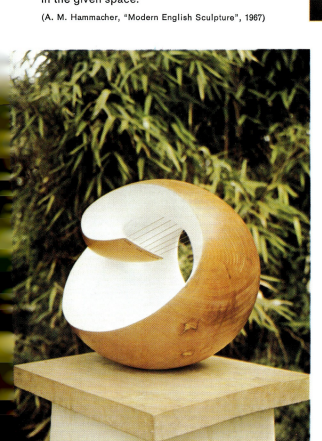

"Barbara Hepworth is five years younger than Moore. She had, especially in the early years, identical sources of training (Leeds, the Royal College, a West Riding scholarship) and periods of travel in Europe (Italy and Paris). For her, too, 'truth to material' and 'direct carving' are fundamental rules, and they remained so even when she started to use bronze as a medium. Now that we are able to survey her work over a period of nearly forty years, we are struck by the fact that in the varying tensions between the involvement with landscape and the human being on the one hand and abstraction on the other, the leaning towards abstraction always preponderates, organic in nature but with an unmistakable inclination to the geometrical."

(A. M. Hammacher, "Modern English Sculpture", 1967)

XVII Barbara Hepworth, "Pelagos", 1946

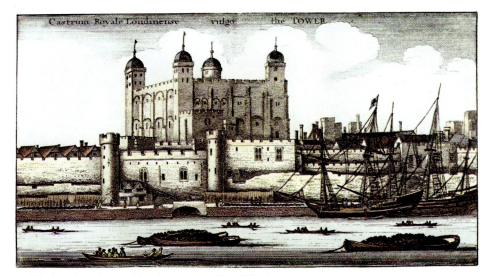

XVIII Hand-coloured Engraving from the 18th Century

XIX J. M. W. Turner, "The Fighting Téméraire", 1839

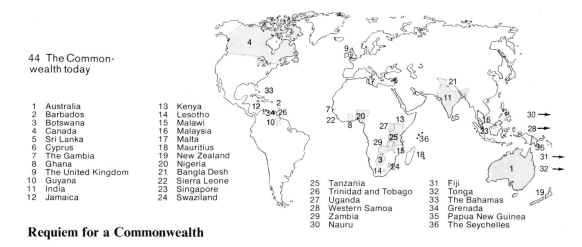

44 The Commonwealth today

1	Australia	13	Kenya
2	Barbados	14	Lesotho
3	Botswana	15	Malawi
4	Canada	16	Malaysia
5	Sri Lanka	17	Malta
6	Cyprus	18	Mauritius
7	The Gambia	19	New Zealand
8	Ghana	20	Nigeria
9	The United Kingdom	21	Bangla Desh
10	Guyana	22	Sierra Leone
11	India	23	Singapore
12	Jamaica	24	Swaziland
25	Tanzania	31	Fiji
26	Trinidad and Tobago	32	Tonga
27	Uganda	33	The Bahamas
28	Western Samoa	34	Grenada
29	Zambia	35	Papua New Guinea
30	Nauru	36	The Seychelles

Requiem for a Commonwealth

The rise of empires, it has been said, is often accompanied by much human misery: their fall, always. The fall of the British Empire was no exception. It brought death to a million people at the partition of India, oppression to racial minorities in many countries, disaster to men who had served the imperial government too loyally: and it brought all 5
the sorrow which comes from the tearing up of roots and traditions. Whether it brought, in any true sense, a better or a freer world, and whether it made anyone happier except the nationalist politicians who were the chief beneficiaries of the change, is very much a matter of opinion.
  Perhaps it was inevitable. Empires are a function of power, and power—and with it 10
the imperial responsibility—has passed across the Atlantic. But, inevitable or not, beneficial or not, the thing has been done. What Churchill called Britain's "self-inflicted mutilation" is nearly complete. The British Empire has joined Niniveh and Tyre. The question now is whether there can be any future, and if so what kind, for the incongruous congregation of countries which has taken its place; countries brought together only by 15
an accident of history which most of them unreservedly condemn and seem anxious to forget.
  The prospect at the moment must strike any candid observer as unpromising. The Commonwealth is being subjected, continuously and cumulatively, to strains which its doubtful structure seems hardly solid enough to bear. It could easily break up altogether, 20
quite soon, or fade into a mere ghost of what its admirers hoped it would be. But if, on the other hand, it can survive this period of stress, if it proves more durable than its critics suppose, then the prognosis could be very different. With old bitternesses forgotten and the transitional stage outgrown, the Commonwealth might find a new spirit and a new role. 25
  The Afro-Asian members are still suffering from disappointment and raw vanity. They are disappointed because independence, far from solving all their problems, merely generated fresh ones. They want to demonstrate their adulthood and they feel frustrated when their views are apparently brushed aside. They had hoped that membership in the Commonwealth would give them real equality in a major league, and they 30
are maddened to find that Britain is still rich while they remain poor, that Britain's voice still seems to carry more weight than all of theirs put together. But this mood will pass, along with the first generation of nationalist leaders and the masses to whom they offered an earthly paradise under the name of independence. More realistic goals, a more sober pride, more lasting values, may then reassert themselves. 35

The influence of British ideas and the example of British standards in public life still pervade the Commonwealth. There are more Englishmen in India today than there were during the Raj, and many Indians and Pakistanis seem more British than the British themselves. The African countries talk about "Africanization", but what they mean is
5 not a return to indigenous African traditions but the training of Africans to take the place of Britons. While the jobs are Africanized, the Africans are being Britishized.
Though the formal links which join the Commonwealth together seem artificial and fragile, new human links are being constantly, unobtrusively forged. The result, in time, could be a much more like-minded Commonwealth than seems possible now.
10 But there may not be time. The likelier development is that some, perhaps all, of the Afro-Asian members will fall away, like alien limbs unsuccessfully grafted on to an old tree, leaving the core of the Commonwealth—Britain, Australia, New Zealand, possibly the West Indies—as a coherent association, prepared to accept mutual obligations, sharing political principles and feeling a genuine kinship with each other.
15 Relations between Britain and the Old Dominions are already very different—different in mood and in the degree of trust—from the relations between Britain and the Afro-Asian members or the Afro-Asian members' relations with each other. The Commonwealth might be healthier, stronger and more influential if its form could be trimmed to accord with this reality. Some such development is what Sir Robert Menzies and many
20 other keen, but currently disillusioned, supporters of the Commonwealth expect, and in their hearts rather hope, to see.

The Commonwealth is worth saving. It still has great potentiality for good. Winston Churchill used to draw three inter-linked circles, representing the Commonwealth, the Atlantic Alliance and Europe. Only Britain, he said, belonged to all three. This concept
25 has been derided as unreal and sentimental by younger politicians with their minds fixed exclusively on burgeoning Europe or the wealth of America and with their hard-nosed skepticism about the Commonwealth.

But it was a noble concept: and there is much to be gained if it can be given new life, if the shifts of power can be accepted without jealousy, if Britain can go into Europe
30 without abandoning the Commonwealth, if different races can find a way of working together, not in blocs and with votes as they do at the United Nations, but in friendly conversation with each other.

When the wind of change has settled down and yesterday's slogans and prejudices have been set aside, the old British Empire may seem no bad foundation for such an
35 attempt.

Anthony Lejeune in "Life", 1966

Canada discovers itself

Larger than China in territory, Canada has fewer people (20 million) than Ethiopia. This small population in a vast, largely forbidding land has created a standard of living second only to that of the U.S. Yet most Canadians are disturbed by the fact that this
40 was made possible largely through a massive influx of U.S. capital.°

45 Toronto, New City Hall

46 Quebec, Rue Saint Louis

Immigration to Canada was much smaller in numbers than in the U.S., and Canada made different use of it. Most U.S. immigrants came not merely to a country, but to an idea. They were thrown into a swirl of enterprise that could be brutal but that was deeply committed to the future and—after the Civil War—to unity. Canada never became a melting pot: its people mixed but failed to merge. In a thinly settled country, dominated by the secular empire of Britain (or, in French Canada, by the clerical empire of the Catholic Church) people identified themselves more by their separate origins than by their common destination.

History deprived Canadians of the customary sources of nationalism. The British North America Act was, in essence, a Confederation not of free provinces but of colonies (Quebec, Ontario, Nova Scotia and New Brunswick). It was a quietly negotiated compact between ruled and ruling. Other colonies and territories joined the Confederation over the years, and Canada slipped toward independence almost effortlessly. At Vimy Ridge in World War I, the courage of Canadian fighting men won Canada the courtesy of a separate signature on the treaty of Versailles. But not until 1931 did Canada achieve genuine independence.

Canada thus won its freedom without rebellion, or without major national heroes. Perhaps it was good (or bad) luck. Perhaps it was more, for after all, character is fate. In the 18th century, as Historian Ramsay Cook points out, English-speaking Canadian settlers had rejected the American Revolution, just as 13 years later, in 1789, French-speaking settlers rejected the French Revolution. As a result, Canada's 1867 charter contained little thought of revolutionary fervor or political ideology. In contrast to the American Declaration of Independence, with its ringing "Life, Liberty and the Pursuit of Happiness", Canada's Constitution enjoins "Peace, Order and Good Government". For a people preoccupied from the outset with conquering a harsh land, that was mandate enough. But it nonetheless has deprived a maturing Canada of what John Porter calls a "myth proclaiming a utopia against which, periodically, progress can be measured. In the U.S. there is a utopian image which slowly over time bends intractable social patterns in the direction of equality, but a Canadian counterpart is difficult to find."

The American Constitution reserved to the states all rights not specifically granted to the Federal Government; yet the reality of union created strong central rule. In Canada, the reverse was the case: the Constitution reserved to the Federal Government all powers not specifically granted to the provinces; yet the reality of disunity created a weak central regime from the start. The most threatening aspect of this disunity was the conflict between French- and English-speaking Canadians.°

Canada's 6,000,000 French are concentrated in Quebec, whose motto is a meaningful *Je me souviens* (I remember). Originally they meant to establish New France in the New World. With the English conquest of a land that French explorers and Catholic missionaries had opened up, they turned fiercely inward to survive as a minority on a vast English-speaking continent. Ill-educated, church-dominated, cut off by language and often by prejudice from improving themselves, the French Canadians grew ever more provincial. Only after World War II did the "quiet revolution" of the French Canadians take form, demanding better schools and opportunity to share equally in the country's growth. In the early 1960s French separatism, including cells of bearded conspiratorial terrorists, was a major threat to Canada's very fabric as a nation. There was serious worry that Canada might disintegrate. The most striking fact about the present Canadian scene is that this threat has for all practical purposes disappeared.°

The rift between English and French Canadians is not over, and probably never can disappear completely, but Canada takes comfort from hopeful symbols such as the new Canadian maple-leaf flag, which does away with both the Union Jack and the French *fleur-de-lis*. Officials in Ottawa are taking crash courses in French paid for by the Government. Listening to their atrociously accented speech, cynics wonder whether there is really much of a future for the French language on the continent. But the linguistic effort is significant.°

What Canada has wrought physically remains its most stunning reason for pride. Montreal, Canada's largest metropolis, with 2,400,000 people, is agleam with new office buildings, hotels, theaters, boutiques. °Toronto (pop. 2,100,000), the Anglo-Saxon's answer to French Montreal, is richer, and rebuilding itself even faster. Both are youthful cities: half of Canada's population is under 25.

For all the new urban sophistication, the most cogent economic fact of Canada today is the push into pioneer land, where technology is taking on nature to create a new frontier unlike anything ever seen before. With vast areas as yet unexplored, only a fraction of the returns are in. The potash finds in Saskatchewan and oil reserves in Alberta are estimated to be equal to all those known in the rest of the world.

There is noticeably less self-denigration and more self-confidence among Canadians today, and not only in the material field. There is a feeling that Canada's way of handling its problems, both internal and with the U.S., could serve as a model for many lesser-endowed countries struggling toward maturity.

"Time", 1967

47 Aerial View of Sydney with Opera House

Australia

Australia today is a rapidly developing land. Founded 180 years ago, it is the home of more than 12,000,000 people who are completing the transformation of a hitherto almost wholly agrarian country to one whose economy is now broadly based as much on the products of its technology as of its farms and mines. By 1988, two centuries after its foundation, Australia's population is expected to reach 18,000,000.°
    Australians enjoy the outdoor life. They like being called an easy-going, happy-go-lucky people; in fact they are hard and highly skilled workers. Now that the demand of industry, commerce and public service is for highly trained technologists, more and more young Australians are attending universities or technical colleges after their secondary schooling. Government scholarships by the thousand have been granted to assist them. Since World War II the number of universities has been more than doubled, and governments are sponsoring a great increase in diploma colleges.°
    Visitors from overseas find Australians a friendly and happily informal people, democratic in their institutions and by nature. The average Australian is tolerant and an easy-going neighbour. He lives and lets live, is quick with his friendship and loyal to his friends.
    Newcomers from overseas find their place in the Australian society and become proud of being Australians, although on special occasions they take out of storage their national costumes and sing songs of faraway places and join in folk dances that are already half forgotten. In more practical ways new settlers from Europe have already

altered the pattern of Australian life. Bistros, barbecues, espresso cafés, salami-bars and smorgasbord tables have sprung up in the cities. An increase in the popularity of Australian wines is partly attributable to the tastes of settlers from Europe.°

From the pioneering days, when life was often hard and men and women had to work together for survival, it has been an Australian tradition for women to stand shoulder-to-shoulder with their men, rarely pampered but never fettered by age-old traditions of subjection and inferiority. Women's suffrage was granted, almost without agitation, long before most other countries. This tradition of working partnership between men and women continues in present-day Australia.°

The aboriginal and part-aboriginal content of the population is now in the vicinity of 100,000, or less than one per cent of the overall total. Little more than 50,000 are full aborigines, and considerably less than half of these now lead tribal or even partly tribal lives. Some live on reserves, on mission stations and on Government settlements, but an increasing number is living in towns. A number of State and Federal laws have been passed aimed at speeding the full integration of all aborigines into the community.°

Since the second world war Australia has enjoyed its greatest period of economic growth. The value of major works, public and private, in hand or planned is more than $ 4,000,000,000. Steelworks, dockyards, dams, bridges, factories, highways, offices, railways, airports, shopping centres and grain-silos—these new projects are expanding all fields of rural, industrial and commercial endeavour in all the States and Territories of Australia.

Australia has built one atomic reactor and is building another. Its Snowy Mountains hydro-electric system in southern New South Wales will be one of the largest in the world. It is estimated to cost $ 800,000,000 and is due to be completed in 1974. Water from Snowy Mountains dams and rivers has opened new land for agriculture; the hydro-electric stations of the same system provide power for industry; thus the Snowy Mountains project embodies the new view of the Australian economy.°

Australia's rural production has paralleled industrial expansion. Wool remains one of the foundations of Australian economic prosperity and its future is of great importance to all Australians. It has been predicted that by 1970 wool may bring in only a quarter of the nation's export income, yet during the past decade Australian wool production and exports have risen by more than three per cent a year and look like continuing to rise at this rate. Wheat, sugar and meat also add substantially to the Australian export income.°

Australia is undertaking increasingly important work and research to assist in the success of outer-space projects. Tracking stations at various points are part of a joint programme of research with the United States National Aeronautics and Space Administration. Already they have yielded valuable observations on American men-in-space flights and on unmanned satellite flights to the moon and Mars. The scientific staff of these stations will also have their part in United States attempts to put a man on the moon.

Australia is also engaged with Britain in the Weapons Research Establishment, with headquarters at Salisbury, north of Adelaide. This organisation is responsible for the guided-weapons range at Woomera where Blue Streak Rocket launchings are preparing the way for the European Launcher Development Organisation space research project.°

Australia is an independent nation in full control of its own affairs and of its dealing with other nations. Australia is also a member of the Commonwealth of Nations. This constantly evolving association of independent nations is drawn together by many ideals and objectives, by historical connections and by the willingness of its members to consult freely and co-operate in their common interests.

Australia is a federation of six States with a Federal Parliament and a Parliament for each of the States. A Governor-General and the Governors of the States represent the Queen. Queen Elizabeth is Queen of Australia as well as of Britain and of some other Commonwealth countries. When she visits Australia the Queen formally opens Federal and State Parliamentary sessions, holds investitures and presides over meetings of Executive Councils and of the Privy Council.°

Australia replaced with decimal currency the old currency of pounds, shillings and pence on February 14, 1966. A new Royal Australian Mint was built in Canberra to provide the new coinage.°

Australian fauna includes many species of animals not found elsewhere. This is believed to be due to the isolation of Australia from the rest of the world in pre-historic eras. Nearly all the indigenous animals are marsupials—mammals which produce their young imperfectly formed and rear them in a pouch covering their lactic glands.

There are about 400 kinds of indigenous animals and 700 species of birds. Apart from the kangaroo family, there are the koala (sometimes called the native bear), wombat, dingo, possum, dugong (a sea mammal), echidna (or spiny anteater), and platypus, an amphibious monotreme with a coat of fur, a duck-like bill and webbed feet, which lays eggs and suckles its young.

The best known birds are the emu, lyrebird, budgerigar, kookaburra (laughing jackass) and many types of brilliantly coloured parrots and cockatoos, as well as hawks and eagles.

"Australian Panorama", 1968

New Zealand—Country at the Cross-roads

The history of New Zealand began before and during the 14th century, when the first Maori people began to settle in Aotearoa ("land of the long white cloud"), after braving the stormy Pacific Ocean in their canoes.

The colonization of New Zealand after 1814 was filled with hardships and difficulties. However, on the whole, New Zealand was very fortunate in the group of settlers who arrived from Britain to begin a new life for themselves. They were people of rugged determination, who were willing to live under severe conditions and to work hard. During the terrible poverty of the "Hungry Forties", many industrial and agricultural workers who could no longer make a living in Britain, arrived in New Zealand. Other immigrants came from middle-class Victorian stock and, though keen to start a new life, still clung to as much of their English culture as possible; we hear of some of these arriving with their family piano! The diaries of some of these newcomers often make interesting and even exciting reading. They are full of the wonders of the new country. The climate seemed kind, there were no extremes of hot and cold, and grain could be grown easily. There were no dangerous animals, and no snakes. There were many delights—rich forests of splendid variety, with birds like the tui and the bell bird, and the flightless weka and kiwi. The pioneers introduced European birds as well as rabbits, but the latter have since become great destroyers of bush and farmland and have to be exterminated.

After many years of lawlessness, when the immigrants were neither responsible to the British Government nor influenced by traditional Maori authority the Treaty of Waitangi was signed in 1840. This event is still commemorated today at the Treaty House in Waitangi in the north of North Island. On that memorable day over 125 years ago, Governor William Hobson presented this treaty for signature to the assembled Maori chiefs. It established the sovereignty of Queen Victoria, and granted the Maori people all the rights and privileges of British subjects. The foundations of peaceful coexistence had been laid, and the genuine integration of the two peoples had already begun. Misunderstandings and even fights still took place between the races, but the aims of the treaty were not forgotten, and today New Zealand can be proud of the harmony which exists between all her people.

The white population of New Zealand is estimated to have been 2,000 120 years ago. At present, the total population is about 2,800,000; only 7% is Maori. New Zealand has always kept the entry of non-British people into the country under strict control. The first concept was that it should be a British colony. In the twentieth century, however, refugees came from Germany, Holland, Poland, and Yugoslavia. The entry of Chinese and other Asian peoples into this underpopulated country was prohibited.

The population of New Zealand is mainly urban, with 63% living in the towns, but the prosperity of the country depends on the export of some 300,000 tons of wool annually, and, since the introduction of refrigeration, on the export of meat, dairy products, and fruit. Until recently, the main market for these products was the mother-country, but with Britain looking more and more towards Europe, New Zealand has now reached a cross-roads. She must move closer to the U.S.A. and her Asian neighbours, especially Japan. Such contacts will not only involve trade, but also political and cultural associations of every kind. The strong ties with Britain will remain, although they will no longer be so exclusive. As in the past, there will probably always be a steady influx of British immigrants. Enterprising people, especially young people, are urgently needed in the teaching and medical professions, as well as for skilled work in industry and commerce. Attracted by the good jobs and the great opportunities for getting on, the immigrant is warmly welcomed by everyone.

The countryside, too, provides a pleasant background to his new life. He cannot fail to be impressed by the variety and grandeur of the landscape, and to marvel at the active volcanoes and boiling geysers among the rugged mountains. Rotorua, a settlement which is half-Maori, half-European, gives the impression of a scene from science fiction, a lunar landscape, dotted with mounds and wreathed in steam. The pungent smell of sulphur is everywhere, and the distinctive "plop-plop" sound of boiling mud makes the visitor cautious about where he treads. The Maori can catch a fish in one lake and cook it in another! G. B. Shaw, standing at the entrance to Tiki Tere, one of the geothermal parks in Rotorua, compared it to the mouth of Hell.

New Zealand has a high standard of living, and it follows the maxim of "The greatest good for the greatest number". It has a more even distribution of wealth than most other developed countries. There are hardly any millionaires, but, on the other hand, nobody goes hungry. The Welfare State provides a free health service, free education, and a school dental service. There is a comprehensive system of state benefits, which aids the old, the sick, and the unemployed. Women were permitted to vote before their English sisters had even begun their long battle for emancipation. Although New Zealanders love to travel to Europe and feel a link with Great Britain especially, they are proud of their country which is beginning to find its own identity, and is producing writers, musicians, and artists of its own. It can be proud of such well-known names as Lord Rutherford, who, at the beginning of this century, paved the way for present-day atomic research, of Sir Edmund Hillary, the first conqueror of Mount Everest, of Katherine Mansfield, a writer of international reputation, and many others. There is still a certain feeling of isolation in New Zealand, which in the past has led her people to take too little interest in the rest of the world. This is changing rapidly now, thanks to broadcasting and television, and to the extensive facilities for air travel. While the older generation still clings tightly to the link with the mother-country, the young New Zealanders are working towards better relations with other countries, especially their Asian neighbours. Thus New Zealand is reaching out towards a new kind of independence.

Enid Bloomfield, Special Contribution for "Britain and America"

The Passing of Mahatma Gandhi

Everyone will have learnt with profound horror of the brutal murder of Mr. Gandhi, and I know that I am expressing the views of the British people in offering to his fellow countrymen our deep sympathy in the loss of their greatest citizen. Mahatma Gandhi, as he was known in India, was one of the outstanding figures in the world of today, but he seemed to belong to a different period of history. Living a life of extreme asceticism he was revered as a divinely inspired saint by millions of his fellow countrymen. His influence extended beyond the range of his co-religionists, and in a country deeply riven by communal dissension he had an appeal for all Indians. For a quarter of a century this one man has been the major factor in every consideration of the Indian problem. He had become the expression of the aspirations of the Indian people for independence. But he was not just a nationalist; he represented, it is true, the opposition of the Indians to being ruled by another race, but he also expressed a revulsion of the east against the west. He himself was in revolt against western materialism and sought for a return to a simpler state of society. But his most distinctive doctrine was that of non-violence. He believed in a method of passive resistance to those forces which he considered wrong. He opposed those who sought to achieve their ends by violence, and when, as too often happened, his campaigns for Indian freedom resulted in loss of life, owing to undisciplined action of those who professed to follow him, he was deeply grieved.

The sincerity and devotion with which he pursued his objective are beyond all doubt. In the latter months of his life, when communal strife was marring the freedom which India had attained, his threat to fast to the death resulted in the cessation of violence in Bengal. And again recently his fast in Delhi brought about a change in the atmosphere. He had besides a hatred of injustice and strove earnestly on behalf of the poor, and especially of the depressed classes in India. The hand of the murderer has struck

The Problems of India today

There can be no mistaking the disenchantment in India today. The euphoria of independence, now in its twentieth year, has evaporated. There have been four bad years, with two wars, the death of two Prime Ministers, a devaluation, and drought two years running. The third of the five-year plans has been a sad disappointment. Growth has been checked for the first time since 1950, food production has been flagging while the population climbs towards 500 million.°

It is easy to make too much of the disenchantment. There have been immense achievements in the past 15 years. Agricultural production has increased by two thirds, industrial output one and a half times. The numbers at school have trebled. Literacy is up from 15 per cent at independence to 30 per cent now. Show pieces such as hydroelectric dams, irrigation schemes, steel plants, oil refineries, nuclear power projects, the airlines, the machine tool industry, and so on, testify along with the statistics to what has been done.

48 Sacred Cows in a Square in the City of New Delhi

Yet it must be admitted that the show pieces are still isolated growth points. The best is fine on any standards, but too much of the primitive lags behind. If anything the gap between the past and the present is widening. India's crisis is a crisis of frustrated expectations, of patience wearing thin in a country where it is unreasonably impatient to suppose that even modest dreams can be fully realised in less than another two generations.

So much is easy for the visitor to see. To suggest what might be done must seem presumptuous. Yet sometimes the fleeting outside glance may be useful simply because it is innocent of preconceptions.

What struck me in a short but crowded tour of some 3,000 miles is the weakness of communication. By that I mean that the message of new farming methods, of family planning, of health and hygiene, is not getting through fast enough or widely enough. It is not getting through, I believe, because there is neither sufficient will nor are there sufficient resources to see that it does.

Take the Indian press. For a fortnight I looked at up to half a dozen of the English language papers every day. Not one of them that I saw carried on-the-spot reporting from the famine areas of Bihar (though one had a page of pictures). The journalists sit tight in their capitals and report political speeches. In Delhi, in particular, the press is parochial and introspective, even though politically acute.

In this it is encouraged by the Government, which complains of sensational and alarmist reporting when the press takes the trouble to find out for itself what is going wrong. The Government would have been taken less by surprise by the famine if the press had done a better job of reporting. As it is, the gravity of the famine seems to have been recognised only when the starving started trekking out of their villages to the towns. For a planning Government the communication with the villages (where three quarters of India's population lives) is, from what I could learn, very far from adequate.

Take broadcasting. The transistor radio is the most powerful agent of social change in the world today. This platitude has not registered with India's planners. The fourth five-year plan (I quote from the official summary) allows £ 22 millions for expanding broadcasting services ("mainly to strengthen external services") in a Budget which provides £ 3,000 millions for industry and mining and £ 2,500 millions for agriculture and related services. Production of radio receivers is currently about 500,000 a year. They are excessively expensive compared with the cheap transistor sets turned out in Japan, Hongkong, or Formosa.

The villages will learn if they get the chance. The Punjab Agricultural University, an impressive centre of agricultural research, sends all its teachers out into the villages. The peasant cultivator, they report, puts shrewd, penetrating questions. And they have been delighted to discover that a black market in improved seed and fertiliser has been growing up. That convincingly proves that their message has got across.

To be illiterate in India is not to be unintelligent. You may not be able to read, but you may be avid to learn. Mass adult education by radio, I suggest, should be in the forefront of the plan for the next five years. The local press could play a part, too, though its performance to date has been poor, and its circulation low because it fails to present to its potential readers what they most urgently want to know.

Education, too, needs to be given more practical objectives. There has been talk of a national student service, with an obligatory term or two of "Peace Corps work" in the villages. It might give the students (there are now one and a half million of them) a sense of purpose and usefulness they seem to lack at the moment.°

A crisis of confidence is hardly surprising. But there have been great achievements, and sufficiently long experience of parliamentary democracy to steady the nerve. "We have been going through a bad patch, but we are sound at heart", a shrewd Indian journalist told me.

I do not doubt it. This is no time for India to lose its nerve, nor for India's friends to lose theirs. We must avoid the temptation to test India's performance by Western standards, or to expect it to Westernise its own culture as the price of aid. India is admirable for its own sake. It has prodigious, sometimes heartbreaking problems. It will disappoint itself and its friends, yet nowhere have I felt more strongly the force of that wise old precept: never despair.

Harford Thomas in "Manchester Guardian Weekly", 1966

The Challenge of Africa

All the new nations of Africa have inherited a legacy of authoritarian political structures from their former rulers. This is a fact worthy of note, especially in relations to the political institutions that are being developed by the nationalist governments that have succeeded colonial rulers.

The development of "strong executives" has been encouraged by investors who insist that, as a guarantee for the security of their investments, they require strong, stable governments, about which they have shown more concern than about the civil liberties of the governed. An African leader who set out resolutely to establish a "strong government" by the ruthless elimination of opposition justified his conduct by saying that he wanted investments, and investors did not ask whether there were civil liberties but whether there was stability and a strong leader capable of ensuring its maintenance.

African communities, or tribes, developed their own political systems before the period of colonization. Every society must have its own institutions for the maintenance of social order and the control and regulation of the use of physical force. With special reference to Africa, indigenous political organizations also gave emphasis to the settlement of disputes and the restoration of harmonious personal relations, on which the communities placed a high value. Some communities and tribes (the Ashanti of Ghana, the Yoruba of Nigeria, the Zulu of South Africa, to mention only a few examples) had highly developed political organizations, with differentiated hierarchies of office-holders, from kings and chiefs to attendants, wielding varying degrees of authority. Each organization was one in which different individuals played different roles. The significant thing was that everyone had a role, and everyone had some degree of participation in political life; for political organization was an aspect of the social life, in which everyone participated.

In Africa, group and tribal ties are still strong. As has been shown, group solidarity was the essential foundation of social life. It is an interesting phenomenon that certain words in the course of time become loaded with irrational emotions and prejudices. *Tribalism* is one such word. *Tribe* and *tribalism* have become so readily and prejudicially equated with whatever is reactionary that few pause to give any further examination to the matter.

Indigenous, or tribal, groups wish to maintain their political identity. Indigenous groups have often refused to exchange European domination for what they fear may be similar control by other indigenous groups.

Among the tribal groups that have demanded constitutional arrangements in recognition of their group solidarity are the Ashanti of Ghana, the Yoruba and the Ibo of Nigeria. Far from being reactionary groups, they are among the most progressive in Africa, and their respective accomplishments give evidence of civic maturity as developed as can be found in any African community. This compels scrutiny of the assumptions that tribalism is reactionary and necessarily incompatible with nationhood.

Despite their respective problems, all the African countries that came under colonial rule had to deal with certain common aspects of the impact of European law. European legal concepts and, along with them, procedures were imposed on all of these countries. Community life, once regulated by customary laws, which were expected to be understood by all adults, was now subject to laws imposed by an alien ruler.

The impact of European law has had not only legal, but political consequences. European law, particularly that of the French and that of the British, carried with it ideas that were bound sooner or later to prove explosive. These concepts rested implicitly, and sometimes explicitly, on doctrines of natural rights, rationalism, and individualism.

The slogan of the French Revolution, "Liberty, Equality, Fraternity", was also inherent in British law and tradition. These ideas were given memorable expression in the American Declaration of Independence of 1776: "We hold these truths to be self-evident, that all men are created equal, that they are endowed by their Creator with certain unalienable Rights, that among these are Life, Liberty and the pursuit of Happiness". Africans demand acceptance as equals, for "all men are created equal", and are "endowed ... with certain unalienable Rights", among them, the right of a people to freedom from colonial domination.

There is a close link between African education and African nationalism. Europe brought to Africa a heritage of education carried on through formal schooling. In the schools that missionaries and European governments established in Africa, Africans were given the key to new knowledge. They learned to read and write and to absorb new ideas—such as those of natural rights, human dignity, and equality.

In Africa, as elsewhere, education is a potent instrument of social change. It has imparted new skills, which aided Africa's economic development. And it has also fostered the emergence of a new class of Africans—a class of literate people. In view of the contributions education is expected to make to nation-building and development, past policies and achievements have been subjected to criticism and reappraisal. Too few people have been educated for the many tasks that now require literate Africans. It is estimated that 100 million adults in Africa cannot read or write. In view of the stress on African culture that African nationalism now demands, it may well be asked if there is anything in African traditional methods of education that is of value, or of relevance, to contemporary issues. There is one thing. And it is an important one. In the traditional forms of education, there was much emphasis on behaviour on good and evil as the society saw it, in terms of its own survival and continuity. Education was for life, for the fulfillment of social obligations. It was rooted in the person, and in his behaviour. This was essentially right. Education must be concerned with what human beings become. The need for technicians and productive skills must not be allowed to obscure this. Training, even for the narrow objective of industrialization, cannot be successful if education is solely in utilitarian terms; for industrial life, like any other, demands standards of discipline and responsibility, attitudes and behaviour, without which it cannot function properly. The quality of life counts.

The challenge of education offered to and by the emergent states of Africa is a challenge to think afresh about what education can do to foster an international community based on men and women who have been adequately prepared not only to be good men and women, but also to be good citizens of a world that consists of many nations, all of which share in mutual sympathy and respect, in a common humanity.

Dr. Aggrey, a great African whose life was devoted to working and living for the brotherhood of man and for cooperation between black und white, left us the beautiful imagery of the black and white keys of a piano. You can, he taught, make some sort of music on the white keys of the piano alone, or on the black keys alone, but for real harmony, you need both the black and the white keys. He believed that harmonious relations between black and white could be achieved, and he held to this belief in spite of humiliating experiences. "I want to sing a song of hope to the despairing", he said, "to breathe the breath of love that will chase away all hating. I believe that right will ultimately conquer wrong, virtue conquer vice, harmony take the place of discords".

The starting point of harmonious race relations is the recognition that each race is like the other—that all men are equal in their humanity.

Kofi A. Busia, Special Contribution for "Britain and America"

The World watches Kenya

The gods tried to give Kenya everything. Its coastline cuts the equator in a girdle of coral reefs and green lagoons that lap miles of glorious white beaches. Inland the country soars 6,000 feet to a dazzling plateau where blue mountains stalk the horizon at sunset and big game wanders free in golden, parklike country. But the accidents of history made this paradise of 225,000 square miles, where 190,000 Asians of Indian origin live among 10 million Africans and some 40,000 whites, slave to all the common problems of Africa.°

Africa wasn't Africa in the heyday of European colonialism but bits of England, France, Belgium and Portugal patched over a captive continent. And no colony had itself more groomed, frilled and disguised in parts than Kenya. Its "White Highlands" swarmed with imitative aspects of British suburbia aided by a cool, wet climate that permitted all roses to bloom. From log fire to fox hunt over Kikuyu hill and dale, the unspeakable galloped in happy pursuit of the uneatable, comforted by the assumption that in Africa at least the empire would last a thousand years. In fact it lasted less than a century, for when Kenya got its *uhuru* in 1963 it was only 68 years since the country had been declared a British protectorate in 1895; it was annexed to the "Crown" as a colony in 1920. And the Asian then as now was its "middleman", but more accurately, the man in the middle, a role not entirely of his own choosing.

How long does it take to belong? In 1859 Burton estimated that 6,000 "Hindus" were settled along the East African coast. Livingstone met Indian traders in Zanzibar and when Stanley went in search of the missionary he got guides and provisions from Indian *dukas*—small, open-fronted stores—along his route.°

The modern development of Kenya began at the turn of the century. In 1895 a railway line started it; 32,000 Indian workers were recruited and brought over in batches to do the job. The line took six years to complete. It winds 8,000 feet into Kenya's lush, green highlands before descending to its terminus on Lake Victoria. Hailed as an engineering feat, it was equally a feat of human endurance and muddled organization. Seven thousand Indians were invalided home, 2,000 died of tropical diseases. Scores were taken by lions prowling outside the workers' tents at night.

European settlement began soon after the railway's completion. Retired British soldiers and a fringe of English aristocracy carved great estates on the cool plateau. Coffee, tea and modern dairy farms flourished on spacious, segregated acres. Beside them stood the crowded "Native Reserves", thickly patchworked with maize fields and banana palms, glaring red-eyed where soil erosion cut a swath through once-green hillsides.

Denied access to these fertile areas cordoned off for "White" and "Native" use, retired Indian workers forged into the wilderness, opening small shops as their forefathers had done, building the nucleus of future towns and cities. Among Indian immigrants, the administration found a ready supply of clerks, builders and stationmasters.

Between two world wars, the 20th Century surged into Kenya with irresistible force. In its wake tribal traditions lay shattered. The peace of a bygone age vanished in the harassing demands of a new and bewildering way of life which paid more heed to a man's marketable value than to human dignity.

A very far-seeing government might have realized soon after World War I the necessity to organize mass education from the start. But this was a colonial regime chiefly interested in helping immigrant white farmers find cheap black labor. It was also an age of *laissez faire* at its most blatant with every community for itself, sanctioned by laws imposed on the country. And at the root of all future trouble lay the nature of the land grab in the "White Highlands". Only 16.7 million out of Kenya's 140 million acres are considered good enough for high potential farming. When European settlers laid claim to the best parts of this, the seeds of Mau Mau had been sown. It erupted in the '50s with all the raging despair of dispossessed Africa.

And yet, now that the debris from that explosion has largely settled, it can hardly be denied, taking into account the era in which all this happened, that Britain left behind good value for its years of exploitation. The country was not ruthlessly plundered. Something viable was created in a lovely country. Kenya's capital, Nairobi, blossomed from a collection of railway sheds planted on the edge of the mighty Rift Valley into one of the great cities of Africa. On the coast, centuries-old Mombasa fulfilled its promise and grew into a modern port that connects much of East Africa to the outside world. In the hinterland agriculture gave the country a sound economic base. From a dugout the old Indian and European settlers fashioned an ocean-going liner. The skill to propel it along now remains in the country.

For little fault of his own the Asian was until recently the clerk in every office, the mechanic in every garage and the familiar Sikh driver on the railways. He is still the accountant in every bank, the builder, plumber, electrician and general handyman in most towns. Asian-owned shops line all the main streets. Most of Kenya's doctors, lawyers, dentists and engineers are descendants of immigrant Indian workers. A large proportion of the country's textile industry, its sugar mills, assembly plants, aluminium and, soon, steel rolling mills, sawmills and the ancillary workshops that go to make a composite secondary industry in a developing country, springs largely from the enterprise of this one community.

It is galling to the African, this awsome degree of Asian competence and endless growth. He is master of a country over which he feels he has no real control. To correct this state of affairs a policy of "Africanization" has been launched making it incumbent on anyone in business to take in local African staff as quickly as possible. Its effects have been rapid and significant.°

The world watches Kenya. And Kenya must succeed in solving its Asian dilemma. Failure to do so will point the finger of racialism squarely into the one corner in Free Africa where race relations are in the hands of black rulers. Given some good will and a little luck the chances are that Kenya's vital experiment could still succeed.

Kuldip Sondhi in "Life", 1968

Arrival in Liverpool

Liverpool next day was grey, cold, wet and foggy; and the promised land looked most unpromising from the deck of the ship. Once ashore, however, the towering buildings, massed traffic, and attractive shops kept us staring and gaping whilst waiting for our trains to various parts of the country. The sight of white people *en masse* was itself something which required some getting used to; but the thing that took us really aback was our first sight of a white man sweeping a gutter. He was a short, seedy-looking, rather dirty man, with heavy working boots and stained, well-worn clothes, but unmistakably a white man nevertheless; and actually standing right down in the gutter sweeping it, collecting the rubbish on a shovel and tipping it into a wheelbarrow. We stood in utter disbelief, at some little distance from him, expecting him at any moment either to vanish like a gremlin down the nearest drain, or else to turn dark brown. I suppose if you had asked us beforehand who swept gutters in England, we should have replied, after a moment or two's reflection, that we supposed some of the English drains, at least, must have the honour of being swept by white men; for even all the stowaways and workless migrants from Africa and the West Indies could not provide enough labour for so many menial tasks. But no one had prepared us beforehand by any such question; and the sight of that man almost felled us.°

We did not lose respect for the white man—very far from it. What we did lose however (and long overdue was the loss), was an illusion created by the rôle the white man plays in Africa: that he is a kind of demigod whose hands must never get dirty, who must not be allowed to carry anything heavier than a portfolio or wield any implement heavier than a pen. Without realizing it, we had come to think of the white man only in the rôle of missionary, civil servant, or senior business executive, one who was always behind the desk, never in front of it. We saw him as one who always gave orders, never took them, who could have any job he liked for the asking. So to realize that that man was perfectly happy working in that gutter (snatches of his melancholy whistling reached us faintly where we stood) was a most salutary experience. It was now possible for us to like the white man. For before you can like (as distinct from merely admiring or emulating), you must feel kinship, a shared humanity, the possibility of common experiences and destinies. As we resumed our walk past the sweeper, he looked up and grinned cheerfully at us, leaning for a moment on his brush. We waved and grinned back; and in that mute exchange of greetings there was erased in a moment the memory of the behaviour of the stewards on board. The latter had acted as if the gods had decreed that the black man should minister and the white man be ministered unto, and that they were stewards and we passengers only by special dispensation. Our friend the roadsweeper, on the other hand, was so far from harbouring any such notions that he had found time to give us, in his own way, a welcome to Liverpool.

William Conton, "The African", 1960

Britain's Coloured Population

The Riot Question is dangerous not because it titillates our latent fascination with violence but because it encourages an already widespread British conviction that the absence of violence indicates good race relations, and that harmony should be our principal goal. It would be tragic if the U.S. race riots made us equate the Equilibrium Society with the just society. We would do well to recall the monstrous stability of the Southern cotton plantation under slavery and the absence of race riots in the cities of South Africa.

The relevant question which is posed for white Britons by the Negro rebellion in the States is not whether there will be violence here, but whether we are now producing the same unjust conditions for coloured people that have driven American Negroes on to the streets in scornful mobs. For, however much we try to think overwise, race riots are not caused by the heat of the July sun, or the club of the odd sadistic policeman, or the speeches of Stokely Carmichael. They incubate for decades. Legal remedies are at hand, but they have come too late to be effective.

49 West Indian Immigrants arriving at Victoria Station, London

Meanwhile, in Britain, it is tempting to regard the present nightmare of race relations in the States as irrelevant to our situation. After all, the coloured community forms only 2 per cent of the total British population (11 per cent in the U.S.). It consists largely of new immigrants, too insecurely based, too ignorant of the outside world, or too grateful for a higher standard of life, to make much trouble. The divisions between and among West Indians, Indians and Pakistanis hamper the development of strong immigrant organisations. It is still too early to prove convincingly to the white community that the children of coloured immigrants will face substantial discrimination when they leave school seeking better jobs and homes than their parents now have. Our welfare system, with all its defects, may yet prevent a coloured under-class from sinking to the depths of the North American ghetto.

Certainly these factors make it unlikely that race riots will break out in Britain's coloured communities during the next few years, unless they are started by whites against blacks, as in Notting Hill in 1958.

It is possible that this will happen. For example, I spoke recently in a West London church where there are two separate youth clubs, one for English and the other for Indian children. When, at my insistence, the Indian children were invited to the meeting and one brave 16-year-old accepted, the police had to be called to keep the peace. The future of race relations in that suburb is in the hands of those children. It may be violent.

However, the general situation here, in contrast with the United States, is likely to remain deceptively calm. We are at a similar stage to New York and Chicago in the 1920's. By a million individual acts of "private preference" we are creating patterns of racial discrimination in housing and employment which it will be increasingly difficult to break. We are educating the children of coloured immigrants, often in substandard schools, for unskilled jobs, which will soon be destroyed by automation. In some places, complaints by coloured Britons of police misconduct outnumber those on any other subject. The hostility which many West Indians in particular feel towards policemen may often spring from previous experiences in the Caribbean rather than here. But what matters is that allegations of police brutality and harassment are readily believed in the coloured community, and that in the absence of any independent machinery to investigate complaints, this vital area of race relations will fester.

Britain's coloured minority is too small to have political significance, except as a potential scapegoat at election time. There is no strong civil rights movement which can effectively represent its interests. Much of the official race relations machinery is devoted more to harmony and social welfare than to promoting racial equality.

The Equilibrium Society is indeed being mistaken for the just society.° The Race Relations Board has already done better, from its position of powerlessness, than its transatlantic counterparts in winning the confidence of coloured people. It must now be allowed to tackle the real problems of discrimination and it must be given the power to enforce the law.

The alternatives are clear. We can provide effective redress for the victim of discrimination, or we can compel him to choose to accept injustice or to take his grievances to the streets. Britain's coloured population is more likely to put up with injustice in the next few years than to riot, but does a civilised society have any choice?

Anthony Lester in "The Sunday Times", 1967

VII American Politics

The Mayflower Compact, 1620

In the Name of God, Amen. We whose names are underwritten, the loyal subjects of our dread Sovereign Lord King James, by the Grace of God of Great Britain, France, and Ireland King, Defender of the Faith, etc.
   Having undertaken, for the Glory of God and advancement of the Christian Faith and Honour of our King and Country, a Voyage to plant the First Colony in the Northern Parts of Virginia, do by these presents solemnly and mutually in the presence of God and one of another, covenant and combine ourselves together into a Civil Body Politic, for our better ordering and preservation and furtherance of the ends aforesaid; and by virtue hereof to enact, constitute and frame such just and equal Laws, Ordinances, Acts, Constitutions and Offices, from time to time, as shall be thought most meet and convenient for the general good of the Colony, unto which we promise all due submission and obedience. In witness whereof we have hereunder subscribed our names, at Cape Code, the 11th of November, in the year of the reign of our Sovereign Lord King James, of England, France, and Ireland the eighteenth, and of Scotland the fifty-fourth. Anno Domini 1620.
"English Historical Documents", IX, 1955

Excerpts from the Declaration of Independence, 1776

When in the course of human events, it becomes necessary for one people to dissolve the political bands which have connected them with another, and to assume among the powers of the earth, the separate and equal station to which the Laws of Nature and of Nature's God entitle them, a decent respect to the opinions of mankind requires that they should declare the causes which impel them to the separation.
   We hold these truths to be self-evident, that all men are created equal, that they are endowed by their Creator with certain unalienable rights, that among these are life, liberty and the pursuit of happiness. That to secure these rights, Governments are instituted among men, deriving their just powers from the consent of the governed. That whenever any form of government becomes destructive of these ends, it is the right of the people to alter or to abolish it, and to institute new government, laying its foundation on such principles and organizing its powers in such form, as to them shall seem most likely to effect their safety and happiness. Prudence, indeed, will dictate that governments long established should not be changed for light and transient causes; and accordingly all experience hath shown, that mankind are more disposed to suffer, while evils are sufferable, than to right themselves by abolishing the forms to which they are accustomed. But when a long train of abuses and usurpations, pursuing invariably the same object evinces a design to reduce them under absolute des-

50 B. Franklin, Th. Jefferson, R. Sherman, and J. Adams (left to right) preparing the Declaration of Independence

potism, it is their right, it is their duty, to throw off such government, and to provide new guards for their future security. Such has been the patient sufferance of these Colonies; and such is now the necessity which constrains them to alter their former systems of government. The history of the present King of Great Britain is a history
5 of repeated injuries and usurpations, all having in direct object the establishment of an absolute tyranny over these States. To prove this, let facts be submitted to a candid world.° *[Here follows a long list of grievances.]*

We, therefore, the Representatives of the United States of America, in General Congress assembled, appealing to the Supreme Judge of the world for the rectitude
10 of our intentions, do, in the name, and by authority of the good people of these Colonies, solemnly publish and declare, That these United Colonies are, and of right ought to be Free and Independent States; that they are absolved from all allegiance to the British Crown, and that all political connection between them and the State of Great Britain, is and ought to be totally dissolved; and that as Free and Independent
15 States, they have full power to levy war, conclude peace, contract alliances, establish commerce, and to do all other acts and things which Independent States may of right do. And for the support of this declaration, with a firm reliance on the protection of Divine Providence, we mutually pledge to each other our lives, our fortunes and our sacred honor.

"*A Documentary History of the United States*", 1965

20 Excerpts from Lincoln's Emancipation Proclamation, 1863

Now, therefore, I, Abraham Lincoln, President of the United States, by virtue of the power in me vested as Commander-in-Chief of the Army and Navy of the United States, in time of actual armed rebellion against the authority and government of the

United States, and as a fit and necessary war measure for suppressing said rebellion,° do order and declare that all persons held as slaves within said designated States and parts of States are, and henceforward shall be, free; and that the Executive Government of the United States including the military and naval authorities thereof, shall recognize and maintain the freedom of said persons.

And I hereby enjoin upon the people so declared to be free to abstain from all violence, unless in necessary self-defense; and I recommend to them that, in all cases where allowed, they labor faithfully for reasonable wages.

And I further declare and make known that such persons of suitable condition will be received into the armed service of the United States to garrison forts, positions, stations, and other places, and to man vessels of all sorts in said service.

And upon this act, sincerely believed to be an act of justice, warranted by the Constitution upon military necessity, I invoke the considerate judgment of mankind and the gracious favor of Almighty God.

"A Documentary History of the United States", 1965

Abraham Lincoln, The Gettysburg Address, November 19, 1863

Fourscore and seven years ago our fathers brought forth on this continent a new nation, conceived in liberty, and dedicated to the proposition that all men are created equal.

Now we are engaged in a great civil war, testing whether that nation or any nation so conceived and so dedicated, can long endure. We are met on a great battlefield of that war. We have come to dedicate a portion of that field as a final resting-place for those who here gave their lives that that nation might live. It is altogether fitting and proper that we should do this.

But, in a larger sense, we cannot dedicate—we cannot consecrate—we cannot hallow—this ground. The brave men, living and dead, who struggled here, have consecrated it far above our poor power to add or detract. The world will little note nor long remember what we say here, but it can never forget what they did here. It is for us, the living, rather, to be dedicated here to the unfinished work which they who fought here have thus far so nobly advanced. It is rather for us to be here dedicated to the great task remaining before us—that from these honored dead we take increased devotion to that cause for which they gave the last full measure of devotion; that we here highly resolve that these dead shall not have died in vain; that this nation, under God, shall have a new birth of freedom; and that government of the people, by the people, for the people, shall not perish from the earth.

"A Documentary History of the United States", 1965

Baron von Steuben

Von Steuben was a trained soldier from boyhood. He learned his profession at the best of schools—that is, in actual warfare, under the direct instruction of the greatest master of the art of war of the eighteenth century.°

Baron von Steuben came to this country, actuated by the highest motives of patriotism, to help us achieve liberty, and he brought with him that which was without money and without price and which he infused into the rank and file of the Revolutionary Army—discipline and organization. He began his desperate task with the Army at Valley Forge in the winter of 1777-78.°

The history of Von Steuben's services shows him a kindly, considerate, brave, and accomplished soldier. As Inspector General, his achievements were not the successes of an independent command, but they were the preparation by persistent but tedious drilling and discipline of men to serve effectively under other commanders and to win for them victory. It seemed a thankless task for it had none of the spectacular in it, none of the glory of military triumph. It was the basic hard work without which such triumphs could not be won, but the results inured to the glory of others.

Steuben asked for no reward, except that if his services were satisfactory, at the end of the war he should be recompensed for the sacrifices he had made in leaving his home and giving up lucrative rank and office. Washington, that calm, sane, just judge of men, recognized fully the debt that he and the Army and the people owed to Von Steuben, and it is gratifying to know that he gave his evidence as he laid down his command of the Army in a letter full of expressions of gratitude to his comrade in arms, whose important aid at a critical juncture he fully appreciated.

When Baron Steuben came to this country he found Germans who had preceded him, and who, like him, had elected to make this their permanent home. Since his day millions of his countrymen have come to be Americans, and it adds great interest to our celebration and emphasizes the propriety of the action of Congress in erecting this statue to know that the German race since the Revolution has made so large a part of our population and played so prominent a part in the great growth and development of our country.° The Germans who have become American citizens and their descendants may well take pride in this occasion and in this work of art, modeled by the hand of an American of German descent, which commemorates the valued contribution made by a German soldier to the cause of American freedom at the time of its birth.

William H. Taft, "Address upon the Unveiling of the Statue of Baron von Steuben", 1910

The New Deal

Roosevelt with his *New Deal,* like Wilson before him with his *New Freedom* sought to remedy the imbalance between governmental functions and private economic power so that the Jeffersonian rights of life, liberty and the pursuit of happiness might be equally realized by all.

Unlike many on the extreme left and right, Roosevelt was the prisoner of no rigid political doctrine. Neither, however, did he have a well-developed economic theory upon which to attack the widespread poverty and desperation of the depression years. But, he did have a liberalist's concern for the common man, a general sense of the direction the government should follow, and a recognition of several problem areas. Furthermore, it was the very essence of his political philosophy not to be doctrinaire, but rather to experiment in the resolution of social ills, to which no doctrine had thus far provided solutions.

TVA (TENNESSEE VALLEY AUTHORITY)

Though the New Deal was not conceived in accord with a single far-sighted plan, it did follow a few general patterns. First, it was accepted that the Federal Government had a large measure of responsibility for the welfare of the people. Secondly, the government must take steps to get the economy moving again. Thirdly, there must be an improved use of the nation's natural resources, the best example of which is the highly successful government-organized Tennessee Valley project.

Alan P. Grimes, "The Political Philosophy of Four American Presidents", 1965

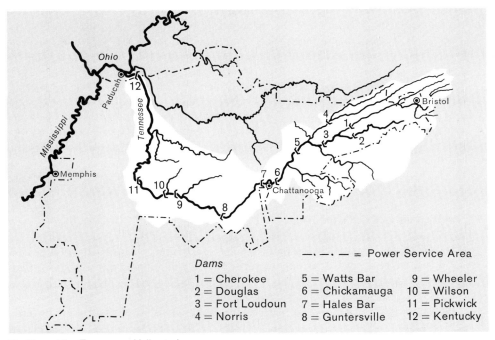

51 Plan of the Tennessee Valley today

TVA (Tennessee Valley Authority)

We are accustomed to look upon the distant past and the wonders of those times with awe and respect. We marvel at the relatively high technical achievements that made possible the Palaces of Mycenae, the Hanging Gardens of Babylon, the Temple of Jupiter in Olympia, and, perhaps the greatest achievement of all, the Pyramids and the Sphinx at Gizeh.

Can our culture, of which we are so proud, show anything comparable to these?

Some people say that we have lost the artistic sense and feeling for the highest aesthetic values. Perhaps this is so. On the other hand, the wonders of the ancient world were all built with slave-labour; we use the machine as our helping hand. Our achievements have been made possible because thousands of earnest men worked and in some cases gave their lives in the endless search to master the secrets of nature, and to harness the almost boundless power of the universe. Thus we have only to think of the dams in

Scotland, the Shannon Scheme (built by German technicians) for the electrification of the Irish Republic, and the Edertalsperre in Germany. Perhaps the greatest, however, is the amazing technical achievement known as the TVA.

This was a great experiment in Government planning. The Tennessee River is one of the most important rivers in the country, its valley covering parts of seven states.

The area round the Tennessee River had been virtually of no use to mankind. There was no proper navigation, the harvests were destroyed by floods, and the soil was being washed away. The Federal Government, being responsible for the control of the rivers, was therefore empowered by Congress in 1933 to set up the TVA. The genius of American technicians and the unlimited wealth poured into the project in the short space of about ten years converted this wilderness into one of the most vital points in the economy of the United States. Several great dams were built preventing floods and making it possible to use the river for transporting goods all the year round. They also make it possible to generate on a large scale electricity which is taken to farms and towns all over the area. This electric power costs only half as much as power supplied elsewhere in the country by profit-making corporations. From being an unhealthy, unproductive and uncultivable territory it has become a most thriving district in which agriculture flourishes and cultural institutions of all kinds abound. Nature has been harnessed to serve the needs of Man.

Special Contribution for "Britain and America"

The Written and the Unwritten

American: If you want to find out how a country is governed, you go to its constitution, and it is some of the differences between the British and American constitutions that we are now going to discuss.

Briton: We in Great Britain are very proud of our constitution because of the principles on which it is based—of the freedom, law, and order which we enjoy because of it. But, astonishing as it may seem, I could not take you into a shop and order for you a printed copy of the British Constitution. The bookseller would smile if you asked him for a copy, and probably reply that he had a number of most excellent books about the constitution, but that he had no copy of the constitution itself.

There are a number of reasons for this, and I am not at all sure that they are easy to explain, but I will try. Our constitution has been compared by someone to a rambling country house that has grown, over the centuries, with a patch here, a new window there, an added wing, a raised roof, and with modernized plumbing. Our constitution has grown and developed, and it is really part of our history. True, certain parts of it are written down in the shape of innumerable Acts of Parliament, passed from time to time—Acts of Parliament like the Habeas Corpus Act (1679), the Bill of Rights (1689), the Reform Bills of the nineteenth century, the Parliament Act of 1911, etc.

All these Acts of Parliament are part of the British Constitution. But there are also a very large number of what we call customs or conventions of the constitution. They are not written down anywhere, but they are generally accepted, and are capable of being changed. For instance, there is no Act of Parliament laying down how our Prime Minister should be appointed, or how many members there should be in the Cabinet;

it is nowhere laid down that the Prime Minister should be a member of the House of Commons and not of the House of Lords.

It is in keeping with our strong British tradition that it is better to keep things elastic. We do not like the rigidity of having things written down. That, as shortly as I can give it, is the position about our constitution, and how we view it. Now what about yours?

American: In the United States, the word *constitution* has a somewhat different meaning, I think. In America, when the word is mentioned, people think of a written document, and we have lots of them. We have a constitution for the United States, we have constitutions for each of the fifty states, and every city has its written constitution. Now it is quite obvious to us as it is to you that no constitution is ever entirely written, and we do have all kinds of customs and usages growing up around these constitutions.

A great many things about the organization of our Government and about its powers are not covered by these documents, but there is nevertheless this short document that we call the Constitution of the United States, drafted by the Constitutional Convention that met in Philadelphia in the summer of 1787. A group of fifty-five men who met there at that time drafted this short document, which every American reads, and which every American knows something about.

Briton: Yes, now let us just slip back to 1787. Possibly the circumstances of the time made it necessary that you should have a written constitution; these different states wanted to be quite certain and clear as to what rights they were surrendering, and what they were not surrendering. Is there something in that?

American: Yes, I think it is impossible to establish a federal system—and that is what these men in Philadelphia were trying to do—establish a federal system that would tie these thirteen more or less independent states together into some kind of unit, without a written constitution, because the members of such a union do want to know what rights are reserved to themselves in the union and what powers they have given up to the central government. It all has to be put down in very definite form; it cannot be kept too flexible because somebody may be going to cheat on the game in the course of time. Well, the fathers of the constitution had to move very cautiously: they could not give the Federal Government a great deal of power because the people from the thirteen states wanted to keep a lot of power to themselves and to their own states.

Briton: What precise powers, then, did they give the Federal Government?

American: The Federal Government—the Congress and the President—have control over foreign affairs, control over trade with foreign countries, also control over trade between the states in the union. The Federal Government has power to provide for a defence organization, an Army and a Navy, and, of course, nowadays an Air Force. That is the kind of thing that is under the control of the Federal Government, and then such things as education are local.

Briton: Let me get this clear: the Federal Government looks after defence, foreign policy, the armed forces, inter-state commerce. And you have one postal system. I suppose that, when this constitution was made, the idea was that, as these were not as important things as they are today, they really thought that they were leaving the majority of power with the states, whereas in actual practice, now, these things are the all-important things which affect the country's life. I would imagine, then, that your Federal Government, in spite of what the Fathers thought, is probably tending to have the lion's share of the power.

American: Yes, exactly! What has happened is that the Federal Government of the United States has grown constantly in power and in importance in our system.

Briton: Now then let us go to the states. What are the sort of powers, then, of which the states still have full control, which possibly may correspond in some degree to our local government powers in this country?

American: You just have to say that the powers which the Federal Government does not have are powers which the state and local governments do have. You cannot go to the constitution and find a list of the powers of the state and local government, but it is very easy to list some of the more important ones of them, e.g. control over education, or the building of highways.

Briton: Let us go on to another point. When we want to change our constitution, it is quite easy. All that has to happen is that the House of Commons or Parliament will pass an Act which can fundamentally alter the constitution so long as they get a majority vote. We have no special arrangements for changing the constitution.

American: It is quite different in the United States: it is very difficult to change the constitution of the United States, and it has not been changed very many times. We have twenty-seven amendments that have been added to the constitution, but ten of these were added at *one* time, immediately after the ratification of the constitution, so, when you take that into account, it reduces the number to seventeen changes in our constitution in about 190 years. The reason for that is clear enough when you look at the procedure that must be followed in changing the constitution. Every change or amendment must be approved by a two-thirds' vote in each House of Congress, and by at least three-fourths of the fifty states.

Despite this, I think the amazing thing is that our constitution does adapt itself to changed conditions. It is in a very real sense a living constitution. Part of that is due to the fact that it is worded in rather general terms, and capable of varied interpretation, but when you realize that the constitution of the United States does not contain such words as *radio,* for example, or *television,* it does not even have such words as *business* and *agriculture* in it, and yet the Federal Congress of the United States does regulate radio and television, and it regulates agriculture in a great many ways. The constitution has been interpreted in such a way as to make it possible for the Government to meet these new conditions as they arise.

The final authority—the final decision on just how much power the President has, how much power Congress has—is the Supreme Court of the United States. Cases will find their way up through the Courts step by step, and end finally in the United States Supreme Court, and that Court then will say, finally, whether or not the action, or whether or not the legislation, is within the constitution—and that is the final word.

Briton: Let me just see that we have got these points clearly in our minds. Our constitution is only partly written: it is flexible. The American constitution is written down, and yet although we pride ourselves upon the ease with which our constitution adapts itself to changing circumstances, we have seen that equally in America—in spite of its being written—it does change, and adapts itself to new conditions. We can change our constitution much more easily than the Americans, and we have nothing quite the same as the Supreme Court.

"London Calling, European Ed."

The American Two-Party System

The most significant fact about the system of political parties in the United States has been the existence of two major parties rather than the half a dozen or more found in other countries.

Why we have just two major parties is not clear. One reason may be the rules of our elections. First, the most important person in our government, the President, is elected by the votes of all the people through their vote, in each state, for members of the electoral college. A majority vote of the electoral college is necessary to elect the President. In that kind of election only two parties could hope to have much chance of winning. Throughout our history, no third party has ever succeeded in winning the presidency.°

Both major parties, today, include a broad representation of almost all groups within our country. If any one factor tends to identify the adherents of the parties, it is most likely to be income. By and large, most of the middle class and the wealthy are Republicans and most of the low-income and poor families are Democrats. There is no uniformity, however, and you can find plenty of rich Democrats and poor Republicans! The geographical patterns of the past can still be observed, though they are changing. Republicans draw their strength from parts of the Northeast, the Midwest, and the Rocky Mountain states. Democrats win regularly in much of the South and in the cities of the North.°

The South has been an exception to the normal workings of two-party politics. The Democrats have so completely dominated party politics there that until very recently no serious Republican opposition arose. Republicans failed even to nominate candidates for most state offices and for Congress. Since the Democratic nominees were assured of election, the only serious contests were waged within the Democratic Party for nominations.°

The two-party pattern of national politics is not necessarily repeated within all of the states. In perhaps a third of the states, the strength of the two major parties is roughly even, and competition between them parallels the national pattern. But in most states one party or the other dominates the political scene. While the opposition party is active, it has only an outside chance of winning the governorship and, in some instances, virtually no chance at all of winning control of the state legislature. That is the normal prospect facing Democrats in South Dakota and Republicans in Georgia.°

A favorite criticism of the American party system is that there are few if any clear points of difference between the two major parties. It is true that American parties are not tightly disciplined organizations in which all of the members of one party think one way on any given issue and all members of the other party think the other way. Both major parties include within their ranks people with all sorts of views on all sorts of issues. There is, however, a consensus within each party on many issues, and the consensus of one party often differs from the other's in philosophy and in specific results.

An essential difference stems understandably from a basic difference in the parties' sources of strength. Gaining large support from the middle classes and the wealthy, some Republicans are generally inclined to support the interests of manufacturing and commercial enterprises. Many Democrats, aware of their support from the ranks of the lower income and the poor, tend to favor the interests of working people and the disadvantaged. This distinction must not be overdrawn. As a party, Republicans often act in the best interests of low-income families, and Democrats often support measures to assist business interests.°

Both parties know that a third party has little chance of gaining substantial strength. The battle in the next election is sure to be between the two parties now in existence. Knowing this, each party feels confident that it can move to the middle ground without serious fear of losing the support of its extreme members. And both parties can see that in a closely divided two-party system, victory will go to the party that can occupy the middle ground. So neither party goes out of its way to emphasize its differences with the other; both prefer to present to the public a claim that they can each satisfy the wishes of a sizable majority of the public.

The blurring of party differences is a disappointment to those political scientists who believe that democracy functions best when voters are confronted with clear-cut choices at election time. They argue that only if the parties are clearly identified with opposing positions on public issues can the voters intelligently express their views on these issues. What they really want is more than just differences between party positions. They would like the elected officials of both parties, especially in the state and Federal legislatures, to be required to give consistent support to party positions with their votes on legislation. They prefer a system of "party responsibility" under which legislators will support their party's position even though it conflicts with their personal judgment. To a large extent that system prevails in the British Parliament.

The absence of such a system in the U.S. Congress is explained not so much by the lack of differences between parties as by the limited ability of our parties to require legislators to support their party's positions. In England, the party has a firm hold on its members in Parliament. There, the party's ultimate weapon is the power to deny a member renomination. If a member fails to support the party's position on important issues, the national party will see to it that someone else is nominated from his district. A member thus disciplined usually has no effective way to win a nomination in his district, or any other, in the face of party opposition.

In this country, however, the national parties have virtually no say in state and local nominations for seats in Congress. States' rights clearly prevail in politics. Nominations are determined exclusively within the states; often, state political parties are powerless to influence nominations in Congressional Districts within the states. Even when a party has control of the White House and has as vigorous a President as Franklin D. Roosevelt, recalcitrant party members who vote against the party's position cannot be denied renomination. Roosevelt tried, in 1938, to engineer the defeat of several Democratic lawmakers who had opposed him. He was almost completely unsuccessful.

Knowing that the national party cannot effectively discipline him to the extent of denying him renomination, the legislator in the U.S. Congress casts his votes on the basis of what he thinks is right and what he thinks is wanted by his constituents. The voters who send a Democrat to Congress from Georgia do not necessarily agree with the voters who send a Democrat from California. Nor do the voters who send a Republican to Congress from Iowa necessarily agree with the voters who send a Republican from New York. With the membership of both major parties spread across a huge country, and lawmakers responsive to local constituencies, it is not surprising that at least at the national level we lack strict party responsibility.

There is, however, a cohesion among party members in Congress, and the national party leaderships can exert some influence on their members to support party positions. Democrats and Republicans in Congress often stick together unless the issue before them is one of compelling personal or local importance.

Abraham Ribicoff/Jon O. Newman, "Politics: The American Way", 1967

Elections in the U.S.A.

Americans are proud of their democratic form of government, and surely the essence of democracy is the direct say that the people have in running their government—national, state, and local. Today, we take for granted the idea that in a democracy everybody can vote. It is true that almost every adult in this country can vote, but we have been a long time making this idea a reality.

The power to decide who can vote rests with each of the 50 states, but this power must be exercised within the limits of both the United States Constitution and the laws Congress has passed to make sure the Constitutional rules are obeyed. For example, the 15th Amendment directs that the right to vote shall not be denied "on account of race, color, or previous condition of servitude", and the 19th Amendment forbids voting discrimination based on sex. As long as the Constitutional rules are followed, however, each state is free to set its own qualifications for voters. Eligibility to vote has been broadened almost continuously throughout our country's history.

In our country's earliest days, the right to vote was sharply limited. In some states the voters amounted to less than 3 percent of the population. Most of the original 13 states required a person to own a certain amount of property or to pay a certain amount of taxes before he was eligible to vote. By 1850, almost all of the states abandoned these qualifications and extended suffrage—the right to vote—to all adult free males.

The next major extension of the right to vote began in 1863 when the Emancipation Proclamation freed the Negro slaves. By the end of the Civil War, some Northern states had voluntarily granted Negroes the right to vote, but the Federal Constitution did not guarantee this right in all the states until the 15th Amendment was adopted in 1870.

While the 15th Amendment proclaimed a national policy against restricting the Negroes' right to vote, Negro suffrage did not become a reality in all parts of the country.°

As World War II ended, the Negroes' right to vote began moving from theory to practice. In 1944, the U.S. Supreme Court ruled that white primaries were in violation of the 15th Amendment. In 1957, Congress passed the first Civil Rights Act since Reconstruction. Part of this law permits the U.S. Attorney General to get a court order to stop anyone who interferes with another person's right to vote.°

In 1965, Congress took the strongest action it had ever taken to make sure Negroes could vote. The Voting Rights Act passed that year cut through the legal technicalities of earlier laws and simply abolished literacy tests in election districts (mostly in the South) where registration was so low that past discrimination against Negroes was obvious. In addition, the U.S. Attorney General was given the power to send Federal voting registrars to these districts. The results were dramatic. In some counties where

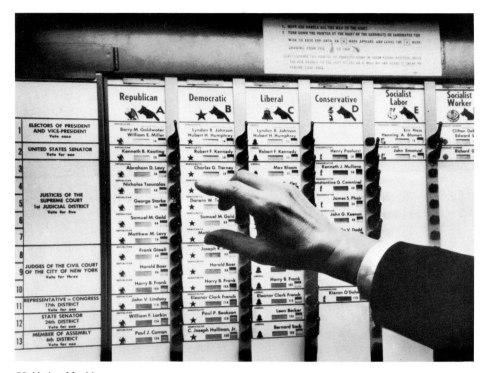

52 Voting Machine

only a handful of Negroes had ever previously been allowed to register with state officials, the Federal registrars quickly enrolled thousands of Negro voters. In 1966, the U.S. Supreme Court took another helpful step by ruling that payment of poll taxes as a condition for voting was unconstitutional in any kind of election.

The result of all these efforts has been an increase in the number of Negro voters in the South from about 250,000 in 1940 to 2,500,000 in 1966.°

These historic developments have moved the nation toward the democratic ideal of universal suffrage. There are, however, several restrictions imposed by the states under their powers to set voter qualifications. These state restrictions, of course, cannot undermine the extension of the right to vote that have been written into the Constitution and the laws of the United States.

The most obvious restriction concerns voting age. Almost all the states accept 21 as the minimum voting age, though Hawaii uses 20, Alaska 19, and Georgia and Kentucky 18.

Efforts to lower the voting age to 18 have won the support of such national leaders as President Eisenhower and Kennedy. A compelling argument is made that those who are old enough to fight and die for their country are old enough to vote for their country's leaders. But most states have been persuaded to keep the voting age at the level of legal adulthood.

Abraham Ribicoff/Jon O. Newman, "Politics: The American Way", 1967

The Future of American Labor Unions

Today, and in the years to come, American labor faces a difficult task of adjustment. Such a task is not unique to this country. Practically every trade union movement in the world is currently challenged by the need to develop new forms, new procedures, and new attitudes to meet changing conditions.°

The most serious problem facing organized labor is present and future automation of the machinery of production. Automation has drastically altered the nature of the American industrial plant, and has brought labor, management, and government face to face with the need to create new jobs and retrain workers in new skills. Union representatives are confronted with the need to bargain for different kinds of jobs, as old jobs are, one by one, replaced by machines. New bargains must be arranged for workers who retain their present jobs under altered working conditions.°

It is predicted that, by 1970, sizable reductions in the number of jobs can be expected in eighteen major areas, including the clothing, food processing, coal mining, oil refining, railroad, and telephone industries. In fourteen others, job increases are expected. These include wholesale and retail trade, banking, insurance, truck and air transportation, electronics and synthetics. Predictions cannot yet be made for the automobile, iron and steel and electric power industries, but changes are bound to come.°

The agonizing problem of adjustment to technological change of all kinds has been carefully considered by the President's Advisory Committee on Labor-Management Policy, established by President Kennedy and continued by President Johnson. This 21-man tripartite body, made up of top leaders of unions, management and public members, stated three "central propositions" in this area:

"1. Automation and technological progress are essential to the general welfare, the economic strength, and the defense of the nation.
2. This progress can and must be achieved without the sacrifice of human values and without inequitable cost in terms of individual interests.
3. The achievement of maximum technological development with adequate safeguards against economic injury to individuals depends upon a combination of private and governmental actions, consonant with the principles of the free society."

But the question of method continually arises. At what point can labor and management reasonably meet, without either giving up too much ground? On the basis of experience gained in selected industries, the answer is sometimes sought in "attrition"—the gradual fading out of jobs. Through attrition, workers remain in their present jobs until normal retirement age and vacancies caused by illness or death are not filled, until, finally, only the number of jobs required under the new technological development will be filled.°

Automation presents still another serious problem for unions: it causes the familiar work group to disintegrate. As new machinery is introduced, as larger and more modern plants are built, workers are physically dispersed. A man sitting alone at a blinking panel, pulling levers and pushing buttons that perform tasks once accomplished by a large group of men, sitting or standing together, means a loss of the "fellow feeling" and solidarity of interest on which union loyalty is based. Jobs in different areas of the same plant may differ widely, so that workers lose the shared possession of common skills.°

The new technology has also begun to have an impact on the effectiveness of strikes. The right to strike remains basic, but the decision to strike is being taken less and less frequently. The possibility of strikes is, however, never absent.°

A union such as the Brotherhood of Sleeping Car Porters has traditionally had an all-Negro membership. Its president, A. Philip Randolph, is a vice-president of the AFL-CIO and a powerful voice in the labor movement. But the problem of integration of races within unions for many years remained a serious one, even though national union leadership has long recognized the Negro's right and need to emerge into full economic citizenship. In the past, many Negroes became union members, but the overall percentage of Negro membership was low. The colored worker was frequently deprived of certain job opportunities because of race prejudice. He was often barred from access to educational advantages which, in turn, deprived him of access to higher grades of employment. In order to correct such abuses, the AFL-CIO undertook a widespread and rigorous anti-discrimination program within its ranks, despite the resistance of certain groups of members and communities in which they lived and worked.

No matter how determined labor is to implement a policy of complete racial equality in unions, they realize that the "civil rights" of Negroes had finally to be confirmed through legislation on a national level. In an address to the AFL-CIO, the American Negro leader, Dr. Martin Luther King, Jr., pointed out the dramatic parallel between the struggle of the unions and the Negro for recognition. To King, organized labor and the Negro represented a common cause: the cause of human rights and dignity.

John Herling, "Labor Unions in America", 1964

John F. Kennedy, Inaugural Address, January 20, 1961

Fellow citizens: We observe today not a victory of party but a celebration of freedom—symbolizing an end as well as a beginning—signifying renewal as well as change. For I have sworn before you and Almighty God the same solemn oath our forebears prescribed nearly a century and three-quarters ago.

The world is very different now. For man holds in his mortal hands the power to abolish all forms of human poverty and all forms of human life. And yet the same revolutionary beliefs for which our forebears fought are still at issue around the globe—the belief that the rights of man come not from the generosity of the state but from the hand of God.

We dare not forget today that we are the heirs of that first revolution. Let the word go forth from this time and place, to friend and foe alike, that the torch has been passed to a new generation of Americans—born in this century, tempered by war, disciplined by a hard and bitter peace, proud of our ancient heritage—and unwilling to witness or permit the slow undoing of those human rights to which this nation has always been committed, and to which we are committed today at home and around the world.

Let every nation know, whether it wishes us well or ill, that we shall pay any price, bear any burden, meet any hardship, support any friend, oppose any foe to assure the survival and the success of liberty.

George Washington   54 Thomas Jefferson   55 Andrew Jackson   56 Abraham Lincoln   57 John F. Kennedy

This much we pledge—and more.

To those old allies whose cultural and spiritual origins we share, we pledge the loyalty of faithful friends. United, there is little we cannot do in a host of cooperative ventures. Divided, there is little we can do—for we dare not meet a powerful challenge at odds and split asunder.

To those new states whom we welcome to the ranks of the free, we pledge our word that one form of colonial control shall not have passed away merely to be replaced by a far more iron tyranny. We shall not always expect to find them supporting our view. But we shall always hope to find them strongly supporting their own freedom—and to remember that, in the past, those who foolishly sought power by riding the back of the tiger ended up inside.

To those peoples in the huts and villages of half the globe struggling to break the bonds of mass misery, we pledge our best efforts to help them help themselves, for whatever period is required—not because the Communists may be doing it, not because we seek their votes, but because it is right. If a free society cannot help the many who are poor, it can not save the few who are rich.

To our sister republics south of our border, we offer a special pledge—to convert our good words into good deeds—in a new alliance for progress—to assist free men and free governments in casting off the chains of poverty. But this peaceful revolution of hope cannot become the prey of hostile powers. Let all our neighbors know, that we shall join with them to oppose aggression or subversion anywhere in the Americas. And let every other power know that this hemisphere intends to remain the master of its own house.

To that world assembly of sovereign states, the United Nations, our last best hope in an age where the instruments of war have far outpaced the instruments of peace, we renew our pledge of support—to prevent it from becoming merely a forum for invective—to strengthen its shield of the new and the weak—and to enlarge the area in which its writ may run.

Finally, to those nations who would make themselves our adversary, we offer not a pledge but a request: that both sides begin anew the quest for peace, before the dark powers of destruction unleashed by science engulf all humanity in planned or accidental self-destruction.

We dare not tempt them with weakness. For only when our arms are sufficient beyond doubt can we be certain beyond doubt that they will never be employed.

But neither can two great and powerful groups of nations take comfort from our present course—both sides overburdened by the cost of modern weapons, both rightly alarmed by the steady spread of the deadly atom, yet both racing to alter that uncertain balance of terror that stays the hand of mankind's final war.

So let us begin anew—remembering on both sides that civility is not a sign of weakness, and sincerity is always subject to proof. Let us never negotiate out of fear. But let us never fear to negotiate.

Let both sides explore what problems unite us instead of belaboring those problems which divide us.

Let both sides, for the first time, formulate serious and precise proposals for the inspection and control of arms—and bring the absolute power to destroy other nations under the absolute control of all nations.

Let both sides seek to invoke the wonders of science instead of its terrors. Together let us explore the stars, conquer the deserts, eradicate disease, tap the ocean depths and encourage the arts and commerce.

Let both sides unite to heed in all corners of the earth the command of Isaiah—to "undo the heavy burdens . . . and let the oppressed go free".

And if a beach-head of cooperation may push back the jungle of suspicion, let both sides join in creating a new endeavor, not a new balance of power, but a new world of law, where the strong are just and the weak secure and the peace preserved.

All this will not be finished in the first 100 days. Nor will it be finished in the first 1,000, nor in the life of this Administration, nor even perhaps in our lifetime on this planet. But let us begin.

In your hands, my fellow citizens, more than mine, will rest the final success or failure of our course. Since this country was founded, each generation of Americans has been summoned to give testimony to its national loyalty. The graves of young Americans who answered the call to service surround the globe.

Now the trumpet summons us again—not as a call to bear arms, though arms we need—not as a call to battle, though embattled we are—but a call to bear the burden of a long twilight struggle year in and year out, "rejoicing in hope, patient in tribulation"—a struggle against the common enemies of man: tyranny, poverty, disease and war itself.

Can we forge against these enemies a grand and global alliance, north and south, east and west, that can assure a more fruitful life for all mankind? Will you join in that historic effort?

In the long history of the world, only a few generations have been granted the role of defending freedom in its hour of maximum danger. I do not shrink from this responsibility—I welcome it. I do not believe that any of us would exchange places with any other people or any other generation. The energy, the faith, the devotion which we bring to this endeavor will light our country and all who serve it—and the glow from that fire can truly light the world.

And so, my fellow Americans: ask not what your country can do for you—ask what you can do for your country. My fellow citizens of the world: ask not what America will do for you, but what together we can do for the freedom of man.

Finally, whether you are citizens of America or citizens of the world, ask of us here the same high standards of strength and sacrifice which we ask of you. With a good conscience our only sure reward, with history the final judge of our deeds, let us go forth to lead the land we love, asking His blessing and His help, but knowing that here on earth God's work must truly be our own.

"*The Inaugural Addresses of the American Presidents*", *1961*

VIII Science

Natural Selection 58 Charles Darwin

We shall, perhaps, best understand how instincts in a state of nature have become modified by selection, by considering° the slave-making instinct of certain ants° ranked by naturalists as the most wonderful of all known instincts.°

This remarkable instinct was first discovered in the *Formica (Polyerges) rufescens* by Pierre Huber, a better observer even than his celebrated father. This ant is absolutely dependent on its slaves; without their aid, the species would certainly become extinct in a single year. The males and fertile females do no work of any kind, and the workers or sterile females, though most energetic and courageous in capturing slaves, do no other work. They are incapable of making their own nests, or of feeding their own larvæ. When the old nest is found inconvenient, and they have to migrate, it is the slaves which determine the migration, and actually carry their masters in their jaws. So utterly helpless are the masters, that when Huber shut up thirty of them without a slave, but with plenty of the food which they like best, and with their own larvæ and pupæ to stimulate them to work, they did nothing; they could not even feed themselves, and many perished of hunger. Huber then introduced a single slave (*F. fusca*), and she instantly set to work, fed and saved the survivors; made some cells and tended the larvæ, and put all to rights. What can be more extraordinary than these well-ascertained facts? If we had not known of any other slave-making ant, it would have been hopeless to speculate how so wonderful an instinct could have been perfected.

Another species, *Formica sanguinea,* was likewise first discovered by P. Huber to be a slave-making ant. This species is found in the southern parts of England. °I opened fourteen nests of *F. sanguinea,* and found a few slaves in all. Males and fertile females of the slave species (*F. fusca*) are found only in their own proper communities, and have never been observed in the nests of *F. sanguinea.* The slaves are black and not above half the size of their red masters, so that the contrast in their appearance is great. When the nest is slightly disturbed, the slaves occasionally come out, and like their masters are much agitated and defend the nest: when the nest is much disturbed, and the larvæ and pupæ are exposed, the slaves work energetically together with their masters in carrying them away to a place of safety. Hence, it is clear that the slaves feel quite at home.°

One day I fortunately witnessed a migration of *F. sanguinea* from one nest to another, and it was a most interesting spectacle to behold the masters carefully carrying their slaves in their jaws instead of being carried by them, as in the case of *F. rufescens*. Another day my attention was struck by about a score of the slave-makers haunting the same spot, and evidently not in search of food; they approached and were vigorously repulsed by an independent community of the slave-species (*F. fusca*); sometimes as many as three of these ants clinging to the legs of the slave-making *F. sanguinea*. The latter ruthlessly killed their small opponents, and carried their dead bodies as food to their nest.°

Such are the facts, though they did not need confirmation by me, in regard to the wonderful instinct of making slaves. Let it be observed what a contrast the instinctive habits of *F. sanguinea* present with those of the continental *F. rufescens*. The latter does not build its own nest, does not determine its own migrations, does not collect food for itself or its young, and cannot even feed itself: it is absolutely dependent on its numerous slaves. *Formica sanguinea,* on the other hand, possesses much fewer slaves, and in the early part of the summer extremely few: the masters determine when and where a new nest shall be formed, and when they migrate, the masters carry the slaves. Both in Switzerland and England the slaves seem to have the exclusive care of the larvæ, and the masters alone go on slave-making expeditions.°

By what steps the instinct of *F. sanguinea* originated I will not pretend to conjecture. But as ants, which are not slave-makers, will, as I have seen, carry off the pupæ of other species, if scattered near their nests, it is possible that such pupæ originally stored as food might become developed; and the foreign ants thus unintentionally reared would then follow their proper instincts, and do what work they could. If their presence proved useful to the species which had seized them—if it were more advantageous to this species to capture workers than to procreate them—the habit of collecting pupæ, originally for food, might by natural selection be strengthened and rendered permanent for the very different purpose of raising slaves. When the instinct was once acquired, if carried out to a much less extent even than in our British *F. sanguinea,* which, as we have seen, is less aided by its slaves than the same species in Switzerland, natural selection might increase and modify the instinct—always supposing each modification to be of use to the species—until an ant was formed as abjectly dependent on its slaves as is the *Formica rufescens*.

Charles Darwin, "The Origin of Species", 1859

Lamps are lighted

The record of Edison's drive toward the lamp after New Year's, 1879, reads like a well-planned military campaign. He marshaled his forces like a Foch; he would not be turned aside from his objective; he hung on with a deathlike grip, grimly determined to conquer not only the unknown, but the scoffers as well. Indefatigable industry was there, refusal to admit defeat, the surmounting of seemingly insurmountable obstacles. As he reached into Nature's storehouse and filched her jealously guarded secrets, he enacted as thrilling a romance as was ever written of human achievement.°

59 Thomas A. Edison

We now move forward to October, 1879. At this time a writer from the *Scientific American* happening to visit the laboratory obtained permission to write a description of the new generator. The article with illustrations was published on the front page of that journal and, as Edison had promised long before, "raised the wind".

On the same day that it appeared on the stands, Edison completed another lamp, in which cotton sewing thread was tried once more. The filament, shaped like an arch or horse-shoe, had been impregnated with carbon by Batchelor, tended in the furnace by Edison and sealed in a glass bulb by Boehm. Sunday morning the lamp was placed on the Sprengel pump for evacuation of the air.

Of the little group who worked with him and witnessed the test, only one survivor remained after Edison's passing in 1931. This was Francis Jehl, the youth from Lowrey's office. Now past his seventieth year and nearing the close of a life-time of service chiefly devoted to the electrical industry, he sat in his study one night and told how on that fateful day he had poured the mercury through the pump to evacuate the bulb and had kept sleepless watch beside his chief after the others had gone for the night. Blessed with an undimmed memory and an intimate knowledge of all that occurred, he recalled every detail of the eventful forty hours. Here are his recollections, which are valuable as being those of the only living eye-witness of the birth of the electric light:

At first (said Jehl) Edison sat back in his chair opposite the pump and watched the air being forced out. He noted how the large cylinders of mercury and air became smaller and smaller. When the stage of metallic clicking arrived, he took a small alcohol flame and began to heat the bulb of the lamp—as in past experiments—in order to expand and dry the air remaining in it. This operation was continued from time to time until the clicking increased in violence. He then attached one of the wires from the battery to one of the lamp terminals and with the other end of the battery wire touched for an instant the other terminal. As a result the vacuum in the lamp became suddenly depressed, large bubbles of air appearing again in the pump tube (due to occluded gases).

He continued to apply the battery current to the carbon lamp filament from time to time, increasing its intensity as well as the time of its application until the occluded gases were driven out and the air pump exhibited the highest attainable vacuum. After the full current had been left on for some time, with the pump still working, Edison requested Boehm to seal off the bulb. The lamp was ready for its life test about eight o'clock in the evening.°

Since the life test alone would decide the question of success or failure, Sunday passed without unusual excitement. We had tested many lamps before, none of which had attained the success expected by Edison; hence the present lamp might yet exhibit some of the antics of its predecessors.

Without much comment Edison now requested me to put the new lamp on the stand and to connect it with the electrical apparatus. After the other men had all gone, he and I kept a death-watch to note any convulsions or other symptoms of impending extinction.

The lamp, however, did not expire! In the morning we were relieved by Batchelor, Upton and Force. The little filament continued to glow brilliantly all that day, passing the twenty-four-hour mark. We were stirred with hope, more and more convinced of progress. Bets were made and general good humor existed all round. Discussions of problems yet to be solved were the order of the day. The night of the twentieth of October again brought quiet to the laboratory as the watch continued, this time composed of Edison, Batchelor and me. During the night between the twentieth and the twenty-first Edison, judging from the appearance of the lamp still burning without flaw, seemed satisfied that the first solid foundation of the future of electric lighting had now been laid. The filament held out heroically that night and the following day until, between one and two o'clock in the afternoon of Tuesday, October 21, 1879, it had attained more than forty hours of life—the longest existence yet achieved by an incandescent lamp. The "boys" from all departments came to take a squint at the little wonder and to express their joy.

William A. Simonds, "*Edison—His Life, his Work, his Genius*", 1934

Science, Technology, and the Human Spirit

The revolutionary consequence of man's increased scientific, technical, and managerial talents is one of the central facts of our time. It touches the lives of all of us, wherever we live. It affects our health, our daily tasks in factory and farm and office, even our spiritual concepts. It profoundly affects our prospects for survival itself.°

There is a relation between man's new vast power to change his environment and his inner life; this seems to me clear. The problems created by atomic energy and other dramatic evidences of man's increased physical powers are so new that he can hardly keep abreast of them.°

As technology has been managed thus far it has, by and large, rather diminished than increased the average man's accountability for and participation in the vital decisions of his daily life.°

No one today can disassociate himself from the spiritual dangers that technology multiplies, nor from every effort to develop methods of administering technology that will magnify, not stultify, the spiritual worth of man. A man wants to feel that he is important. He wants to be able not only to express his opinion freely, but to know that it carries some weight; to know that there are some things that he decides, or has a part in deciding, and that he is a needed and useful part of something far bigger than he is.

This hankering to be an individual is probably greater today than ever before. Huge factories, assembly lines, complex and seemingly mysterious mechanisms, and standardization in general all underline the smallness of the individual, because they are so fatally impersonal. If our intensive technical development could be made personal to the lives of most men; if they could see themselves (because it was true) as actual participants in that development in their own communities, on their own land, at their own jobs and businesses—there would be an opportunity for a fortifying kind of individual satisfaction, and there would be stronger and happier men.

Here is democracy's great advantage in a technical world over communism and other forms of centralized and monolithic systems. It is the unique strength of genuinely democratic methods that they provide a way of stimulating and releasing the individual resourcefulness and inventiveness, the pride of workmanship, the creative genius of human beings whatever their station or function. A world of science and great machines is still a world of men; our modern task is more difficult, but the opportunity for democratic methods can be even greater than in the days of the ax and the hand loom.

A method of organizing modern technical development so that it draws in the average man and makes him a part of the great job of our time—in the day-to-day work in the fields and factories and laboratories and the offices of business—will tap riches of human talent that are beyond the reach of any highly centralized, dictatorial, and impersonal system of development based upon remote control in the hands of a business, a technical, or a political elite.

David E. Lilienthal, "This I do believe", 1949

Work and the Automatic Factory

"Automation" is the latest and perhaps the culminating phase of the American technological revolution. The essence of automation is the replacement of the worker who operates the machine by the machine that operates machinery. During the earlier phases of the continuing revolution the elements of production were broken down and assigned to machines that had to be regulated and controlled by workers. In the case of automation the productive system has developed built-in mechanisms of regulation

60 Automated Steel-Mill, Operator's Control Desk

and control. Its ultimate goal is the almost workerless factory, office, and salesroom. The characteristic of the old machine was its repetitive capacity: raw materials were fed into it while it repeated the same operation endlessly, but it had to be overseen and its products had to be assembled. What is fed into the automatic machine is not raw material but "information". The machine then operates by the principle of "feedback", and the results are communicated to the entire process, whether it be the generation of electric power, or the mixing of chemicals, or the making of synthetic fertilizers, soaps, and detergents, or the numberless uses of telecommunication.

Since the principle involved is similar to the mechanism of the human nervous system and even of the human brain, these machines have been spoken of as "thinking" machines, and some commentators have been moved to suggest that the machine can now replace the human brain, while the brain is little more than a machine. Such an approach misses the difference between machinery and the human spirit, between the brain itself and what the brain contrives in order to rid itself of routine burdens, and it is therefore itself a symptom of the age of automation. What concerns us here, however, is not so much the fallacy that the machine can duplicate man, but the fact that the new machinery is coming to function without the men and women who used to watch over the operation of the old machines.

The old Malthusian fear—that there would be a surplus of population over the available food supplies (and therefore jobs)—has been replaced by an anxiety about whether there will be enough jobs (and therefore food supplies) to go around when the machines have taken over the empire of industry. In the mid-1950s America was still exploring the answer to this problem. But in essence it was no different a problem from the one that had faced Americans throughout their technological revolutions. There had always been anxiety about the displacement of men by machines, and in the end the machines had always created new jobs by broadening the scope of the industrial process, by creating new income and new consumer demands, and by shifting the emphasis to distributive, social-welfare, and leisure-time services. The consequences of automation were likely to be of the same sort, but to a higher degree. Americans would need a large number of technicians to plan, make, and drive the machines. They would need fewer workers in industrial production and more in meeting the leisure needs that would flow from the reduced working day. The economy was shifting from one organized around the use of natural resources and human labor to an economy organized around the use of time and the access of more people to what the culture offered.

As another consequence of automation, Americans are looking forward to the end of drudgery-on-the-job. The trivial tasks are being turned over wholly to the machines, without the need for the strained pace-setting of the assembly line and the attention it required. What remains are what Adam Abruzzi calls the "distinguished" as against the "undistinguished" jobs—the planning for what the new machines will do, the study of the situations in which they are likely to break down, the imaginative and the contemplative challenge of thinking out the total design for work and leisure of which the machines form a part. An era was opening in which the worker might again have restored to him his skill and responsibility, and the control of his working pace. The dogma that idleness is somehow a sin was part of an age that is passing. An age of automatic machines would put a premium on leisure in which the mind would not be idle.

This has already transformed America into a nation of amateurs. If one phase of the work revolution was summed up in "automation", another was expressed in the phrase "do-it-yourself". Nourished by the fact of the vanishing domestic servant and of skyrocketing costs, "do-it-yourself" was primarily an effort to recapture in the leisure hours the sense of the wholeness of a piece of work that had been lost in the plant and office when work was transformed into the "job". The same worker who hurried away from his plant because his job offered few psychic satisfactions was likely to spend hours tinkering with carpentry, adding an attic to his house, or painting a canvas, putting into his amateur work the emotional energy he could not express on his job. Here he could see the relation between the initial idea and the finished product; here he could follow his own pace and be his own boss. Without intending it Americans found that they were swinging back at home to the kind of work relation that had been lost somewhere in the course of building up a factory system and the job-wage nexus.

America found itself in the mid-1950s with three streams of tendency in relation to work: a factory system which was still the heart of industrialism but was losing its workers and being run by machines; a growing working population of engineers and of nonindustrial technicians, with an ever greater role for education in the further changes of the productive process; and a trend toward do-it-yourself amateurism which helped to fill the void left in work-hungry human beings by the dehumanizing of the "job".

Max Lerner, "America as a Civilization", 1957

Are Machines getting smarter than Men?

Question: *Dr. Wiener, is there any danger that machines—that is, computers—will someday get the upper hand over men?*
Answer: There is, definitely, this danger if we don't take a realistic attitude. The danger is essentially intellectual laziness. Some people have been so bamboozled by the word "machine" that they don't realize what can be done and what cannot be done with machines—and what can be left, and what cannot be left, to the human beings.
Is there a tendency to overemphasize the use of computers?
There is a worship of gadgetry. People are fascinated by gadgets. The machines are there to be used by man, and if man prefers to leave the whole matter of the mode of their employment to the machine, by overworship of the machine or unwillingness to make decisions—whether you call it laziness or cowardice—then we're in for trouble.
Do you agree with a prediction, sometimes heard, that machines are going to be constructed that will be smarter than man?
May I say, if the man isn't smarter than the machine, then it's just too bad. But that isn't our being assassinated by the machine. That will be suicide.
Is there actually a trend for machines to become more sophisticated, smarter?
We're making much more sophisticated machines and we're going to make much more sophisticated machines in the next few years. There are things that haven't come to the public attention at all now, things that make many of us believe that this is going to happen within a decade or so.

Can you give us a look into the future?
I can. One of the big things about machines has been miniaturization—cutting down the size of the components. Where, at the beginning of the development of computers, a machine would have to be as big as the Empire State Building, it can be reduced now to something that you could fit into a rather small room. One of the chief factors in this miniaturization has been the introduction of new types of "memories", memories depending on solid-state physics—on transistors, and things of that sort.

Now, it's becoming interesting to ask: "How does the human brain do it?" And for the first time within the last year or so, we're getting a real idea of that.

You know, genetic memory—the memory of our genes—is largely dependent on substances which are nucleic-acid complexes. Within this last year it's coming to be pretty generally suspected that the memory of the nervous system is of the same sort of thing. This is indicated by the discovery of nucleic-acid complexes in the brain and by the fact that they have the properties that would give a good memory. This is a very subtle sort of solid-state physics, like the physics which is used in the memory of machines now. My hunch is—and I'm not alone in this—that the next decade or so will see this used technically.

In other words, instead of a magnetic tape as a memory core of a computer, you will have genes—
You will have substances allied to genes. Whether you call them genes or not is a matter of phraseology, but substances of the same sort.°

Is this a prospect that should frighten people?
Any prospect will frighten people. It should frighten people if it is applied without understanding. With understanding this can be a very valuable tool.°

What would the capability of this machine be, compared to the computers you have today?
It might be enormously greater. The machine could be much smaller, it could carry a much larger set of data. But anything that I would say about this would be not only premature but hopelessly premature. But work is to be done in those fields, I'm certain.

People are already saying the computers "think". Is this so?
Taking things as of the present time, computers can learn. Computers can learn to improve their performance by examining it. That is definitely true. Whether you call that thinking or not is a terminological matter. That this sort of thing will go much further in the future, as our ability to build up more complicated computers increases, I should say is certain.

Is there a chance that machines may learn more than man? Are they doing this now?
Certainly not now and certainly not for a long time, if ever. But if they do, it's because we have ceased to learn. I mean, it's easier for us to learn than for the machine. If we worship the machine, and leave everything to the machine, we've got ourselves to thank for any trouble we get in.

Here is the point: The computer is extremely good at working rapidly, at working in a unique way on well-presented data. The computer doesn't compare with the human brain in handling data that haven't yet jelled. If you call that intuition—

I won't say that intuition is impossible for the computer, but it's much, much lower and it isn't economical to try to make the computer do things that the human being does so much better.
What exactly is a learning machine?
A learning machine is one which not only, say, plays a game according to fixed rules, with a fixed policy, but periodically or continuously examines the results of that policy to determine whether certain parameters, certain quantities, in that policy should be changed to advantage.
The example that always comes to mind is machines that play checkers—
Well, take checkers. The machine was good enough to be able, after a while, to systematically defeat its inventor until he learned a little more about checkers.
Why is this not so with chess?
Because chess is more complicated. It will be so with chess, but it's a much bigger job.
Are machines being taught to write?
Yes. There are machines which will take a code and put it into handwriting, or take handwriting as well as printing and put it into a code. Oh, yes, that's being worked—you can even take speech and put it into a code.
Is it science fiction to talk about "thinking robots" taking over the earth?
It is science fiction, unless people get the idea "Leave it all to 'Tin Mike'". I mean, if we regard the machine not as an adjunct to our powers but as something to extend our powers, we can keep it controlled. Otherwise we can't. The gadget worshipers who expect the machine to do everything, and let people sit down and take it easy, have another think coming.
Are computers being used intelligently today?
In ten per cent of the cases, yes.
This is a startlingly low figure. Why do you say that?
Because it takes intelligence to know what to give to the machine. And in many cases the machine is used to buy intelligence that isn't there.

The computer is just as valuable as the man using it. It can allow him to cover more ground in the same time. But he's got to have the ideas. And in the early stage of testing the ideas, you shouldn't be dependent on using computers.
Is this true also in the use of computers as the basis for automation? That is to say, is automation in some cases being unintelligently employed?
It most definitely is. But, as for examples, this is not my field.
What are some of the things that computers can be used for intelligently, and do better than humans?
Bookkeeping, selling tickets, and keeping a record of that sort. When you've got your plan of computation, machines can carry it out much better than man can. And computers of the future will do these things very much better. They will have enough variety so they can afford to do what the brain does—waste a lot of effort and still get something.
Are these machines of the future going to take away a lot more jobs from humans?
They will.
That will sharpen a problem that already exists. What is the solution?

The answer is that we can no longer value a man by the jobs he does. We've got to value him as a man.

Here is the point: A whole lot of the work that we are using men for is work which really is done better by computers. That is, for a long time human energy hasn't been worth much as far as physical energy goes. A man couldn't possibly generate enough energy today to buy the food for his own body. The actual commercial value of his services in modern culture isn't enough. If we value people, we can't value people on that basis.

If we insist on using the machines everywhere, irrespective of people, and don't go to very fundamental considerations and give people their proper place in the world, we're sunk.

Is it too late to halt this drive toward more and more automation?

What has been done is irrevocable. I saw this at the very beginning. It isn't merely the fact that the computers are being used. It's the fact that they stand ready to be used, which is the real difficulty. In other words, the reason we can't go back is that we can never destroy the possibility of computers' being used.°

So people can look for machines to play still more of a role in automation, in running business, in education—

We can. And, at any rate, whether we use machines or not—which is a decision which we have to make one way or another—the fact that they are there to be used cannot be turned off.

Are you saying that it might be a wiser decision not to make use of some of these machines?

It may be wiser in particular situations. I'll give you a simple example: It is very easy now, with automatization, to make a factory which can produce more than the whole market can consume. If you go and simply push production up, you may hit the ceiling. Competition, as it has been understood in the past, has been greatly changed by the existence of automatization. Automatization no longer fits in with laissez faire.°

Do you mean it is possible for machines to declare war and doom all mankind?

If we let them. Obviously they won't declare war unless we create a setup by which they will.

Dr. Wiener, is man changing his environment beyond his capacity to adjust to it?

That's the $ 64 question. He's certainly changing it greatly, and if he is doing it beyond his capacity, we'll know soon enough. Or we won't know—we won't be here.

From an interview with Norbert Wiener in *"U.S. News & World Report"*, 24.2.1964

A New Era in American Agriculture

Some envisage the year 2000 as the time when the American farmer finally is freed from the arduous and time-consuming demands of planting and harvesting, a time when he, too, enjoys leisure for the pursuit of recreation, entertainment, advanced learning, and he and the world he inhabits can provide true parity of education and opportunity for his children.

Some see him sitting in an air-conditioned farm office scanning a print-out from a computer center, typing out an inquiry on a keyboard which relays the question to the computer. The computer center, which he may own in partnership with other farmers, perhaps through his cooperative, helps him to decide how many acres to plant to what crop, what kind of seeds to sow, what kind and how much fertilizer to apply, exactly what his soil condition is, and what day to harvest what crop.

The experts say the fields on this hypothetical farm will bear a surface similarity to the fields of today, but a surface similarity only. They see a land carefully graded and contoured to control erosion and the use of precious water. They see a soil bearing nutrients to meet the specific needs of each crop, and treated to control harmful organisms, weeds and plant diseases. They foresee virus-free plants, bred by geneticists to give higher yields in a much shorter growing period and to mature at the same time. The stalks on these plants, they say, will lend themselves to mechanical harvesting, and new uses will be made of the parts of the plant once discarded at harvest.

The experts envision all the field work on this farm carried out by automated machinery, directed by tape-controlled programs, and supervised by television scanners mounted on towers. They predict that weather will no longer be the incalculable threat it remains in our time, for satellites will provide long-range forecasting—providing time to prepare for, divert or dissipate damaging storms. They say robot harvesters will complete the farming operation with high-speed picking, grading, packaging and freezing and will then transport the produce to transportation depots for distribution to retail warehouses.

While many find this picture of the future exciting, others find it depressing. Some contend that automation and the computer will excise the soul from farming, will destroy its joy, dull its satisfactions, and chill the ageless intimacy between man and his land. But others say no. They say the farmer of the 21st century will be more deeply, intricately, and learnedly involved with the land than ever before. They point out that no computer can give a learned answer until it is asked a learned question, that no robot tractor can operate until a skilled human being programs it to operate. And they contend that the joy and satisfaction of farming will come—as always—from the successful interplay between the farmer and his soil.

"*Agriculture/2000*", ed. by the U.S. Department of Agriculture, 1967

"Open Skies" – Satellites in the Sixties

It was in 1965 that a decade of gigantic effort reached a climax when a rocket thundered into orbit and a human being stepped into a wholly new environment. Cosmonaut Alexei Leonov had shown that a space-suited man could survive in space and now Astronaut Edward White demonstrated that he could maneuver freely in it. Thus mankind left his world and entered a new era. Now° the world is forever changed. And as for man, his horizon has become infinite.°

The human interest element involved in all manned space flights tends to relegate the scientific and "application" satellites to the back page—except when they are as spectacular as Early Bird. But at least once a week some new satellite joins the halo of

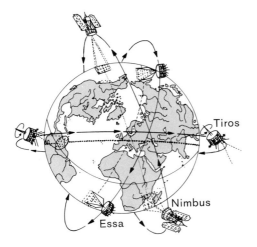

61 Weather Satellites

hardware now orbiting Earth, and many of these are quietly changing the patterns of world society.

Freedom of space is now an accepted doctrine. Reconnaissance vehicles of the U.S. and U.S.S.R. now crisscross each other's territory with perfect legality. Some of these
5 radio TV pictures back to Earth; others return capsules containing high-quality photographs. It may be that they have already exerted a stabilizing influence on the world's political situation, for the great powers can no longer surprise each other, or conceal large-scale military preparations. In a manner that could hardly have been conceived at the time, President Eisenhower's imaginative "Open Skies" proposal has
10 become reality. This situation must be singularly galling to the mainland Chinese, who invented the rocket almost a thousand years ago but now have their nuclear installations pinpointed and their shots called in advance by the U.S. State Department.

The military reconnaissance satellites may have helped to preserve peace; there is no doubt that their civilian counterparts have preserved lives and property, and will
15 do so on an ever increasing scale. Even the U.S.'s very first Tiros satellite, launched April 1, 1960, produced cloud pictures of the earth which, as one meteorologist put it, converted his struggling science from rags to riches overnight. The ninth in the uniformly successful Tiros series was orbited on Jan. 22, 1965, and for the first time gave a complete coverage of the planet from pole to pole.

20 It is now impossible for hurricanes, gathering strength in the empty wastes of the Pacific, to catch the meteorologists unaware. For the latest weather satellites, even when they circle above the oceans in the darkness of a moonless night, can still watch the cloud formations a thousand miles below by the infrared rays they emit. Now indeed, in a manner beyond the wildest dreams of Tennyson, lies the earth all Danäe to
25 the stars.

Hundreds of lives and millions of dollars may already have been saved by the Tiros satellites; far more will be, as the meteorologists learn to read their messages. There are many other justifications for the space program, but this one is quite sufficient in itself.

30 The most socially far-reaching, and perhaps economically most important, application of space research was also demonstrated in 1965, when the Communications Satellite Corporation's Early Bird went into service. Although the earlier Telstars and Relays had shown what comsats could do, these were unable to provide continuous coverage between any two points on the globe. Being at relatively low altitudes, and
35 hence orbiting in the stronger regions of the earth's gravitational field, they had to

move swiftly to remain aloft. Thus they traveled from horizon to horizon in a matter of minutes, and so provided only intermittent and limited service.

The answer to this problem, it had been realized for years, was the synchronous or hovering satellite, moving above the equator at such an altitude that it would take exactly 24 hours for one revolution, and so would remain poised permanently over the same spot. Three such satellites, spaced equally round the earth, could provide global coverage of TV, high-quality radio, or any other type of electronic communication.

Syncom 3, launched in August 1964, showed the feasibility of the system by its sharp live TV transmissions from the Olympics in Tokyo; then, in May 1965, Early Bird bridged the Atlantic with pictures—a century after the "Great Eastern" had laid the first successful telegraph cable between Europe and America. Shortly the TV networks were quarreling with Comsat about what rates they should pay, and another miracle had become an ordinary item in the market place.

Far more important, the unification of the world had entered upon its final phase. The politicians may still shout and shoot across their borders, but history has passed them by. The engineers and the scientists have made their frontier problems obsolete.

Arthur C. Clarke in "Life", 1965

Promise and Menace of the Nuclear Age

The future depends on people. People are unpredictable. Therefore, the future is unpredictable. However, some general conditions of mankind depend on things like the development of technology, the control won by man over nature and the limitations of natural resources. These can be predicted with a little greater confidence. The future is unknown but in some respects its general outline can be guessed.

Such guesses are important. They influence our present outlook and our present actions.°

Some technical predictions seem safe: Nuclear energy will not render our older power plants obsolete in the near future. But nuclear energy will make it possible to maintain the pace—even the acceleration—of the industrial revolution. It will be possible to produce all the energy we need at a moderate cost. Furthermore—and this is the important point—this energy will be available at any place on the globe at a cost which is fairly uniform. The greater the need for power, the sooner will it be feasible to satisfy the need with the help of nuclear reactors.

62 Atom Bomb Test at Eniwetok Atoll, Marshall Is.

Nuclear energy can be made available at the most outlandish place. It can be used on the Antarctic continent. It can be made to work on the bottom of the ocean.

The expanding front of industrialization has been called the "revolution of rising expectations". That nuclear energy should be involved in the current and in the turbulence of this expanding front, is inevitable.

One can say a little more about the effects of scientific and technological discoveries on the relations among the people of the globe. With added discoveries raw materials will no longer be needed with the old urgency. For most substances substitutes are being found. This may make for greater economic independence.

On the other hand, new possibilities will present themselves. We shall learn how to control the air and how to cultivate the oceans. This will call for cooperation and more interdependence.

The dangers from radioactive by-products will act in a similar direction. The radioactive cloud released from a reactor accident may be more dangerous than a nuclear explosion. Such a cloud will not stop at national boundaries. Some proper form of international responsibility will have to be developed.

What effect the existence of nuclear weapons will have upon the coexistence of nations is a question less understood and less explored than any other affecting our future. Most people turn away from it with a feeling of terror. It is not easy to look at the question with calm reason and with little emotion.

A few predictions seem disturbing but are highly probable: Nuclear secrets will not keep. Knowledge of nuclear weapons will spread among nations—at least as long as independent nations exist.

Prohibition will not work. Laws or agreements which start with the word "don't" can be broken and will always be broken. If there is hope, it must lie in the direction of agreements which start with the word "do". The idea of "Atoms for Peace" succeeded because it resulted in concrete action.

An all-nuclear war between the major powers could occur but we may have good hope that it will not occur if we remain prepared to strike back. No one will want to provoke the devastation of his own country.°

In a limited nuclear war the radioactive fallout will probably kill many of the innocent bystanders. We have seen that the testing program gives rise to a danger which is much smaller than many risks which we take in our stride without worry. In a nuclear war, even in a limited one, the situation will probably be quite different. That noncombatants suffer in wars is not new. In a nuclear war, this suffering may well be increased further due to the radioactive poisons which kill friend and foe, soldier and civilian alike.

Fortunately there exists a way out. Our early nuclear explosives have used fission. In the fission process a great array of radioactive products are formed, some of them intensely poisonous. More recently we have learned how to produce energy by fusion. Fusion produces fewer and very much less dangerous radioactivities. Actually the neutrons which are a by-product of the fusion reaction may be absorbed in almost any material and may again produce an assortment of radioactive nuclei. However, by placing only certain materials near the thermonuclear explosion, one may obtain a weapon in which the radioactivity is harmless. Thus the possibility of clean nuclear explosions lies before us.°

All this is of course only a small part in the process of the increasing power of man and the increasing responsibility of man. As the impossible of yesterday becomes the accomplished fact of today we have to be more and more aware of our neighbors on this shrinking planet. The arts of peace may lead to conflicting interest as easily as they may lead to fruitful cooperation. If we ever learn to control the climate of the world, a nation may find itself in the same relation to another nation as two farmers who have to use the waters of the same river.

Rivals are men who fight over the control of a river. When the same word "rivals" comes to mean cooperation for the best common use of the river or any other resource —that will be the time of law and of peace. Surely this sounds like Utopia and no one sees the way. But the general direction in which we should go is not to consider atomic explosives and radioactivity as the inventions of the devil. On the contrary, we must more fully explore all the consequences and possibilities that lie in nature, even when these possibilities seem frightening at first. In the end this is the way toward a better life. It may sound unusually optimistic in the atomic age, but we believe that the human race is tough and in the long run the human race is reasonable.

Edward Teller / Albert L. Latter, "Our Nuclear Future—Facts, Dangers and Opportunities", 1958

Landing on the Moon

Our astronauts' first landing on the moon is now probably less than a thousand days away. What will they do when they get there?

Even the earliest and briefest missions will begin an exciting program of exploration to solve long-standing mysteries of the moon. This many-faceted program will later reach full swing when more-advanced spacecraft enable explorers to remain longer on the moon and to make extended journeys across its surface.

New details of what our first Apollo landing party will do, when the two astronauts have left their three-man mother ship in lunar orbit and set down their landing craft on the moon, have been made public by NASA.

From touchdown to lift-off they will remain on the moon for eighteen hours. Twice, both astronauts will emerge from a hatch of the Lunar Module, their landing craft, and venture together over the lunar surface—for three hours each time. The rest of their stay will be taken up in checkouts of their craft and life-support gear, communications, and a six-hour period for eating and sleeping between trips outside.

Collecting samples of moon rocks and soil to bring back for study will be a major activity of their six hours of exploring. They will take photographs of the lunar terrain, too, and inspect and measure the "footprints" of their own craft in the lunar soil. Finally, they will spread out on the lunar surface, a safe three hundred feet away from their point of take-off, an array of scientific instruments that will automatically radio information back to earth for at least a year after they have left the moon.°

From this modest beginning will unfold a vast project of lunar exploration designed to answer questions as varied as these:

Are there living organisms on the moon—perhaps completely different from any on earth? Microbiological experiments on lunar samples, from the surface and below, should tell. Likewise to be sought in the samples are primeval organic substances,

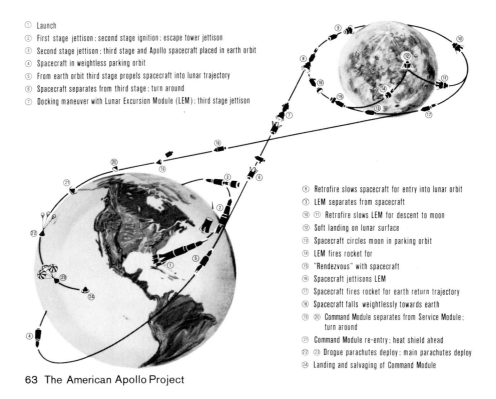

63 The American Apollo Project

like those from which life originated on earth, and oxygen and traces of water that might be extracted from lunar materials to help support future bases on the moon. Geologists will be eager to identify the lunar minerals themselves, and deduce the manner in which they were formed.

Is there a trace of a lunar atmosphere and how much? Since it must be so tenuous that even Lunar Module rocket engines may contribute substantially to it, scientists urge beginning its study as near as possible to the start of the Apollo program.

What is happening in moon craters, like Alphonsus, that show signs of activity? These "thermally active" craters, the maria or "seas", and the cratered highlands will be the three main types of lunar terrain of interest to explorers.

How was the moon born? Was it torn from the molten earth by solar gravity or did it and the earth condense from the same rotating gas cloud, or were moon and earth both built up from solid fragments orbiting the sun in disarray—the "accretion" theory now favored? Investigating the moon's history figures largely in a list of fifteen key moon questions that the National Academy of Sciences, in close cooperation with NASA, has prepared. For this may tell us more about the earth's own past. While our planet's birthmarks have been virtually eradicated by erosive forces like wind, rain, floods, and vegetation, those of the airless moon should be preserved.°

Early Apollo moon landing, limited to about 250 pounds of scientific gear, will not go far beyond the first landing in surface activities. These Lunar Modules will be unable to support a stay of more than forty-eight hours on the moon, and much of this time must be used to check out the craft for the flight back. Also, the stay must be limited to avoid fatigue. At the end of their two-week voyage to the moon and back, the crew will face the most strenuous, exacting, and critical maneuver of all—the precision approach and re-entry into the earth's atmosphere at a blazing 36,000 feet a second, more than 24,000 m.p.h. Main emphasis will be on demonstrating the feasibility of the flight itself.

Follow-on flights with more-advanced spacecraft will permit much longer stays on the moon. Increased payloads will provide moon explorers with really sizable tools (like deep-drilling rigs) and with vehicles to make extended trips afield from the landing sites. Then will come the heyday of lunar exploration.

One of two moon-landing concepts that look particularly promising is called the Augmented Lunar Module (ALM). It applies the fact that the Saturn V launch vehicle seems capable of hurling toward the moon a somewhat higher payload than was originally specified. This would allow some increase in the propellant capacity of the LM and, in turn, an increase in the useful load landed by the LM. Thus the life support for the astronauts—oxygen, water, food—could be extended for several days. More scientific equipment could be carried along to make those extra days worth-while.

Wernher von Braun, "Space Frontier", 1963

The Laser's Bright Magic

In *The War of the Worlds,* written before the turn of the century, H. G. Wells told a fanciful story of how Martians invaded, and almost conquered, earth. Their weapon was a mysterious "sword of heat", from which flickered "a ghost of a beam of light".

Radiation from this Martian ray gun, focused by a curved mirror, dropped men and horses in their tracks, made lead run like water, and flashed anything combustible into masses of flame.

In Wells's days, such ideas were pure imagination. Today his "sword of heat" comes close to reality in the laser, the marvelous new device that shoots out narrow, highly concentrated beams of light—the sharpest, purest, most intense light ever known.

The blinding radiation from the more powerful lasers can indeed melt lead so that it runs like water. When focused to a sharp point at very close range, it can vaporize any substance on earth. Within extremely small areas—incredibly—it burns billions of times brighter than the light at the sun's surface.

The laser is far from being a practical death ray, although scientists are at work developing it as a weapon. In my opinion it may become the answer to the missile problem—the swift, powerful ray capable of knocking enemy missiles from the sky.

Meanwhile, the peaceful purposes to which the laser may be put are so many and so varied as to suggest magic. For example, laser light can bore holes through steel in the wink of an eye, detect art frauds, make three-dimensional photographs, subdue

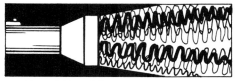

64 Normal Light Waves

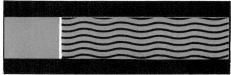

65 Laser Waves

some cancers. In the future it may lead the blind, detect earth quakes, prevent tooth decay. Potentially it can illuminate the ocean depths, avert plane crashes, carry millions of simultaneous telephone messages, and perhaps revolutionize surgery. And this is but the beginning of a lengthy catalogue.

Small wonder that the laser's potential has created a tremendous stir in the industrial and scientific world.°

If you were to come into my laboratory to watch a ruby laser operate, you might be surprised at the apparent simplicity of a device capable of such power. Essentially you see only two enameled steel boxes: a relatively small one holding the laser itself, and a larger one, with a control panel, holding capacitors, or condensers, to store a heavy charge of electric current.

As you watch, a technician throws a switch, and a whine fills the room while the capacitors charge up. Then the technician points to a sign on the door saying "Caution —Eye Hazard", and hands you a pair of dark goggles to filter out the greater part of the light. A direct hit in the eye by a strong laser beam can cause instant blindness, and even reflected laser rays can burn holes in the retina of the eye. For this reason laser laboratories sometimes have walls painted a dull black, to cut down on reflection.

Now the laser is ready. When we press the firing button, you hear a vicious crack, like a rifle shot. At the same time, a small but incredibly dazzling red spot flashes momentarily on the wall at which the laser is aimed.

To demonstrate the power of the laser, the technician aims it at a piece of steel the thickness of a quarter, using a lens to focus the beam to a fine point. Again you hear a whine, a sharp report. This time a shower of incandescent sparks flies from the piece of steel. It has been pierced all the way through by that awful blast of light.°

To understand why laser light is so concentrated, you must recall that light travels in waves, like ripples on a pond. The number of waves that pass a given point in a second determines the frequency of the light. The distance from the crest of one wave to the crest of the next is the wavelength.

Ordinary white light, such as that from an incandescent light bulb, is made up of many wavelengths (which is the same as saying many colors) all jumbled together and traveling in every direction. That is known as incoherent light.

Laser light, on the other hand, is coherent. It is essentially of one wavelength (that is, one color), with all the waves moving in one direction. Moreover, all the waves are in phase, or in step, reinforcing each other like soldiers marching in lock step, or like voices singing in unison. They can remain in an unbelievably straight, narrow beam for long distances, instead of fanning out like a flashlight beam.

As we shall see, it is precisely because laser light is coherent that it is capable of performing such a bagful of tricks.°

A variety of medical boons will likely come to mankind from the laser. One of the most promising applications is the laser photocoagulator, now being used by a growing number of eye surgeons to repair torn retinas and prevent blindness.

Thousands of persons a year in the United States develop holes or torn places in the retina—the membrane of nerve cells lining the back of the eye that detects light and sends visual messages to the brain. If these rents go unattended, the retinal membrane separates from the wall of the eye. Blindness results unless the patient submits to difficult and painful surgery and a weeks-long convalescence flat on his back.

Before the laser photocoagulator, the only means of forestalling a detachment involved much more cumbersome, painful techniques that were in varying degrees severe and that sometimes made things worse.

In Palo Alto, California, Dr. H. Christian Zweng of the Stanford University School of Medicine and the Palo Alto Medical Research Foundation showed me how easily the laser photocoagulator works. His patient, a Stanford physics professor, sat in a chair with his head tilted while Dr. Zweng aimed a small hand-held instrument at the dilated pupil.

With light from a tiny laser in the handle of his instrument, Dr. Zweng flashed a series of very weak pulses directly around the torn edge in the retina. The lens of the patient's eye focused the beams on pinpoint areas, and they coagulated the tissues at those points, creating miniature scars that "welded" the torn retina back into place. The whole affair was over in 20 minutes.

The patient had not been anesthetized, yet he never flinched. "In fact, I felt practically no pain, just a very slight sting", he told me afterward as he put on dark glasses and climbed into his car to drive himself home.

Dr. Zweng, a pioneer in use of the laser photocoagulator, reports similar operations on more than 130 patients, only two of them unsuccessful.°

It may be that, after much more experimentation, the laser will join X-ray and surgery as part of the arsenal against cancer. In the meantime, Dr. Goldman emphasizes, laser treatment is strictly experimental—for cases in which other methods cannot be used.°

At this point, to speak of a laser eraser may sound faintly ridiculous. Yet Dr. Schawlow is patenting such a device. Its very weak beam literally burns away the black, heat-absorbing pigment of a typed character without even scorching the white heat-reflecting paper beneath.

Will it sell? Dr. Schawlow just laughs, but he adds: "Don't forget—there must be five million typewriters manned by five million secretaries who can't spell!"

All of which prompted the *Electronics Weekly* of London to say: "With all the talk about death rays, it's nice to know that the Americans have decided the laser can be used to erase typing errors. It gives a less frightening meaning to the verb, 'to rub out'".

From death ray to eraser—that's a long jump. But if anything can make it, the laser, with its infinite magic, will.

Thomas Meloy in "National Geographic", 1966

Genetic Intervention

"Tampering with human genes" is a lurid cliché I have encountered over and over again in discussions of the prospective applications of molecular biology. It has been brought about to some extent by those of my colleagues who, quite rightly, wish to encourage wider public appreciation of the importance of the new biological science.

In a sense, we may be competing with the physicists, whose importance for society is emphatically punctuated by the imminence of the Bomb. "Tampering" is, however, a rather loaded and irritating way to describe an intervention as likely to be constructive or harmful as any other technical advance. We might as well call education the process of "tampering with a child's mind", or building a house, "tampering with the human environment".

Why this special anxiety about genetic intervention? If it is irreversible, we should of course worry about the implied commitment of the evolution of the species. But when we reach that stage of scientific sophistication, there should be no greater difficulty about reversing the evolutionary mistakes than there was in making them in the first place.

Nor can we trust natural processes always to produce the most admirable of biological types. Indeed it is hard to point to any part of the human scene which is not thoroughly permeated with completely artificial stresses on the evolutionary process, the byproduct of civilization. Without rational intent, we influence the environment to change our mutation rates, and much more important, to create rapid convulsions of different rates of reproduction of different kinds of people.

Furthermore, human self-consciousness may often operate to inhibit natural evolutionary change. Thus if a child were to display a conspicuous but fundamental "favorable" mutation he might be so rejected as to overwhelm his advantage. Imagine, for example, a child with four functional arms and hands, and the brain to manage them. A parent might well be advised to have the extra limbs amputated, despite their biological advantage, so the child could grow up as an accepted member of the community. The example merely illustrates the way in which striking deviancy is outlawed in the context of human culture, though it might have served as an important advance at an earlier stage of human evolution.

In fact, since socially coordinated people (not mad scientists) will be the decision-makers in genetic intervention, there is no reason to expect them to ignore these influences of the community. Such interventions will have to be gradual to be acceptable and hence useful. A few points in IQ for a generation is as much as we can stand in a realistic system of human improvement, and this gives the time needed to reflect on what progress really consists of.

In fact, the anxiety about genetic intervention is almost certainly not directed at anything really likely to happen. We probably will welcome any chance to alleviate the impact of mongolism, schizophrenia, diabetes or dwarfism. Probably what is more alarming is the abstract concept that "man will control his own destiny". Man as manipulator is too much of a god; man as object, too much of a machine.

Freud once commented that a grave difficulty in the acceptance of psychoanalysis was universal human narcissism, the infantile self-love that defies the scientific dissection of human nature. To understand this makes man less magical to the primitive mentality. He pointed out three major historical assaults on that self-concept, each of them violently resisted in their time: the cosmological, when the earth was displaced from the center of the universe; the Darwinian, when man was shown to be part of all living nature and to have evolved from it; the psychological, when man was shown to be unable to know all that transpired in his own mind, so many transactions being unconscious.

Some of the more panicky reactions to genetic engineering, and their characterization as "tampering", are, no doubt, very closely akin to the anxiety and derision that greeted Darwin's formulation of man's evolution from ape-like forerunners. How would an ape-prophet's relatives have greeted his predictions about the upsets their species would soon experience?

Joshua Lederberg in "The Washington Post", 1967

Sketches of the Future

Artificial organs, and synthetic life in the 1980s. Weather control and immunization against all infectious diseases in the 1990s. Soon after 2000: drugs to increase intelligence, direct coupling of brains to computers, breeding of animal "slaves". These are some predictions which emerged by using a technique called "Delphi", to foresee the future at the RAND Corporation in California.°

Several crystal-gazing techniques are developing. Delphi is a kind of elaborated Gallup Poll of experts. There is projection of existing trends (with various refinements). "Morphological research", which its pioneer, Fritz Zwicky, calls "an orderly way of looking at things", tries to assemble "all possible solutions to a large-scale problem". There is "scenario writing", developed by Herman Kahn, whose chilling sketches of future thermonuclear catastrophes became notorious a few years ago. The aim is to imagine various ways in which the future could develop, and so identify crucial choices. Finally, there are "goal-oriented" techniques which set a goal like landing on the moon and then analyse what new things have to be invented to succeed.

The experts polled by RAND using the Delphi technique all agreed that weather control would become feasible between 1987 and 2000, while artificial organs of plastic and electronic components would come into use between 1975 and 1988. There was considerable agreement that drugs for changing personality would be in use in 1984, but drugs for increasing intelligence would be most likely to emerge around 2010. Some thought that by 1997, education would proceed by impressing information direct into the brain; after 2020, it would be possible to put people into a "long duration coma to permit a form of time travel"; telepathy might begin to be used in a serious way by 2022, while direct control of the force of gravity might come in about the same time. "Two-way communication with extra-terrestrials" might be under way by 2020. However, some experts thought all these latter possibilities would never be realised.°

The most dismaying analysis, by Roger Revelle, who directs the Harvard Centre for Population Studies, shows how the world population has multiplied ten times since the birth of Christ, but five times in the last 350 years, and is likely to double between now and the year 2000, reaching some 6000 million. At this time, according to a Swiss expert, Gabriel Bouladon, who considers the future of transport, people will be hurtling from London to Sydney in hypersonic ramjets in 60 minutes while there will be 360 million private cars in the United States and the same number in Europe (seven times the present amount).°

Curiously, few of these prophetic experts apart from Kahn make much attempt to foresee social and political evolution, the effects of wars, or changes in the kinds of things people think important. Most predictions seem to add up to a gigantic electronic toyshop in the year 2000, with the same deep gulf between the owners of the toys and the starving remainder. But the interesting new emphasis is on prophecy as a means of creating the world one wants. Many large firms are now asking themselves, not what will the world be like in 2000, but what do we want it to be like. It is then possible to analyse ways of making the dream come true. The disturbing thing is that many of the dreams are more like nightmares.

John Davy in "The Observer", 1967

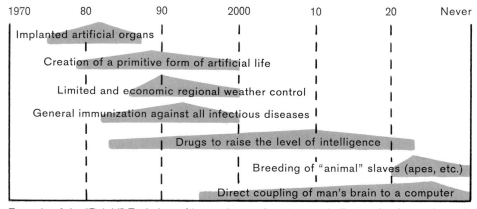

Example of the "Delphi" Technique (the maximum of each curve indicates the time estimated as most probable by the experts asked).

Further Predictions from the "Delphi" Enquiry

(with the most probable time of their realization)

1970	Manned lunar landing and return
	Rescue of astronauts stranded in orbit
1975	Automation of office work and services
	Education becoming a respectable leisure pastime
1978	Automatic language translator—correct grammar
	Manned Mars and Venus fly-by
1979	Widespread use of automatic decision-making at management level
1982	Permanent base established on Moon (ten men, indefinite stay)
	Manufacturing of atmospheres suitable for human beings on Moon or planets
1985	Manned landing on Mars and return
1988	Widespread use of robot services, as household slaves, sewer inspectors, etc.
1990	Manufacturing of propellants and raw material on the Moon
2000	Economically useful exploitation of the ocean through farming
	Evolution of a universal language from automated communication
2006	Establishment of a permanent Mars base (ten men, indefinite stay)
2020	Chemical control of the aging process, extending life span by fifty years
	Manned landing on Jupiter's moons
and later	International agreements providing a certain basic standard of living for the world's population as a result of high production from automation
	Pluto fly-by
	Inter-galactic communication
	Manned multi-generation mission to other solar systems
	Extra-terrestrial farming
	Regular commercial traffic to lunar colony
	Manned Venus landing
Never	Lunar-based laser beam for use in space vehicle propulsion
	Heliocentric strategic fleet

IX Arts

The Norman Abbey of Tewkesbury

Tewkesbury is a rather higgledy-piggledy, sprawling little town built at the junction of the rivers Severn and Avon, in Gloucestershire. Like most English country towns, the place has grown up gradually through the centuries, so that big and small houses huddle together along the main street. But there is one central feature which looms over all, and round which the whole place seems to be built. This is Tewkesbury Abbey, with its enormous square tower, nearly 150 feet high, which is supposed to be the finest Norman tower in the world.

More than a thousand years ago, there was a monastery at Tewkesbury—and not much else, I dare say: just a few miserable huts round about the monastery gates, and a lordling's castle on a nearby small hill. Then, there came a good soldier, Robert Fitz Hamon, a friend and relative of William the Conqueror. He had led a rough, turbulent sort of a soldier's life; he had killed a great many people and even burned a church or two; but he wanted to make his peace with God before he died. He liked the situation of the monastery at the junction of the rivers, and he decided to build a great church there and dedicate it to Our Lady. It was twenty years' building. In 1123, the masons laid the last stone on top of its noble tower, and the job was done.

66 Tewkesbury Abbey

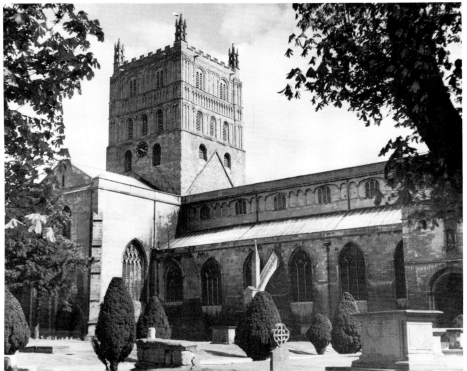

The building is 300 feet from end to end, and along the nave fourteen stone pillars hold up the splendid arch of the roof. Towards the east end, four massive stone piers support the tremendous weight of the tower itself.

I have never really understood how those Norman builders did it—how, with only primitive machinery, they lifted the heavy pieces of masonry into position; how, without logarithms, they made their complicated calculations about stresses and strains. I can only tell you that they did build well and truly, and they calculated correctly.

I wish I could make you see how huge and glorious the tower looks, rising over the little town; but I cannot even tell you what colour it is, because its weathered stone takes the light from the sky, and seems to change as the weather changes.

I wish I could describe to you the cool, dim-lit splendour of the interior of the church, that lofty nave with its elaborate vaulting, its round arches and its massive columns with simple capitals. The exquisite, airy little chapels are built round the east end as memorials to the great folk who are buried there.

The names of these people are the names which made England's history before and during the Wars of the Roses—the names of the barons who made and un-made our kings: e.g. Warwick and Beauchamp.

Cromwell's Puritans did bad things in Tewkesbury Abbey; you can see that to this day. They struck off the heads and arms and legs of many of the beautifully carved stone figures; anything that they could describe as a "graven image" was the target of their haphazard hammers.

The wicked work of these barbarians did not stop there. They stripped the colour from the walls, the pillars, and the roof, and whitewashed the whole church from floor to ceiling. We do not know—and now, alas, we can never know--what the interior of the abbey looked like when it was all a blaze of colour, a riot of all the rarest and loveliest colours which the monkish painters could gather out of Europe. But little bits of the original colours are left here and there which help us to imagine how glorious the whole must have been.

John Moore in "London Calling, European Ed.", 1949

The Spire of Salisbury Cathedral

Salisbury Cathedral has what is generally looked upon as the most beautiful of Gothic spires. It is octagonal in plan, and rises from a square tower, which, although it cannot actually be traced to the very ground, clearly gives the feeling that it does rise from it and not from the roof of the cathedral. The design for the spire must be read as though the base of the tower were actually visible. The junction between spire and tower is most beautifully concealed by pinnacles, so that the spire seems to grow from the base of the tower in the most natural manner.

The tower has windows to break up its surfaces; but the spire has none. It is only ornamented by three bands, one set above the other and each lightly "diapered". These bands play almost exactly the same rôle as bracelets on an arm. They are purely for decorative purposes, and are placed with a delightful sense of taste. The spire expresses a spiritual longing only, it serves no utilitarian purpose whatever. Consequently there was nothing to tie the hands of its designers. It is a little over 400 feet high, and is visible

67 Salisbury Cathedral

for miles from the surrounding plain as a spiritual sign to all men that here is the House of God. It is extremely austere, as it should be, and, with the exception of the three aforementioned "bracelets", without any other ornament. The total height from the ground to the extreme top of the spire is divided up roughly by the tower occupying three-fifths and the spire two-fifths. The whole unit is marvellously moulded into the forms and masses of the body of the cathedral, and is a most perfect example of the meaning of proportion as being an exquisite sense of the relation of the parts to the whole.

    In Salisbury, at least as far as its exterior is concerned, there is unity in every line. Look at the strongly moulded base which runs the whole way round, quite unbroken, linking all the different masses formed by nave, double transepts, and choir. See what firmness it gives to the rising masses above it, how it pulls them all together into one indivisible whole, which is the meaning of unity. Once the base is established, all the masses rise upward from it until they end in the glorious climax of the spire. There is nothing to contradict this feeling of aspiration. Such is Salisbury Cathedral.

Darcy Braddell, "How to look at Buildings", 1932

England at the Time of Queen Elizabeth

The subjects of Elizabeth had a gaiety of mind that the next reign lacked. The Englishmen of her age felt that they did indeed belong to "spacious times". They had a sense of release, of new horizons suddenly opened up, which must have been extraordinarily
5 exhilarating. The Renaissance was essentially an assertion of the spiritual emancipation of man from the religion, the social structure, the scholasticism of the middle ages. And in England during the second half of the sixteenth century special circumstances gave the movement a peculiar quality. The establishment of a strong central government, brought peace and order into a land which had groaned under the anarchy of the Wars
10 of the Roses—and the fear of a return to such anarchy lies at the back of all Shakespeare's historical plays. The breach with Rome, although half the people still hankered after the forms and doctrines of the "old religion", typified the immense quickening of national self-consciousness that culminated in the triumphant defiance of the Spanish supremacy.° The rapid development of internal trade and overseas commerce gave
15 increased power and wealth into the hands of an expanding middle class. The drawing aside of the curtain of mystery veiling the stage of the Atlantic revealed to man's astounded and delighted gaze a whole New World for discovery, plantation, and plunder. And all these varied threads were woven together on Time's loom to fashion a texture of thought and society, which seemed at once durable and pliant, shot with swiftly
20 changing hues and yet serviceable for daily wear, offering on the one hand security and on the other adventure. It was this combination—almost unparalleled in history since the days of Pericles—of social stability with illimitable opportunity for the individual, which gave the Elizabethan age its sense of balanced flight, its unique quality of happiness and spontaneity. The whole world was in flux, and yet by some trick of magic men
25 trod on solid ground.

Nor were the Elizabethans in any doubt who the magician might be. They turned, and rightly turned, in gratitude to their Queen. Their grandfathers had endured the social anarchy which marked the end of the middle ages. Their fathers had drunk to the dregs the cup of Geneva under Edward VI and the cup of Rome under Mary, and found
30 neither to their taste. Yet no third alternative had appeared possible. Elizabeth, the procrastinator, the crowned sphinx who could never make up her mind, who reigned forty-five years perpetually hesitating between Protestantism and Catholicism, between peace and war, between marriage and virginity, provided the alternative—a breathing-space of nearly half a century for the English people to discover a middle way and to
35 grow contented, prosperous and respected throughout the world. England at that time was the one peaceful country in a Europe ravaged by religious wars, in which she was willing enough to take part on French or Flemish soil; and the epoch lies like a miraculous season of calm weather between the Wars of the Roses and the Puritan Revolution. The Virgin Queen was worshipped by her subjects because she gave them stability, and
40 when foreign ambassadors enquired the secret of it she danced before them. The stability of Elizabethan England was a balance.

Her court, too, was both the keystone and the symbol of the national life. The headquarters of a strong executive under the permanent direction of the Cecils, it was also a stage on which almost any young man who took the Queen's fancy might cut a figure
45 and if he were lucky make a fortune. Fortunes were to be had because the Crown not

only controlled the distribution of lucrative monopolies and such properties as came to it through intestacy, but also itself took part in those expeditions, half-commercial and half-piratical, to the New World and elsewhere which were so frequent at this time. Elizabeth lived on the Thames; her five chief palaces, Whitehall, Hampton Court, Greenwich, Richmond and Windsor, all gave on to the river; and she passed from one to another in her royal barge. The goings and comings, therefore, of the great sea-captains Frobisher, Hawkins, and Drake, took place under her very windows; and when the last-named returned to Deptford in 1580 after his famous voyage round the world, she boarded the *Golden Hind* and knighted him on his own deck, beneath which, as she pretended not to know, lay ballast in the form of ingots plundered from the Pacific coast of Spanish South America.

Nor was the traffic confined to America. Any day a vessel might appear in the Thames laden with merchandise from Africa, from Muscovy, from the Levant, even from India or the Far East. For London, which had been an obscure port at the northwest corner of the medieval map, suddenly found herself the centre of the world. And during the last fifteen years or so of Elizabeth's reign, eyes and ears greater than hers drank in the sights and sounds of the little-great river. Shakespeare's plays are drenched in sea-spray and shot with the coloured thread of mariners' tales, from the pitiful story of old Aegeon in *The Comedy of Errors* to *Pericles, The Winter's Tale* and *The Tempest*, while the Venice of his *Merchant* is only London in masquing attire.

John D. Wilson, "The Essential Shakespeare", 1946

An Inspiring Painter of Atmosphere

J.M.W. Turner made the British School supreme, and its supremacy was won, not by historical painting, but by landscape. He revealed a new world in nature.

We may hardly grasp the magnitude of the revolution in painting that Turner brought about. Fostered by his special training and enormous industry, his genius perceived depths in nature hitherto unrealized, and to some extent made them seen by everybody. "Genius bloweth where it listeth", but yet is conditioned by its place in time. For his revelation of a new world in landscape, Turner was fortunate in coming at a time when romantic interest in nature and "picturesque beauty" was abroad. His progress was continuous until he came as close to expressing the elemental infinity of nature as mortal is ever likely to. And that, I take it, is the highest function of landscape painting.

Turner's sketch books show that—when still a boy of about fourteen—he was painting straight from nature, copying the subtleties of out-of-door colour, light and air.

More and more Turner's chief concern was how to render the transfiguring effect of light-filled air. He saw that he must lighten the entire key of tone and colour, not only in the lights but in the shadows as well.

Turner's recognition by his contemporaries is shown in his election as Royal Academician at the age of twenty-seven. Those who understood his paintings called him the most vital and inspiring figure in European Art since Rembrandt. He touched a depth and truth of perception and poetic sentiment that have not been excelled.

Hazlitt noted that Turner's paintings represented not the objects of nature so much as the medium through which they are seen—they are pictures of the elements, of air, earth, and water. They reveal a new glory in the world.

A. G. Dumfries, Special Contribution for "Britain and America"

J. M. W. Turner's "The Fighting Téméraire"

I must request you to turn your attention to a noble river-piece by J. M. W. Turner, Esquire, R.A., *The Fighting 'Téméraire'*—as grand a painting as ever figured on the walls of any Academy, or came from the easel of any painter. The old *Téméraire* is dragged to her last home by a little, spiteful, diabolical steamer. A mighty red sun, amidst a host of flaring clouds, sinks to rest on one side of the picture, and illumines a river that seems interminable, and a countless navy that fades away into such a wonderful distance as never was painted before. The little demon of a steamer is belching out a volume (why do I say a volume? not a hundred volumes could express it) of foul, lurid, red-hot, malignant smoke, paddling furiously, and lashing up the water round about it; while behind it (a cold grey moon looking down on it), slow, sad, and majestic, follows the brave old ship, with death, as it were, written on her. I think, my dear Bricabrac (although, to be sure, your nation would be somewhat offended by such a collection of trophies), that we ought not, in common gratitude, to sacrifice entirely these noble old champions of ours, but that we should have somewhere a museum of their skeletons, which our children might visit, and think of the brave deeds which were done in them.°

It is absurd, you will say (and with a great deal of reason), for Titmarsh, or any other Briton, to grow so poetically enthusiastic about a four-foot canvas, representing a ship, a steamer, a river, and a sunset. But herein surely lies the power of the great artist. He makes you see and think of a great deal more than the objects before you; he knows how to soothe or intoxicate, to fire or to depress, by a few notes, or forms, or colours, of which we cannot trace the effect to the source, but only acknowledge the power.

William M. Thackeray, "A Second Lecture on the Fine Arts", 1839

Henry Moore

Yorkshire is a bleak and rugged place, with vast empty open moors which throw up bleak and rugged humps of granite into the cold grey northern light. Another great living sculptor comes from Yorkshire, too—Barbara Hepworth. It is possible, then, that granite and northern light are as sculpturally inspiring as marble and Mediterranean sunshine are said to be. Henry Moore is amazingly like a rugged piece of Yorkshire granite: there might almost be an affinity between man and stone.°

Significantly, Henry Moore's father was a coalminer, with a lifetime spent in hewing rock and proud of his skilled and dangerous calling. His mother, one of those massive workingclass matriarchs with eight children, suffered from rheumatism. As a child, Henry Moore had to rub her back with liniment. The physical sensation of his fingers in contact with the subtleties of yielding flesh and resisting bone was a uniquely sculptural one.

A Sunday School story about Michelangelo sent the little boy away with the words, "the greatest sculptor in the world", ringing in his ears. The whole thing reads like a success story of a young artist making good, with that fairy godmother of fiction, the enlightened schoolmistress, seeing genius in a gawky Yorkshire lad and giving encouragement and help when and where they were needed.°

The influences at work in the young artist: Michelangelo and Rodin, Epstein and Gaudier-Brizeska, African art and, perhaps above all, Mexican art.

The Mexican influence reached its most seminal in *Chac Mool,* the recumbent Rain God whose raised knees and enquiring eyes were to inspire the archetypes of so much of Moore's sculpture, translated from male god into female human, with the austere made sensuous and committed to a sharing and identity with the contours of the earth itself. The sensuous with Moore is never frivolous. His work is always invested with an enormous dignity, a feeling of contained power, a sort of immemorial patience, and endurance.

Part of the fascination of Moore's work° is the way in which he pursues that relentless search—which is one of the essential qualities of genius—for fresh discovery, for new exploration into the nature of his art. Again and again it has seemed that Moore has "arrived", as in the famous Northampton *Madonna and Child.*

Again and again he has gone off on a new quest. After beautiful rounded groups of family relationship, he rushed off to enquire into the meaning of lonely skeletal forms, a complete break-up and almost sinister shattering of the old motifs. Then came a fresh synthesis with the pairs of *Kings and Queens* in which form flows over the skeletons, acquiring a new power and authority, and a sharply accentuated tragic sense. Again, this tragic sense flowed into a new vein of warriors and Greek-inspired draperies.

Then suddenly all these human plastic values seemed to be thrown overboard in geometric abstractions or primitive totem poles—much to the despair of Moore's more conventional admirers who would like to see him settle down. Yet on each occasion, there seems to have been a reversal here and there of the old and tried discoveries which emerged again richer and more subtle than before.

Anne Symonds in "London Calling, European Ed.", 1966

The Edinburgh Festival

Summer 1946! After long years of war and insularity, Scotland came alive again, calling to people of other nations, kept apart, alienated, to join with her own in celebrating the arts. The Festival was born. Music, drama, these were the aspects of European culture which were emphasized, and indeed the official title is still "The Edinburgh Festival of Music and Drama", but right from the beginning other arts were included. The first of a great series of art exhibitions was one of van Gogh's paintings, brought together from all over the world. A film festival joined up with the others, later on, and the military tattoo, a spectacular exhibition of military manœuvres in a spectacular setting (the Castle Esplanade) became a feature of the Festival which visitors find enthralling. Exhibitions of ceramics, of photographs, a consortium of authors discussing their craft, folk-song ideas proliferated, and Edinburgh began to have itself a yearly jamboree!

Everything has been made possible by the vision and generosity of the City Fathers (the Council) whose original idea it was. So now—for three weeks—the city goes gay. If the weather is kind—and it often is at that time of year, late August and early September—the old grey town is transformed: flags flying, pipers piping, fireworks flashing—all add to the special Festival flavour. Not the least part of this "flavour" is the cosmopolitan atmosphere imparted by the influx of visitors from all over the world.

And what have they flocked to see, to hear? The best. We have had famous orchestras from Vienna, Berlin, Paris, New York, Leningrad, Moscow; opera from Prague, Holland, Stuttgart. Comedy and tragedy have been brought to us by the Comédie Française, the Greek National Theatre, the Piccolo Teatro Milan. Music has included chamber music, solo performances. We have seen and heard men and women of international renown—great conductors like Klemperer, von Karajan, pianists like Svlatoslav Richter, Claudio Arrau, violinists like Isaac Stern, David Oistrakh, cellists like Rostropovitch, singers like Fischer-Dieskau, Elisabeth Schwarzkopf, Joan Sutherland, Maria Callas—even modern popular idols like Marlene Dietrich.

One of the charms of the Festival is the way in which it changes from year to year and yet remains enchantingly the same. The variety is due mainly to the Festival Directors. One man holds this part, generally for three or four years. It is an exacting but no doubt rewarding task. For the public, a change of director means a distinct change of emphasis. The taste of one will be eclectic, seeking to gather and fuse many strands; another, for example Lord Harewood, will try to find a unifying theme, e.g. Greek tragedy, Czech culture, and introduce different aspects of the theme through the different mediums of music, play, opera, art.

The exhibitions of art have been one of the great successes of the Festival. But for that, so many people in this country would never have seen even one original painting by van Gogh, Gauguin, Renoir, Cézanne, Corot, Delacroix, let alone whole roomfuls of them, nor seen the impressive sculpture of Epstein, nor been introduced to the mysteries and glories of Byzantine Art.

And I have not even mentioned the "Fringe"! Fringe? The queer title belongs to the great number of "unofficial", unsubsidized Festival shows which enterprising, mainly young, artists and performers have brought to Edinburgh, and which now exist alongside the official Festival and are thought by many to be more interesting and alive than their "parent". Every hall, of every shape and size, is a bustle of activity; we have even had a huge stadium of canvas erected over an ice-rink, to house the performance of a medieval fable-pageant, *Les Quatre Fils Aymon*.

Then, too, local talent is encouraged and emboldened. Young Edinburgh artists show their paintings outside, on the steps of the "Scotsman" offices. Scottish genius has been fostered, e.g. in the revival of the great medieval play *The Three Estates* and the creation of the new Scottish Opera.

What, for one individual, have been the highlights of the Festival through these many years? The moving moments I recall are hearing Fischer-Dieskau sing *Das Lied von der Erde* strong and sweet; Sutherland soaring as Lucia; the love duet from *Tristan;* and the first time I saw a real, three-dimensional Cézanne.

Rita MacDonald, Special Contribution for "Britain and America"

"Punch" in the Sixties

One of the problems is that to-day most of the newspapers have become comic magazines. We have no monopoly of humour, and as artists in particular have such a huge market—not only in Britain but in America and sometimes on the Continent—a lot of them aren't willing to discipline themselves or be guided towards the *Punch* standard. We have to comb the world for artists who show the right quality and the right kind of wit for us. °And we have to make sure that we get the right balance of different kinds, so that we mix quickies which give you one brief chuckle with drawings into which you can look and which you can turn back to, detail that makes you smile till the smile broadens into a laugh.

Then there's the problem of topicality. This wasn't so important for some of my predecessors, because for something like a hundred years there was really little difference between a *Punch* in June and a *Punch* in January. Now we try to produce a topical weekly magazine. In the matter of political cartooning conditions have worked our way. The dailies, of course, have all got their own cartoons, but what they comment on usually won't stand up for more than a few hours. It's hurriedly thought out, hurriedly drawn, it's bunged into the paper, it's there on your breakfast table, and two hours later the comment is as dead as a dodo. Now here on *Punch* we have time to look at the world for at least a week, and we try to take a broad view and find out what people are really thinking about. I'd like to bet that in 52 issues of *Punch* you get a much better picture of what's going on in the world than you'd get from 310 issues of any daily.

Nowadays we include a certain amount of serious writing in the paper, apart from the criticism of books and the arts. This is not only valuable in itself, but it helps to bring new blood into *Punch* and it helps the purely comic writers to look better, by contrast. I don't believe you can produce a magazine of unrelieved comic writing, and I think it's fatal to ask writers with reputations to be funny in print—to order.°

Another innovation in *Punch*—which, I suppose, people will always accuse of never changing—is the section for women which I introduced recently. For many years women were discouraged from writing in *Punch;* but then, in the nineteenth century, as far as I know, very few of them tried their hand at humour. They might legitimately laugh at men's jokes, but it wasn't done to make their own—especially for money. Now over half the unsolicited prose and verse is sent in by women, but the odd thing is that they never submit drawings. That's something I cannot understand. The only woman drawing for *Punch* at the moment is Anton.°

Is anything beyond a joke? I can only tell you that we have no hard and fast rules, no black list or anything like that. What I go on is my own taste. For example, I don't like jokes about tramps these days—partly because I don't believe that there are many tramps left. I don't like jokes about physical infirmity. If jokes are going to hurt a lot of people, then they are out. Sex jokes? If we published anything faintly suggestive, I'd be bombarded with protests from people who'd say: "Hullo, *'Punch'* has gone over the weir. Lost its soul." But sex is not ignored. I don't see how you can possibly avoid it. What people don't realize is the amount of sex in the old *Punch*—very much more than there is to-day. Because sex is sometimes treated vulgarly in other papers readers are apt to think that any reference to sex—even in *Punch*—is

Queen Elizabeth just runs through a little thing of her own composition to William Shakespeare. (1896)

Dropping the pilot (1890)   (1954)

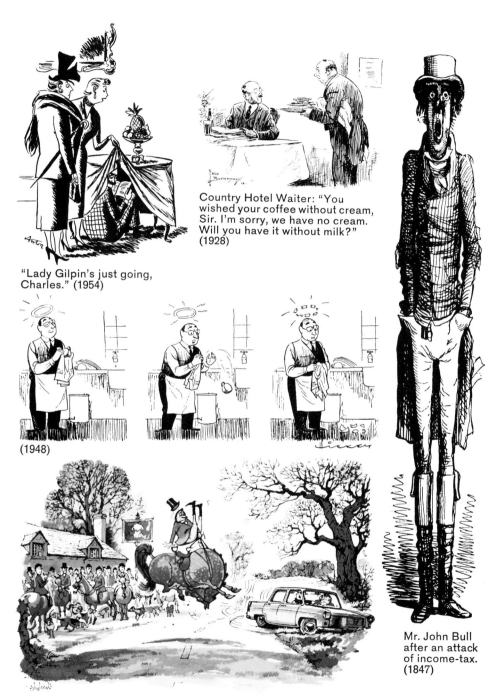

"Lady Gilpin's just going, Charles." (1954)

Country Hotel Waiter: "You wished your coffee without cream, Sir. I'm sorry, we have no cream. Will you have it without milk?" (1928)

(1948)

"You never hear anything about testing t h e i r breath." (1967)

Mr. John Bull after an attack of income-tax. (1847)

tasteless. I usually tell my critics in this matter that it is *Punch's* duty to prove that the delicate subject of sex can be handled with wit and good taste.

In politics everything is wide open. A lot of papers claim to be independent, but I do believe that we really *are*. I can only judge this by the composition of the *Punch* Table—which decides the subject of the weekly political cartoon. The members range from dyed-in-the-wool Tories to very advanced Liberals and further Left than that. As for me, I'm very much of a middleman. I don't think that a comic paper should adopt set political attitudes. Where we see glaring wrongs, we'll come out fighting. We have very strong views on all manner of things. For instance, we were much more opposed to De Gaulle than any of the dailies, chiefly because we are scared stiff of anything resembling dictatorship. If people say that *Punch* is too cosy and not aggressive enough, that it doesn't ever take the world seriously, then I'd say they haven't read the paper recently. They're picking up gossip about the past.

If there are trouble spots in the world and ugly sores in our own social life, then humour is one of the weapons against them. If we don't use it in that way, then we're falling down on our job. But I can see no sign whatever of the supply of targets drying up at all, and I don't believe that the comic writer is in any danger of occupational exhaustion, from the strain of trying to make people laugh in a world that often seems to be decidedly unfunny. Wherever there is news, there is humour to go with it. To be funny, you need fact. One of my star writers seldom sits down to write an article without a dozen books of reference around him, and his hands on half a dozen more. Some people think that humour should be spontaneous, and that if you've got to look something up then you can't be funny, but that's not true.

Punch has gradually inched its way up in the last few years, without violent splashes in any direction, until we've reached about 126,000. If we can do that at a time when other papers are going to the wall, it seems to me that *Punch* is good for another 120 years at least.

Bernard Hollowood in "The Twentieth Century Magazine", 1961

American Architecture

At any time in history, the number of truly creative people is a small part of the total population, and the number of great achievements in architecture, as in any of the other arts, is also small. It is remarkable that so many structures of genuine worth, that are likely to endure in the histories of world architecture, have been designed and built in the short life of the United States. America is still continuing its explosive growth, begun in Colonial times, and its history remains a dynamic one. The very vigor of its expansion

▲68 Modern Suburb, South of Golden Gate Park, San Francisco

▶69 Independence Hall, Philadelphia

▼70 Guggenheim Museum, New York

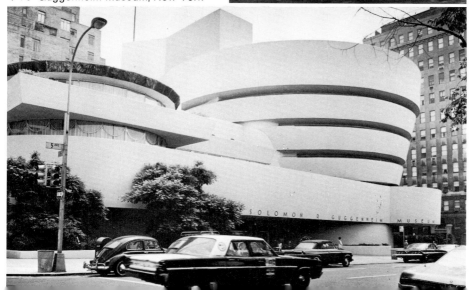

◀71 A Typical 18th Century Residence in Virginia

▲72 Los Angeles Air-Port, Central Building

◀73 Seagram Building, New York

seems to have provided a sympathetic environment for creative architectural accomplishment—both by native-born architects and by those who have come to its shores from other, older lands.

American architecture is more than a synthesis of designs conceived in other times and other places, and yet it has built proudly on the backgrounds of its people. Whether their ancestry was English and the architecture they drew from was that of the late middle ages and the Renaissance, as in the beginning; or French and *Beaux Arts* influenced, as later; or middle European and inspired by the excitement of the early modern movement in the arts—in continuing, successive numbers, architects from the Old World have arrived and transfused the talent that was developing in the new country.

Never has the fusion of backgrounds been more clear or more effective than at the present moment. Consider first some names: Belluschi, Breuer, Gropius, Gruen, Kiesler, Lescaze, Neutra, Pei, Saarinen, Sert, van der Rohe, Yamasaki. These and many others have enriched an architecture that could also draw on the work of those whose ancestry was longer in the United States—people such as Richardson, Hunt, Sullivan, Maybeck, Goodhue, Wright. And yet, to carry the point further, even the "native" architecture in the United States has often had a strong influence from other places. Wright and Maybeck, each in his own way, were influenced by designs from the Orient; Hunt and Richardson were romantically aware of the medieval Periods of Western Europe.

This is not to say, however, that architecture in the United States has been uniformly eclectic or merely a synthesis. The excitement that it produces in those who see it today, and the influence it is having on other lands, in its turn, could come about only through originality and creative strength. Something has been added to what was there in the beginning. The great addition, probably, has been technological accomplishment. Methods of engineering design and techniques of construction have been developed rapidly and efficiently. In addition, there has been a refining process on the one hand (Mies's glass-walled office building is surely a refinement of his earlier, European work), and an infusion of boldness on the other hand (the audacity of Eero Saarinen's forms are an interesting contrast to the urbane modernism of his father's work).

As a picture of its society, then, architecture in the United States reflects a land into which have flowed many streams of creative development, and where they have all been gathered together into a strong, forward-moving current. Today it is a picture of growth, vigor, imagination, and an ability strong enough to direct the current to new ends—new social goals, new esthetic principles, new technological possibilities.

Thomas H. Creighton, "American Architecture", 1964

Minoru Yamasaki

Yamasaki, searching for a quality of "humanism" in his buildings that stimulates a climate of rapport with man, voices strong discontent with forceful buildings that lack compassion towards man. °He cites Mies's Seagram Building, with its dignity and majesty, as the one building in the United States he would most liked to have designed. Admiring the order and calm of Mies's architecture he says, "Mies showed us that machine-made buildings can be as beautiful as the hand-made buildings of the past".

Minoru Yamasaki was born in Seattle, Washington, in 1912. His was not the idyllic boyhood that his buildings might suggest. The son of a poor, immigrant family, he had to spend five gruelling summers in Alaskan fish canneries to pay for his architectural education.°

In 1954, the assignment to design the United States Consulate in Kobe took Yamasaki first to Japan and subsequently around the world. His impressions on this first time out of America were to set his direction. He found that there was great emotional experience and involvement possible with buildings of the past; he felt this was achieved, not necessarily through form or ornamentation, but from a clear, cultural concept executed in the building technique and technology of the times.

The wonderful change of pace and the element of surprise in moving through spaces in the buildings of Japan impressed him as it had Wright.°

"An architecture to implement our way of life and reflect it must recognize those human characteristics we cherish most: love, gentility, joy, serenity, beauty and hope, and the dignity and individuality of man. This idea in its essence is the philosophy of humanism in architecture. We must strive to enhance life through beauty and delight, and reflect the nobility to which man aspires. We must provide—through order—a background of serenity for today's feverish activity, and scale architecture to frame man happily in his environment. Finally, we must be truthful in expression of structure and purpose, and advance today's industrialized technology for the benefit of society.

Many of the qualities basic to older architectures—good proportion, elegance of detail and nobility—exist in distinguished, historic European buildings. These qualities must be translated into our idiom, and we can be inspired by and learn much from European examples. However, in the understanding of serenity and scale, I believe we must turn to Japanese architecture.°

The chaos brought on by political turmoil, mobility, the population explosion, and by the tremendous impact of the machine, demands that man—if he is to retain his sanity—must have a serene environment. But with serenity we must have delight—the delight of the interesting silhouettes, of waterplay, of variety in outdoor and indoor spatial experience. But serenity, the physical manifestation of the belief that man can live in quiet dignity, must unify the whole".°

The pleasure in architecture for Yamasaki is discovering a specific concept. This was Saarinen's concern too. "If you can find the concept which is appropriate to a particular problem, then you can devise an architecture appropriate for it", he says.°

74 Model of the World Trade Center, New York

Yamasaki's commission to design the World Trade Center° may prove as significant for him as it inevitably must for New York. To be located on Manhattan's Lower West Side, it will house anyone and anything connected with world trade. The program presented to Yamasaki, who was selected over a dozen other American architects, was quite explicit: twelve million square feet of floor area on a sixteen acre site, which also had to accommodate new facilities for the Hudson tubes and subway connections—all with a budget of under $ 500 million. The vast space needs and limited site immediately implied a high-rise development that will make the adjacent drama of Manhattan's business tip seem timid in comparison. It also raises all the old questions of concentration—is it just too big? Can the city cope with the ensuing congestion?

After studying more than one hundred schemes in model form, Yamasaki decided on a two-tower development to contain the nine million square feet of office space. One tower became unreasonable in size and unwieldy structurally, yet several towers became too approximate for their size and "looked too much like a housing project"; whereas two towers gave a reasonable office area on each floor, took advantage of the magnificent views, and allowed a manageable structural system. The twin towers, with 110 floors rising 1,353 feet, will be the tallest in the world. From observation decks at the top of the towers it will be possible to see for forty-five miles in every direction. Apart from sheer height, the visual impact on the skyline of twin towers, on what is essentially a one-towered island, will make them really count. One distinct advantage of the project's enormity is the architectural opportunity to advance the art of building. Yamasaki re-examined the skyscraper from first principles, considering no ground so hallowed that it could not be questioned, especially in view of the potential of modern technology.

Paul Heyer, "Architects on Architecture", 1960

A Real American Style of Music

The point I want to make with all my might is that America right now seems to me to be, musically, just about where Germany was around the seventeenth century. Deep in the singspiel. (We mustn't talk about present-day church music: that must be traditional, and has all been inherited.) But our secular music is just about where German music was fifty years before Mozart. Only *our* singspiels are called *Oklahoma!*

75 Leonard Bernstein behind the Scenes

and *Can-Can*. This is a period we must pass through before we can arrive at a real American symphonic form, or a real American style of whatever kind of concert music. It may not be the symphony as we have known it: we may produce something very different. But the musical language it will speak must first be created in our theater; then one day it can be divorced from "meaning" and stand alone, abstract. Do you see what I mean? For all our technical mastery and sophistication we are not really ready yet to produce our own concert music. As a result, all the stuff that is being turned out by the mile every day for concert performance in American halls is really European, and *old* European at that, with perhaps some American spice added by way of cowboy tunes or blues harmonies or jazz rhythms. But the music remains essentially European, because the whole notion of the symphonic form is a German notion, and don't let anybody tell you anything else. All the Russian symphonies are really German ones with vodka substituted for beer; and Franck's is German with some cornets making the difference; and Liszt's are German with nothing making the difference, and so are Elgar's and Grieg's and Dvořak's. Whatever national touches have been added, it's all German deep down, because the line of the symphony is a straight one smack from Mozart to Mahler.

Now, here we are, remember, a brand-new country, comparatively speaking, a baby only a hundred and seventy-five years old. Which is nothing at all when you think of the old empires that produced that straight line I just mentioned. And actually we have been writing music in this country for only fifty years, and half of that fifty years the music has been borrowed clean out of the pockets of Brahms and Company. Of course we have the disadvantage here of having been born already grown-up, so we don't start with folk dances and prayers for rain. We started with the leavings of the European development, handed to us on an old cracked dish. But then, we have an advantage after all: we have jazz. Which is the beginning of some other straight line which will grow here as certainly as the symphonic line grew out of another folk-strain for about a hundred years in Germany. Whatever jazz is, it's our own folk music, naive, sophisticated, and exciting. And out of it has been born something we call the musical comedy. Well, 175 years isn't very long for that to have happened (and it really took only the last fifty years) compared to the centuries it took for the singspiel to arrive. And here we are at the point of building that singspiel into real opera—or, in our terms, developing *Pal Joey* into whatever American music is going to become. We are all ready and waiting for the Mozart to come along and just simply do it. °I'm taking bids on the new Mozart. Any comers?

Leonard Bernstein, "The Joy of Music", 1959

The New Jazz

On Nov. 17, 1959, a bearded prophet from Texas named Ornette Coleman carried his white plastic alto saxophone into New York's Five-Spot Café and blew the jazz world to pieces. The molten, unchained improvisation of Coleman and his waistcoated trio of young musicians confused many listeners and even infuriated many jazzmen. Some walked out in disgust. English critic Kenneth Tynan cried, "They have gone too far". But Leonard Bernstein leaped to the stand to embrace the new

76 Ornette Coleman

musicians, and advanced jazzmen such as conservatory-trained John Lewis proclaimed Coleman the apostle of a new age. The most violent, ambitious revolution in the history of jazz had begun.

    The rhythms of jazz have always been the rhythms of revolution, a personal revolution beyond all ideology and dogma. They were created by the American Negro who could find freedom only in such private and personal rhythms. Ironically, this was his greatest cultural gift to his country and became the most characteristic expression of that country. The history of jazz itself is a history of personal revolutions—the clear, classic, galvanizing trumpet calls of Louis Armstrong; the proud, complex elegance of Duke Ellington; the melodic eruptions of the Bird, Charlie Parker; and now Coleman's searing self-revelations that triggered what has come to be known as the New Thing. The New Thing is the dominant movement in jazz today, enlisting the energies of a whole generation of remarkable young Negroes and reflecting, as jazz always does, the surrounding tensions of urban America.

    Its forms have been hammered out by the urgencies of a new Negro sensibility—which can produce the anguished sensitivity of a James Baldwin, the civilized sagacity of a Ralph Ellison, the proud dignity of a march on Washington—or the blind fury of a Watts riot. Racial pride, black consciousness, the frustrated anger of the exploited, the cry for equality and dignity and the demand for artistic legitimacy are the new music's themes. "The jazz revolution is not a programmatic black-power movement", critic Nat Hentoff points out. "It believes in soul and law and freedom. There's almost a touching belief in music as a cleansing, purifying, liberating force, as if jazzmen were the unacknowledged legislators of the world. They all want to change the social system through their music".

    The esthetics of the new music is also its politics—freedom. The new jazzmen have ripped jazz from its formal moorings. Like their contemporaries in painting, theater, films and poetry, their art has become nothing but itself—pure sound, spontaneously created under the pressure of feeling and thought—not variations on a theme, not ruminations on a harmonic structure, but pure melody driven by inspiration.

"Newsweek", 1966

The Comic Strip—A Mirror of the American Way of Life

The comic strip of the American daily press long ago achieved the status of a folk movement, and it is perfectly acceptable, in almost any company, to admit that you follow the fortunes of Dick Tracy or Steve Canyon. Indeed, the strips do have honourable popular origins. They first appeared in more or less their present form in the 1860s, when a tremendous flow of immigrants was arriving from Europe, and for many poor strangers who spoke no English they served as an introduction to American ways of thought and life.°

The early strips thus reflected many facets of American living, and it is perhaps not fanciful to suggest that they still express, often unconsciously, many of the chief characteristics of the nation—or at least that part of it, approximating most closely to the urban Middle West, that has come to be accepted as standard America. The diversity of the United States is still immense, in custom as in country, but that unpleasant alleged "norm" called the American Way of Life—drug stores and dating, profit motives and women's clubs—is spreading relentlessly, and has about it a deadening and intolerant sameness. We may trace its traits and prejudices closely in the world of the strip cartoon.

For example, the visitor to a Middle West manufacturing town is almost sure to notice the predominance of women. This is a powerfully matriarchal society. In the home, the self-possessed, well-read, relatively leisured housewife has innumerable advantages over her generally plodding husband; in civic affairs the women's organizations, from opera societies to church clubs, are always potent; and in politics such groups as the League of Women Voters have much influence. In any family party dining out, a woman is likely to pay the restaurant bill. In economic affairs the purchasing power of the housewife is all important, and the whole structure of American commercial life is designed largely to satisfy the demands of women.

This maternalism is accurately portrayed (without bitterness) in the strip cartoons. A favourite situation is that of Dad and Junior slipping away from the women for a weekend's fishing, pursued by admonitions about warm underwear. Dagwood, in Chic Young's admirable cartoon *Blondie,* is always getting into trouble with his wife for stealing a sandwich from the kitchen or muddying the hall floor. "We are going visiting today", announces the dictatorial wife in *Bringing Up Father:* and Father puts his hat on. Women are often ignorant in the strip cartoons, often drive their cars foolishly or make inane remarks, but they are always in command.

Many such cartoon episodes concern a wife's desire for a mink coat, the supreme American symbol of opulence, for the American has never lost his respect for wealth, however acquired, and still passionately enjoys the office-boy-to-millionaire saga. A man is judged by the make of his car, and there is scarcely a club or a hotel in the nation that will exclude any rich man from its custom. If you have money, you are consequently esteemed (only in certain parts of the country, outside the cartoon standard, does birth assume an equally absurd importance).°

The American home of the strip cartoons is that of Dixie Dugan and her family in a famous series: it is a weatherboard house with a small garden running down to the street, with a mailbox by the gate, a hammock for Dad to swing in by the porch, and indubitably a refrigerator and a television set inside. For the comic strip, as for the Voice of America, this is the U.S.A.

When somebody appears who is not a complete American, by these rigid standards, he is generally regarded as a figure of fun. More than one cartoon deals with hillbilly folk, the men heavily covered with tangled beards, the women wearing poke bonnets and smoking pipes. They talk in the quaintest of dialects and live in mountain shacks. One strip deals with an immigrant family still not totally Americanized, and demonstrates their origin by spelling English words in the German manner. When Englishmen turn up (often as a subject of ambition for socially conscious mothers) they speak with a wildly exaggerated drawl and generally wear dinner jackets.

Perhaps allied with its maternalism, perhaps stemming from the heritage of the frontier, is America's overwhelming love of children. It is a pleasant experience to walk with a small boy along an American street, and to find both men and women enthralled and delighted by the very presence of a child. American children must be the most violently loved on earth. As a result, some of the happiest and best of the comic strips are those that deal with children. Generally, in art as in life, the protagonists in these adventures are freckled, tousled, slightly spoiled boys, or small girls of precocious tendencies. It is an odd fact that American children, in spite of their pioneering background, are closely home-bound in their enterprises. Sail along the Mississippi for a month and you will scarcely see a Huck Finn playing along its banks (if you do, he is in rags and lives in a shanty-boat, and may even be a halfcaste, and is therefore outside the cartoon pale). Young Americans will play daring and imaginatively in their own backyard, but they seldom venture into the woods. So, in the strips, Mom is never far away, and the place is warm with security. Two situations often recur. Boys are depicted selling soft drinks for cash, thus displaying an early and commendable instinct for profit. Girls are forever interrupting their elder sister's moments of courtship with remarks that sometimes seem to show an astonishingly early onset of puberty.°

For years the genius of Walt Disney has been exerted in the comic strips, both through Disney characters like Donald Duck and Goofy, and through the efforts of many plagiarists. His own cartoons are nearly always good and gay.°

Nor, indeed, within the presently accepted pattern, are the vices of the newspaper strip cartoon really very vicious. The so-called "comic books", sold separately and irregularly, often contain material of nauseating fancy, but the press cartoons are usually innocuous enough.°

Inasmuch as they reflect materialism, contempt for the individualist, cloying sentiment, and parochialism, they do no more than express general American tendencies, and however much the foreigner may dislike such trends, whatever pride he may take in his own national superiorities, he must in fairness admit that the American Way of Life, like the American comic strip, brings happiness to many, and no great evil. In any case, as the Chicago bartender said to his disgruntled customer, "If ya don't like the saloon, why doncha go fishing?"

"The Funnies—An American Idiom", 1963

X Literature

Standard English

An Englishman's "accent" is the noises he makes when he pronounces English. A speaker from Suffolk will not use all the same noises as a speaker from Lancashire, and thus one is said to have a Suffolk accent and the other a Lancashire accent. The differences between two accents are partly a matter of the pronunciation of individual sounds: thus a northern speaker pronounces the *a* sound in the word *ask* like the *a* sound in *mad*, whereas a southern speaker makes it resemble more the *a* in *car*.°

Though there are many different accents of English they are mostly used to speak the same English: that is, "Standard English".° If the first sentence of this chapter were read aloud by someone from Yorkshire, someone from Devon, and someone from Kent, the words would of course be the same, but the pronunciation would vary in each case. The speakers would not therefore be speaking "dialect". We use the word "dialect" to describe the special words and word order which a particular brand of English uses, and we associate this with a particular locality. °Of course, particular accents go with particular dialects; but we often hear someone described as "speaking dialect" when what we mean is that he has an *accent* of some kind.

In the sense described above, Standard English is itself a dialect. English was brought over by the Angles, Saxons and Jutes, and as they settled in different parts of the country, over a period of time their forms of English and their pronunciation of them began to vary. This is the origin of dialects; and thus it is wrong to claim, as is sometimes done, that one is "older" than another. The dialect of south-east England, because it was in use in London and the court, and because books began to be written in it, became accepted as "standard". Accent, however, was not standard. We know that Sir Walter Raleigh kept his Devonshire accent at the court of Elizabeth I.

From Raleigh's time the accent of the south-east gained greater prestige because of its associations with the capital, the court, the old universities and the public schools. It became a class accent—that of an educated ruling class. More recently, the BBC added to the status of this accent by choosing it as the one for news bulletins and announcements on official occasions. It is now known as "Received Pronunciation", commonly abbreviated to "R.P." To some people it seems the only "correct" pronunciation of English. They even call other pronunciations "lazy", and "slovenly" as though there were some moral disgrace in not using Received Pronunciation. How absurd this attitude is can be seen when we consider not only the history of other accents in this country, but also the status of English as a world language. An American New England pronunciation is in no sense "inferior" to R.P., and one would not find the American who thought it was. In fact, many Americans are as irritated by R.P. as some English are by what they call the American's "drawl". This English attitude to accent is a matter of amazement to many overseas peoples who find nothing like it in their own countries. In the U.S.A. for instance, while there are certain unacceptable pronunciations, there is no *one* correct one; what are called Eastern, Southern, and General American are equally acceptable. Of course, there must be some standards of pronunciation, otherwise we would not understand one another. The purpose of speech is after all *to communicate*. If an accent is so broad that it makes understanding difficult, then the speaker is at a disadvantage when talking to people from elsewhere. This does not mean that everyone should have the same accent (which would be impossible to achieve anyway) but that accents should be sufficiently alike to be mutually intelligible.°

Fortunately, the old attitude that there is *one* correct accent is changing. With the spread of higher education, educated people today speak with a variety of accents. In the professions and public life more different accents are heard than ever before. A Prime Minister may have a Yorkshire pronunciation, a Minister of Health a touch of Birmingham in his voice, and we often find such speakers are amongst the most effective.

Nowadays the air is full of voices from radio and television. They often have different accents, but we have the evidence of our ears that they are communicating effectively. That, after all, is one of the reasons they are asked to broadcast. This is another factor making for greater tolerance of accents other than R.P. It is undeniable that there is still a good deal of social prejudice about some accents, particularly town accents—but this also is changing. The Beatles did a good deal for Liverpudlian.

Andrew Wilkinson, "In your Own Words", 1967

The Cultural Background of Shakespeare's Time

The British Empire was founded by private adventurers exploiting the outlying parts of the world, with the unofficial encouragement of Elizabeth. Modern English literature had a similar origin. The Renaissance, though a learned movement, had its true centre not in universities but at courts grown rich with commerce. In the fourteenth and fifteenth centuries it became the fashion for the merchant princes of Italy to devote their surplus wealth, the banking system being then still in its infancy, to the encouragement of art and literature, much of which possessed the double attraction of offering at once a permanent investment and a means of personal display. This fashion spread to the rest of Europe, and Chaucer was already benefiting from it before 1400. Elizabeth, therefore, inherited a long tradition of royal patronage of art and letters, and as a daughter of Henry VIII and Anne Boleyn she was fond both of learning and of pageantry. But she inherited also an exhausted treasury and a full share of her grandfather Henry VII's passion for economy. Thus she contrived to obtain as much entertainment as possible without spending a penny more upon it than she could help.

The arrangement as regards plays was that towards Christmas, at which season and up to Twelfth Night the court held high festival, the Master of the Revels, whose office was a special department of the royal household under the immediate charge of the Lord Chamberlain, invited the acting-companies of London to submit plays for selection, very much as Philostrate does in *A Midsummer-Night's Dream*. The players, of course, received a fee for performing the chosen play or plays; but the Queen had

77 A Wedding Feast at the Time of Queen Elizabeth

no direct financial responsibility for their maintenance, any more than she had for the expeditions of Drake and Hawkins. Indeed the public theatres of the metropolis came into existence during the second half of her reign in order, at any rate in theory, to give scope for the companies to rehearse before performing at court, without being
5 at the charge of Her Majesty. And the theory that the players existed for the Queen's "solace", as the phrase went, was of vital importance in other respects. The growing puritanism of the City rendered the Lord Mayor and Corporation bitterly hostile as a rule to the theatre, so that but for the protection of the Court the stage would have been suppressed long before Shakespeare reached London.
10 The poets, like the dramatists, looked to Elizabeth as towards the sun in their heaven; but she had in general small comfort to offer those who courted her in verse and were unable to support themselves by public means. Moreover, she herself took much greater delight in music than in poetry, and had as we have seen a passion for dancing. In this, as in so many other ways, she was typically English of the time.
15 During the latter part of her reign music and dancing were even more popular than the drama itself, and a puritan writer in 1587 complains that "London is so full of unprofitable pipers and fiddlers that a man can no sooner enter a tavern than two or three cast of them hang at his heels, to give him a dance before he depart". In those days you were entertained to music while your barber shaved you, and it was counted
20 a shame for a lady or gentleman to be unable to "bear a part" when, as the custom was, the music-books were brought in after supper and the company sat round the table to sing madrigals. This indeed was the golden age of English music, and especially of English vocal music, the age of the great polyphonic composers William Byrd, Thomas Campion, Orlando Gibbons, and a host of others. That Shakespeare was
25 himself passionately fond of music is witnessed by the countless references to music and singing in his plays.

Most of the well-known composers were in the service of noblemen, and every Elizabethan gentleman of standing maintained musicians as part of his household, "the music of the house" as Nerissa calls it being as necessary to greatness in that day
30 as gardeners and chauffeurs are in this. The Tudor peace transformed the private

armies of the barons, the bane of medieval England, into retinues of servants which included musicians, players and entertainers of other kinds; and instead of fighting each other the nobility, like Duke Theseus, occupied such time as was not given to the chase and other sports,

> With pomp, with triumph and with revelling.

John D. Wilson, "The Essential Shakespeare", 1946

The Shakespearian Theatre

Acting at the houses of private persons was generally in the evening, because public performances took place in the afternoon. It must not, however, be supposed that noblemen did not attend the public playhouses, though it was unseemly for ladies to show themselves there. A special "room", or as we should say "box", was reserved for lords, and we are told that during part of 1599, Shakespeare's patron, the Earl of Southampton, with his friend the Earl of Rutland, "passed away the time merrily in going to plays every day". Furthermore, the seats in the galleries, which were of varying prices, were largely occupied by gentlemen and professional men of different sorts, a large number of them being students of the Inns of Court, who, as one of them, the poet Donne, tells us, were

> Of study and play made strange hermaphrodites.

Much has been heard of the "groundlings", for the most part prentices, who paid a penny to stand on the floor of the house. It has been too little recognised that the public theatres were in the main dependent upon the cultured classes of London.

What would strike a modern eye most about Shakespeare's theatre was its smallness. The auditorium of the Globe was probably about 55 feet square, that is approximately the size of a lawn tennis court; and this included the stage, which jutted right out among the audience, and was some 43 feet wide by about 27 feet long. The play was therefore performed almost in the middle of the theatre, the groundlings standing on

78 The Swan Theatre, London   79 The Globe Theatre, London

three sides of the stage, which was raised three or four feet off the floor, while the seats for those who could afford them were ranged in three tiers of galleries round the walls, and in some theatres stools could even be hired for accommodation on the stage itself. The whole atmosphere must have been extraordinarily intimate and domestic, especially when we remember that the personnel both of the company and of the audience was far more permanent than anything conceivable in modern London. Each member of the cast would be as familiar to the spectators as the individuals of a local football team are to-day to a crowd on the home ground. Under such conditions acting and drama were very different from anything we know now. And to understand Shakespeare, to follow the swiftness of his thought, the delicacy of his poetic workmanship, the cunning of his dramatic effects, the intricacy of his quibbles, to appraise in short the infinite riches of his art, we must think ourselves back into that little room at the Globe or its predecessors, in which his dramas were first given by a team of players, moving and speaking on a bare platform surrounded by a ring of faces only a few yards away, faces in front, to right, to left, above, faces tense with interest at the new miracle that awaited them, the faces of the brightest spirits and keenest intelligences of his time.

Did space permit, I might say much of the instrument for which he composed his mighty dramatic symphonies, that threefold instrument, the Elizabethan stage, the full significance of which Shakespearian criticism is only now beginning to appreciate. I will instance but one of its features, by way of showing how it moulded the art that belonged to it. The absence of stage scenery meant that Shakespeare had to create it in the verse he wrote.

But look, the morn, in russet mantle clad,
Walks o'er the dew of yon high eastward hill,

said an actor playing Horatio, pointing across the Globe theatre one sunny afternoon in 1601; and the spectators were entirely unconscious of any incongruity. Can we do better with all the resources of a mechanical age? Rather, does not the shining splendour of those lines make even the best contrivance of illuminated back-cloth look garish and absurd? Lacking scenery, again, Shakespeare lacked visual aids to the localisation of his scenes. Where does *Macbeth* open, on earth or in hell? or the third act of *Julius Caesar,* before the senate house or within it? or the first and second scenes of the second act of *Romeo and Juliet,* inside the orchard of Capulet or beyond the wall? The answer to all these alternatives is that the action of Shakespeare's plays proceeds within the bare framework of the Elizabethan theatre, which just because it is delocalised allowed the dramatist a freedom denied to his modern successors. And if such bareness be thought a primitive crudity, let the military plays be considered, plays whose short fighting scenes followed each other on the Elizabethan platform with all the bustle and excitement of a battle-field seen simultaneously at many points, but are so sadly hampered by a drop-curtain as to be almost unplayable under our theatrical conventions. The supreme example of the kind is, of course, *Antony and Cleopatra,* in which the whole globe itself could be the scene because it was written for the Globe. In that theatre a dramatist was bounded in a nutshell and could count himself king of infinite space.

John D. Wilson. *"The Essential Shakespeare",* 1946

Shakespeare, the Poet of Nature

Shakespeare is above all writers, at least above all modern writers, the poet of nature; the poet that holds up to his readers a faithful mirrour of manners and of life. His characters are not modified by the customs of particular places, unpractised by the rest of the world; by the peculiarities of studies or professions, which can operate but upon small numbers; or by the accidents of transient fashions or temporary opinions: they are the genuine progeny of common humanity, such as the world will always supply, and observation will always find. His persons act and speak by the influence of those general passions and principles by which all minds are agitated, and the whole system of life is continued in motion. In the writings of other poets a character is too often an individual; in those of Shakespeare it is commonly a species.°

Shakespeare has united the powers of exciting laughter and sorrow not only in one mind, but in one composition. Almost all his plays are divided between serious and ludicrous characters, and, in the successive evolutions of the design, sometimes produce seriousness and sorrow, and sometimes levity and laughter.°

The work of a correct and regular writer is a garden accurately formed and diligently planted, varied with shades, and scented with flowers; the composition of Shakespeare is a forest, in which oaks extend their branches, and pines tower in the air, interspersed sometimes with weeds and brambles, and sometimes giving shelter to myrtles and to roses; filling the eye with awful pomp, and gratifying the mind with endless diversity.°

It is not very grateful to consider how little the succession of editors has added to this authour's power of pleasing. He was read, admired, studied, and imitated, while he was yet deformed with all the improprieties which ignorance and neglect could accumulate upon him; while the reading was yet not rectified, nor his allusions understood; yet then did Dryden pronounce "that Shakespeare was the man, who, of all modern and perhaps ancient poets, had the largest and most comprehensive soul. All the images of nature were still present to him, and he drew them not laboriously, but luckily: When he describes any thing, you more than see it, you feel it too. Those who accuse him to have wanted learning, give him the greater commendation: he was naturally learned: he needed not the spectacles of books to read nature; he looked inwards, and found her there. I cannot say he is every where alike; were he so, I should do him injury to compare him with the greatest of mankind. He is many times flat and insipid; his comick wit degenerating into clenches, his serious swelling into bombast. But he is always great, when some great occasion is presented to him."

Samuel Johnson, "Preface to Shakespeare", 1765

Human Relationships in Shakespeare

Elizabethan drama grew in no-man's-land between the two historical epochs that we call the feudal and the capitalist. All around it old habits and ways were crumbling, new ones beginning to take shape, in a medley of fragmentary relics and experiments. In the medieval society that was falling to pieces the individual had been enclosed, snugly though crampingly, inside a narrow framework of institutions and beliefs, like an apprentice safe and warm in his airless cupboard-bed in one of the old houses of the Hanse merchants still to be seen in Bergen. Now the snug crib which was also a prison was releasing or ejecting him into a strange environment where he must learn to find his way about, among others groping likewise.

Life was thus both exhilarating and frightening. The epoch of free competition was coming in, the world was an oyster waiting for anyone's sword to open it.°

In a season of change one artist will fasten chiefly on what is bad in the situation, decline and decay, another on what is good, birth and growth. Shakespeare belongs emphatically to the second sort. It is hard to resist the temptation to read a symbolic meaning into the words of a speaker in one of the late Romances, which sound so full of prophecy and vision—"Thou met'st with things dying, I with things new-born" (*Winter's Tale,* III,3,108). Most of his rivals in the theatre belong as unmistakably to the first sort.°

Over a great part of Elizabethan and especially Jacobean drama hangs a cloud of gloom and embitterment. Its preoccupations are with death and with madness, the two things that separate the human being most totally from the rest of humanity. Its characters tend to be hard, distinct, unmingling entities, repelling like billiard-balls, imparting to one another only a mechanical kind of movement. Most typical among the bad ones are the "Machiavels", self-proclaimed villains emancipated from all bonds of conventional virtue.°

Contemporaries appear to have thought of Shakespeare and his poetry as "sweet"; an epithet which may not at first sound very appropriate, but which ceases to surprise as soon as we compare him with almost any of the other playwrights.°

It has been often enough or too often said that Shakespeare had a horror of anarchy, of social disorder; what really horrified him was not any breakdown of "order" in the policeman's understanding of the word, but something more fundamental, the destruction of men's faith in one another that is always liable to accompany the break-up of an old social pattern whether authority remains intact or not. He was always struggling to banish the chilling distrust that invaded his England in the later Histories and the following plays. Disloyalty and ingratitude are two of the sins he condemns most eloquently, and if he so habitually censures men by comparing them with brute beasts, what he has against the animals is, surely, their incapability of fellow-feeling. Tragic emotion in his plays springs, more generally than in those of other Elizabethans, from a sense of men's best feelings for one another being alienated or violated.

Victor G. Kiernan in "Shakespeare in a Changing World", 1964

On Poetry

The functions of the poetical faculty are twofold; by one it creates new materials of knowledge, and power, and pleasure; by the other it engenders in the mind a desire to reproduce and arrange them according to a certain rhythm and order, which may be called the beautiful and the good. The cultivation of poetry is never more to be desired than at periods when, from an excess of the selfish and calculating principle, the accumulation of the materials of external life exceed the quantity of the power of assimilating them to the internal laws of human nature. The body has then become too unwieldy for that which animates it.

Poetry is indeed something divine. It is at once the centre and circumference of knowledge; it is that which comprehends all science, and that to which all science must be referred. It is at the same time the root and blossom of all other systems of thought; it is that from which all spring, and that which adorns all; and that which, if blighted, denies the fruit and the seed, and withholds from the barren world the nourishment and the succession of the scions of the tree of life. It is the perfect and consummate surface and bloom of all things; it is as the odour and the colour of the rose to the texture of the elements which compose it, as the form and splendour of unfaded beauty to the secrets of anatomy and corruption. What were virtue, love, patriotism, friendship—what were the scenery of this beautiful universe which we inhabit; what were our consolations on this side of the grave—and what were our aspirations beyond it, if poetry did not ascend to bring light and fire from those eternal regions where the owl-winged faculty of calculation dare not ever soar? Poetry is not like reasoning, a power to be exerted according to the determination of the will. A man cannot say, "I will compose poetry". The greatest poet even cannot say it; for the mind in creation is as a fading coal, which some invisible influence, like an inconstant wind, awakens to transitory brightness; this power arises from within, like the colour of a flower which fades and changes as it is developed, and the conscious portions of our nature are unprophetic either of its approach or its departure. Could this influence be durable in its original purity and force, it is impossible to predict the greatness of the results; but when composition begins, inspiration is already on the decline, and the most glorious poetry that has ever been communicated to the world is probably a feeble shadow of the original conceptions of the poet.

Percy B. Shelley, "A Defence of Poetry", 1821

On Books

All books are divisible into two classes, the books of the hour, and the books of all time. Mark this distinction—it is not one of quality only. It is not merely the bad book that does not last, and the good one that does. It is a distinction of species. There are good books for the hour, and good ones for all time; bad books for the hour, and bad ones for all time. I must define the two kinds before I go farther.

The good book of the hour, then,—I do not speak of the bad ones—is simply the useful or pleasant talk of some person whom you cannot otherwise converse with, printed for you. Very useful often, telling you what you need to know; very pleasant often, as a sensible friend's present talk would be. These bright accounts of travels; good-humoured and witty discussions of question; lively or pathetic story-telling in the form of novel; firm fact-telling, by the real agents concerned in the events of passing history;—all these books of the hour, multiplying among us as education becomes more general, are a peculiar characteristic and possession of the present age: we ought to be entirely thankful for them, and entirely ashamed of ourselves if we make no good use of them. But we make the worst possible use, if we allow them to usurp the place of true books: for, strictly speaking, they are not books at all, but merely letters or newspapers in good print. Our friend's letter may be delightful, or necessary, to-day: whether worth keeping or not, is to be considered. The newspaper may be entirely proper at breakfast time, but assuredly it is not reading for all day. °A book is essentially not a talked thing,

but a written thing; and written, not with the view of mere communication, but of permanence. °A book is written, not to multiply the voice merely, not to carry it merely, but to preserve it. The author has something to say which he perceives to be true and useful, or helpfully beautiful. So far as he knows, no one has yet said it; so far as he
5 knows, no one else can say it. He is bound to say it, clearly and melodiously if he may; clearly, at all events. In the sum of his life he finds this to be the thing, or group of things, manifest to him;—this the piece of true knowledge, or sight, which his share of sunshine and earth has permitted him to seize. He would fain set it down for ever; engrave it on rock, if he could; saying, "This is the best of me; for the rest, I ate, and drank, and slept,
10 loved, and hated, like another; my life was as the vapour, and is not; but this I saw and knew: this, if anything of mine, is worth your memory". That is his "writing"; it is, in his small human way, and with whatever degree of true inspiration is in him, his inscription, or scripture. That is a "Book".

Perhaps you think no books were ever so written? But, again, I ask you, do you at all
15 believe in honesty, or at all in kindness? or do you think there is never any honesty or benevolence in wise people? None of us, I hope, are so unhappy as to think that. Well, whatever bit of a wise man's work is honestly and benevolently done, that bit is his book, or his piece of art. It is mixed always with evil fragments—ill-done, redundant, affected work. But if you read rightly, you will easily discover the true bits, and those *are* the
20 book.

Now books of this kind have been written in all ages by their greatest men:—by great leaders, great statesmen, and great thinkers. These are all at your choice; and life is short. You have heard as much before;—yet have you measured and mapped out this short life and its possibilities? Do you know, if you read this, that you cannot read that
25 —that what you lose to-day you cannot gain to-morrow? Will you go and gossip with your housemaid, or your stable-boy, when you may talk with queens and kings; or flatter yourselves that it is with any worthy consciousness of your own claims to respect that you jostle with the common crowd for *entrée* here, and audience there, when all the while this eternal court is open to you, with its society wide as the world, multi-
30 tudinous as its days, the chosen, and the mighty, of every place and time? Into that you may enter always; in that you may take fellowship and rank according to your wish; from that, once entered into it, you can never be outcast but by your own fault; by your aristocracy of companionship there, your own inherent aristocracy will be assuredly tested, and the motives with which you strive to take high place in the society of the
35 living, measured, as to all the truth and sincerity that are in them, by the place you desire to take in this company of the Dead.

John Ruskin, "Sesame and Lilies", 1865

The Modern English Play

Nineteen-fifty-six was the year of the Hungarian Revolution and the year of England's shameful adventure in Suez. It was also the year when young Englishmen and women
40 started to pour into plays and films the energies that have changed the mood of their country, the year of John Osborne's *Look Back in Anger* and Brendan Behan's *The Quare Fellow*, the year when Brecht's Berliner Ensemble played in England for the first

time, the year of the Free Cinema experiments that were the first work of the men who later made *Saturday Night and Sunday Morning, This Sporting Life, Taste of Honey, Tom Jones*.

Before the historic opening of the English Stage Company at the Royal Court Theatre in April 1956, the country with the greatest body of dramatic literature in the world possessed a theater that had turned into a stuffed flunkey. At that time there wasn't a contemporary English play worth discussing. The available choices came in two broad categories, generally described by salespeople in theater-ticket agencies as "entertaining" and "something to think about."° "Entertainment" consisted of revues, drawing-room comedies and thrillers; "Something to Think About" generally had a knight or a dame playing in it, and the only recognizable problem it ever raised was the problem of parking the car. If it was a really high-flying example it would be in bad verse. Highbrow theater was a mandarin bolt-hole, a place where effete literati could run to earth and hide themselves from the world, and the best actors understandably worked hardest at the classics. The London theater list in 1956 was full of famous old plays decked out with stars; theater-going then was often a little like going to *Swan Lake*. You knew the work backwards, and went only to fall out of the gallery clapping.°

Shakespeare in general was elaborately and rhetorically done, using fussy sets that were not so much pieces of stage architecture as examples of interior decoration. There was no National Theatre, and no Royal Shakespeare Company at the Aldwych. The Old Vic did Shakespeare with a second-best company, and the Stratford-on-Avon team was grand but *ad hoc;* there was no ensemble work on a serious, long-term, state-supported basis.°

And on May 8, 1956, the anniversary of victory in Europe after the Second World War, there was the first night of a play that held that the Establishment's England wasn't really victorious about anything at all, being slothful, craven, ruled by played-out snobs, in thrall to a fatuous monarchy, and so mannered in its style of public expression that for a man to declare openly what he meant was liable to have the effect of a brawl in church. The play was John Osborne's *Look Back in Anger*. The next morning the critics treated it like a bad smell, but the two serious Sunday papers recognized it for what it was: a flagrantly unacceptable statement of affairs that those under 30 would accept on the spot, written in their own mutinous, free-wheeling, coolly unofficial English, with a fierce gaiety that had been lost from the stage for a long time and a theatrical gift that at last dared to go too far.

And then, in the same month, Joan Littlewood staged Brendan Behan's *The Quare Fellow*, a tragedy set in a prison before the hanging of a condemned man and delivered with dauntless humor. Behan lodged his protest against capital punishment in a voice of Irish disengagement and with a surface of unnerving jokes. The play began with a ballad that was roared out under a Victorian notice lettered Silence. There was lewd romping between the convicts who were digging the unseen man's grave, and the hangman was presented as a benign and boozy bourgeois who prided himself on always being ready to get out of a sickbed to do a hanging. I remember both these first nights very well, including the furious support in the next-door pubs of the people who responded to them, mostly leftish and young, and the frosty dislike of the other camp, whose worst fears for the future sanctity of the flag-wagging old Britain were confirmed later that year by the uproar against the Tory government's action in Suez.

For the first time since Shaw, the theater in Britain grew dangerous and offensive. The gathering attention paid to the new plays that now appeared reasserted a lost social truth: that art has the power to be a serious threat to the status quo if the status quo is one that the majority doesn't believe in, because art can provide people with the symbols by which they can make changes.

This fact is always in dispute by scoffing neutralists, who argue circularly that socially meaningful art is propaganda art, therefore Soviet tractor art, therefore not art, therefore not socially meaningful. I think the trouble lies in the word "socially"; perhaps it should be "humanly". The reason why the events of the English theater since 1956 have had such a powerful effect on a society is that they were powerfully recognizable to a very large number of human beings. It would be interesting to collect the hundreds upon hundreds of popular newspaper pieces that, during the past 10 years, have taken their tone and their attitudes directly from what began as the nation's minority theater. The archetypes created in Osborne's *Look Back* and *The Entertainer* and *Inadmissible Evidence,* in Shelagh Delaney's *A Taste of Honey,* Harold Pinter's *The Caretaker* and Arnold Wesker's trilogy about a working-class Jewish family, turn up in features aimed at people who can be assumed never to have been to the theater in their lives.

Penelope Gilliatt in "Life", 1966

American Literature now stands in its Own Right

American literature, as it does in most countries, grew up twofold; the early, scholarly, traditional, and correct writers imitated English writing of the time and their thinking followed European trends and held in contempt the starveling, semiliterate organism that was growing up under their eyes. This attitude still obtains in many American writers, particularly in those critics who are descended from recent immigrants. On the other hand, the exotic nature of the new continent, with its unexplored and mysterious areas and its noble but savage Red Men, engaged the interest of some European writers who reported us with the childlike inaccuracy we now address to Africa and the upper ranges of the Amazon. However, we were fortunate quite early in developing some mature writers of eye, ear, and enthusiasm; Washington Irving, for instance, looked with joy on our people, our speech, stories, and patterns of thought; Cooper made up a fund of misinformation about the American Indians; while Longfellow searched for Hellenic meter and meaning in the life and history of Americans. Meanwhile, the true seedlings of our literature were sprouting in the tall tales, the jests, the boasting, and the humor of the storytellers in the forests and on the plains. Their product was printed in local newspapers and in publications fiercely ignored by the princely intellectual Brahmins of the East Coast, who felt that the indigenous must somehow be tainted. Even Edgar Allan Poe, who surely wrote more like a European than an American, had to be acclaimed in France before he was acceptable to upperbrow Americans. But the writers of America for Americans survived and expanded and, perhaps because their only outlet was in obscure and local journals, created a situation which even today exists only in America.°

Perhaps someone knows how the great change came which elevated American writing from either weak imitation or amusing unimportance to a position of authority in the

whole world, to be studied and in turn imitated. It happened quickly. A Theodore
Dreiser wrote the sound and smell of his people; a Sherwood Anderson perceived and
set down secret agonies long before the headshrinkers discovered them. Suddenly the
great ones stirred to life: Willa Cather, then Sinclair Lewis, O'Neill, Wolfe, Hemingway, Faulkner. There were many others, of course—poets, short-story writers, essayists
like Benchley and E. B. White. Their source was identical; they learned from our
people and wrote like themselves, and they created a new thing and a grand thing in the
world—an American literature about Americans. It was and is no more flattering than
Isaiah was about the Jews, Thucydides about the Greeks, or Tacitus, Suetonius, and
Juvenal about the Romans; but, like them, it has the sweet, strong smell of truth. And
as had been so in other ages with other peoples, the Americans denounced their glory
as vicious, libelous, and scandalous falsehood—and only when our literature was
accepted abroad was it welcomed home again and its authors claimed as Americans.

John Steinbeck, "America and Americans", 1966

The Contemporary American Short Story

The United States has stood high in the short story form almost from the birth of the
nation. It is doubtful if any other country has produced a more distinguished body of
stories or so many artists writing the story. In the pre-modern period the great names
include Irving, Poe, Hawthorne, Melville, and perhaps Bierce. The modern period
begins with Henry James and Stephen Crane and may be thought of as flowering in
Sherwood Anderson, Ernest Hemingway, and William Faulkner. It also flowered in
the work of Willa Cather, Ring Lardner, Dorothy Parker, F. Scott Fitzgerald, Katherine
Anne Porter, Caroline Gordon, Eudora Welty, John Steinbeck, and Robert Penn
Warren. These and numerous others had made their names prior to World War II.

Since World War II the volume of good short stories has if anything increased. This
is not surprising. Strong, virile traditions do not collapse overnight. Although the
stories possibly do not measure up to the work of Crane, Anderson, Hemingway, and
Faulkner, they do speak with authority for the post-War period. They not only reveal
a diversity of technical achievement, but they also give us artistic insight into modern
man's relationship to an increasingly industrialized society. In fact, so many writers

Henry James   81 Stephen Crane   82 Katherine A. Porter   83 William H. Faulkner   84 Ernest Hemingwa

85 John Steinbeck 86 Jerome D. Salinger 87 Robert P. Warren 88 Jack Kerouac 89 Truman Capote

have produced at least several superior stories that it will be possible in this article to consider only a sampling of their work.

In general, the successful writers of the post-War period can be thought of as following in the aesthetic footsteps of their predecessors, but an important minority have sought new forms of aesthetic expression or even rebelled. The period has been marked by a strong university and college influence. Many of our post-War authors have been trained in creative writing classes taught by teachers who themselves are authors. The stories have often appeared in literary quarterlies supported by universities. Peter Taylor, to cite one example, studied with Allen Tate and Caroline Gordon at Southwestern at Memphis and with John Crowe Ransom at Vanderbilt and Kenyon. Since finishing college Mr. Taylor has partly supported himself by teaching creative writing in several colleges and universities.

The academic orientation has been both a strength and a weakness. The strength is that one expects technical competence, and one gets it. In fact, the very volume of good short stories in the post-War period is partly accounted for by the training of the writers. They not only have read their predecessors on their own but they have studied them in the classroom. The weakness is that the writer tends to get caught up in a kind of academic inbreeding. Everybody looks back to Chekhov, to James, to Joyce, and to the other masters. He learns that there is a way to do things and hesitates to find his own way. He is a follower, not a pioneer.

It is a healthy sign then that there has been a reaction against the carefully wrought story, an effort by some writers to break through the old forms. The loudest rebellion has been that of the Beat Generation writers. They have sought complete freedom from form and a completely free expression of language.

But good stories, whatever the theory or lack of theory behind them, have one bond in common: They produce an impact upon the reader. The reader comes from them feeling that he has discovered something significant about life. This is true of the carefully wrought story, and it is also true of the so-called "uncooked" story. Anton Chekhov, a pioneer in his own time, speaks well for the conservative position of today. "When I write", says Chekhov, "I reckon entirely upon the reader to add for himself the subjective elements that are lacking in the story".

Chekhov's point about the story is that the artistic writer should present outward and inward events in the lives of his characters in such a subtle way that the reader makes discoveries about them and about the life they represent. The writer works objectively but with purpose. He leads the reader to a moment, even a shock, of revelation. The artistic reader in turn reads with the intent of achieving discovery or revelation, or, in the language of modern psychological theory, *gestalt*. In some stories the discovery is experienced by the protagonist, but it comes in such a way as to seem understated. The reader, in the end, pulls things together for himself.

Chekhov's point, which has the backing of Aristotle, of Flaubert, of Henry James, of Joyce, has been perhaps the most adhered to canon of writers of the modern short story. Technically, it has meant close but suggestive (often ironical) specification of physical detail, of physical action, of dialogue, of interior monologue. It has meant the effacing of the author, and eliminating any comment by him upon the story. However, there have always been writers, sometimes ignorant of theory, sometimes indifferent to it, who have stated or explained their themes—Theodore Dreiser, for example. And even when the reader is told what he is to discover, he may be so carried away by the story and the characters, so interested in the theme, so convinced of the author's authority, as to receive a strong impact. By the same token, the reader may come away from a consciously artistic story with such a pinprick of recognition as to feel cheated. This undoubtedly is the reaction of the Beat Generation writers to the stories of the more conservative authors.

Jack Kerouac, foremost among the Beat Generation fiction writers, speaks for the Beat position in the following passage: "Not 'selectivity' of expression but following free deviation (association) of mind into limitless blow-on-subject seas of thought, swimming in a sea of English with no discipline other than rhythms of exhalation and expostulated statement, like a fist coming down on a table, bang! (the space dash)."°

In the stories of the Beat Generation one gets an almost hysterical emphasis upon emotional impact. The characters developed by the conservative writers usually are people who express little emotion or if they express emotion they seem to do so pathologically—the emotion of an alcoholic, for example. This is one of the big problems of our age, to express emotion in an adequate, normal way. The Beat writer in a way reflects an effort to solve the problem. He puts so much emphasis on the emotion of his characters that abnormal emotion, even raw sensation, becomes normal to him. He champions the very exaggerations that the conservative writer presents only as symptoms. Moreover the freedom from restraint also carries over into his language.°

It is not always easy to draw a sharp line between those writing in the Chekhovian tradition and those taking a different approach. John O'Hara, John Cheever, Irwin Shaw, J. F. Powers, Walter Van Tilburg Clark, Peter Taylor, Flannery O'Connor, and Mary McCarthy show at least some characteristics of the Chekhovian story. Carson McCullers and Truman Capote push toward more personal expression and toward less rigorous attention to form. J. D. Salinger is an extreme individualist and does not hold himself to any one approach. Jack Kerouac and R. V. Cassill represent the Beat Generation.

Danforth Ross, "The American Short Story", 1964

XI Religion

The Church of England

British people are perhaps not much more or less religious than others, but religion is now, as it has always been, an important factor in the national life. There is, of course, complete religious freedom, and anyone may belong to any religious faith that
5 he chooses or to none at all. The Church of England is the established Church of the English nation, though perhaps a quarter of the people belong to other religious denominations and many others cannot be said to have any religious attachment. The established Church of Scotland is quite separate, having a different organization without bishops, and in Wales there is (since 1914) no established Church at all. It would
10 be wrong to begin a discussion of religion in Britain, or even in England, without some mention of these important facts. Nevertheless, it is natural and appropriate to concentrate mainly on the Church of England. The Queen is its head and was crowned, like her predecessors, by the Archbishop of Canterbury in Westminster Abbey, and the Church has a continuous history going back before the Reformation to the earliest
15 days of English Christianity. The establishment is part of the law, and important changes concerning the Church cannot be made without the consent of Parliament— though many people in the Church wish that this were not so.

    First of all, something must be said on definitions. In England the terms "Anglican Church" and "Church of England" are almost interchangeable, though in practice the
20 term "Anglican" tends to be more favoured among "high-church" than among "low-church" people. But there are also other Churches of the same type, and sharing the same origins and the same apostolic succession, outside England. In Scotland and the U.S.A. these churches are called "Episcopal" or "Protestant Episcopal", but it is also quite common in these other countries to use the term "Anglican", meaning in
25 this case apparently "like the Church of England". So the particular form of Christianity which has been adopted by England as a nation is also a world-wide form, though outside England it loses its English national character.°

    The doctrine of the Church of England was set out in the Thirty-nine Articles, agreed upon by a convocation of clergy in 1562 and finally ratified in 1571, and this statement
30 of doctrine is still authoritative, without alteration, today. It is essentially a "Protestant" statement.°

    At about the same time the Book of Common Prayer was devised, using the English language instead of Latin and giving an important place to the reading of the Bible in regular worship. It owes much to Archbishop Cranmer, who was later burned at the
35 stake at Oxford in 1556 during the reign of the Catholic Queen Mary.

    The Prayer Book now in use is the version approved in 1662, which is little different from that of Cranmer's time. Like the English Bible, it contains some of the best prose in the English language. It includes services for regular use day by day and others for special occasions. The regular services are the Holy Communion, adapted from the
40 Mass, and Morning and Evening Prayer, which are also called Matins and Evensong.

By 1900 there was a widespread demand for some flexibility in the permitted usages, and after years of work the Convocations of Canterbury and York and the three Houses of the Church Assembly (bishops, clergy and laity) agreed on an alternative version. This had to be submitted to Parliament, where it was not treated as a party-political question, but it was rejected by a small majority in the House of Commons in 1927 and again, after some revisions had been made, in 1928. The majorities included Members of Parliament who did not belong to the Church of England, and the affair led to much dissatisfaction with the constitutional position of the Church and its dependence on Parliament. Many churches use parts of the 1928 Prayer Book today, although strictly speaking they are breaking the law by doing so.

Another great reform of the sixteenth century allowed priests of the Church of England to be married, and today the clergyman's wife is a most valuable helper in his work. But the Church is still steadfastly opposed to the idea of having women as priests. There are, however, nearly fifty Anglican religious orders for women, besides a few for men.°

The Anglican Church is said to be both Catholic and Protestant, though until the early part of the nineteenth century the Protestant tendency was on the whole predominant. About that time two new movements became important. The Evangelical movement united some members of the Church who were much concerned with the Christian duties of the Church towards the world. It was very influential in securing the purchase of the freedom of the slaves in the British colonial possessions, and in following Wesley in seeking to improve the lives of the people in industrial England. It was in the Puritan tradition, concerned with strict personal life and condemning self-indulgence. The other movement was in a different direction; some teachers at Oxford, notably Keble, Newman and Pusey, were anxious to restore some of the order of religious observance associated with Catholicism, and the movement which they started was called "tractarianism" or the "Oxford Movement". (It should be carefully distinguished from the much later movement which was for a time called the "Oxford Group"; that movement, now usually called "Moral Rearmament", was founded by an American, the late Frank Buchman, and never had anything to do with the Anglican Church.) The Evangelical Movement and the Oxford Movement still have their influence today, and the colloquial terms "low-church" and "high-church" now correspond with the Protestant and Catholic tendencies which are to be seen side by side in the contemporary Church.

Peter Bromhead, "Life in Modern Britain", [6]*1968*

The English Bible

But though Shakespeare may be in the retrospect the greatest glory of his age, he was not in his own day its greatest influence. By the end of Elizabeth's reign, the book of books for Englishmen was already the Bible, although the Authorized Version that is still in use was only drawn up by James I's Bishops in the years immediately following her death. For every Englishman who had read Sidney or Spenser, or had seen Shakespeare acted at the Globe, there were hundreds who had read or heard the Bible with close attention as the word of God. The effect of the continual domestic study of the

book upon the national character, imagination and intelligence for nearly three centuries to come, was greater than that of any literary movement in our annals, or any religious movement since the coming of St. Augustine. New worlds of history and poetry were opened in its pages to a people that had little else to read. Indeed it created the habit of
5 reading and reflection in whole classes of the community, and turned a tinker into one of the great masters of the English tongue. Through the Bible, the deeds and thoughts of men who had lived thousands of years before in the eastern Mediterranean, translated into English during the period when our language reached its brief perfection, coloured the daily thought and speech of Britons, to the same degree as they are coloured in our
10 own day by the commonplaces of the newspaper press. The Bible in English history may be regarded as a "Renaissance" of Hebrew literature far more widespread and more potent than even the Classical Renaissance which, thanks to the reformed Grammar Schools, provided the mental background of the better educated. The Bible and the Classics together stimulated and enlarged the culture of the British, as their ocean
15 voyages stimulated and enlarged their practical outlook on life.

George M. Trevelyan, "History of England", [3]1958

The Common Prayer Book

It is more than 400 years since the first Prayer Book that could be "understanded of the people" was published—in English—and it remains the English Prayer Book, conveying to new ages the truths that are never old.
20 When the first Prayer Book of Edward VI—the foundation of our present Book of Common Prayer—was published, England was passing through a very violent religious, political, and economic revolution. No wonder the Litany prays: "From battle and murder and from sudden death, good Lord, deliver us". For battle, murder, and sudden death were rather familiar in the sixteenth century.

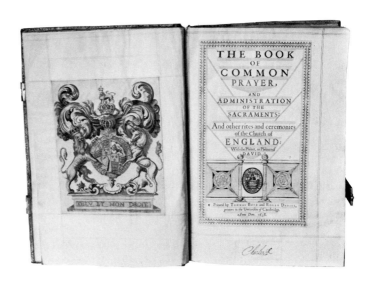

90 Title Page of the Signed Common Prayer Book of King Charles I

This first Prayer Book accomplished the fundamental revolution: it was in English, not Latin, and it could be "understood of the people". Then came the stormy five years' interlude of Queen Mary's reign, during which the Latin service returned, and Archbishop Cranmer, author of some of our most magnificent collects, was publicly burned alive at Oxford. During the reign of Queen Elizabeth, the Prayer Book was revised, and this version, with some small alterations, is still in use.

Now, first and foremost, this Prayer Book is English—English, of course, to begin with, in the obvious sense that it is written in the language of the people, and in the language of the people at its very noblest. What an incalculable debt English literature must owe to the grand, old sentences which have sunk deep into the consciousness of successive generations: "The changes and chances of this mortal life", "That peace which the world cannot give".

But the Prayer Book is English in another and, perhaps, a deeper sense. Like much else that is essentially English, it is based on compromise. It excludes certain medieval doctrines and practices which the reformers condemned as superstitious, but it embodies in translation much of the ancient Latin liturgies.

And so, in the reign of Elizabeth, it was enabled to survive the attacks of Roman Catholics on the one hand and of Puritans on the other, and, ever since, it has served and helped to hold together a Church which has always comprehended members of very diverse ways of thought.

Now compromise—generally accepted, I suppose, as a great virtue in politics—is often derided in religion, and, perhaps, what began as compromise is now better described as "comprehension", for comprehension suggests both inclusiveness and understanding.

But the Prayer Book has become comprehensive in a sense altogether undreamed of by its first compilers. In the reign of Elizabeth, the Prayer Book was a question only of the homeland. Francis Drake had not yet sailed round the world, the first English colonies were not yet founded. But, through the centuries which followed, the English people and the English tongue, and with them, of course, the English Common Prayer Book, were spreading across the five continents.

So the Prayer Book has taken root across the world because it could be "understood of the people"—in fact, it has been translated into nearly 150 different languages.

John Elton in "London Calling, European Ed.", 1949

Puritanism in England

The growth, triumph, and transformation of the Puritan spirit was the most fundamental movement of the seventeenth century. Puritanism, not the Tudor secession from Rome, was the true English Reformation, and it is from its struggle against the old order that an England which is unmistakably modern emerges. But, immense as were its accomplishments on the high stage of public affairs, its achievements in that inner world, of which politics are but the squalid scaffolding, were mightier still.°

In the mysticism of Bunyan and Fox, in the brooding melancholy and glowing energy of Cromwell, in the victorious tranquillity of Milton, "unshaken, unseduced, unterrified", amid a world of self-seekers and apostates, there are depths of light and darkness which posterity can observe with reverence or with horror, but which its small fathom-line cannot plumb.

There are types of character which are like a prism, whose various and brilliant colours are but broken reflections of a single ray of concentrated light. If the inward and spiritual grace of Puritanism eludes the historian, its outward and visible signs meet him at every turn, and not less in market-place and counting-house and camp than in the student's chamber and the gathering of the elect for prayer. For to the Puritan, a contemner of the vain shows of sacramentalism, mundane toil becomes itself a kind of sacrament. Like a man who strives by unresting activity to exorcise a haunting demon, the Puritan, in the effort to save his own soul, sets in motion every force in heaven above or in the earth beneath. By the mere energy of his expanding spirit, he remakes, not only his own character and habits and way of life, but family and church, industry and city, political institutions and social order. Conscious that he is but a stranger and pilgrim, hurrying from this transitory life to a life to come, he turns with almost physical horror from the vanities which lull into an awful indifference souls dwelling on the borders of eternity, to pore with anguish of spirit on the grand facts, God, the soul, salvation, and damnation.°

Overwhelmed by a sense of his "Ultimate End", the Puritan cannot rest, nevertheless, in reflection upon it. The contemplation of God, which the greatest of the Schoolmen described as the supreme blessedness, is a blessedness too great for sinners, who must not only contemplate God, but glorify him by their work in a world given over to the powers of darkness.°

The spirit bloweth where it listeth, and men of every social grade had felt their hearts lifted by its breath, from aristocrats and country gentlemen to weavers who, "as they stand in their loom, can set a book before them or edifie one another". But, if religious zeal and moral enthusiasm are not straitened by the vulgar categories of class and income, experience proves, nevertheless, that there are certain kinds of environment in which they burn more bravely than in others, and that, as man is both spirit and body, so different types of religious experience correspond to the varying needs of different social and economic *milieux*. To contemporaries the chosen seat of the Puritan spirit seemed to be those classes in society which combined economic independence, education, and a certain decent pride in their status, revealed at once in a determination to live their own lives, without truckling to earthly superiors, and in a somewhat arrogant contempt for those who, either through weakness of character or through economic helplessness, were less resolute, less vigorous and masterful, than themselves.°

Their triumphs in the past, their strength in the present, their confidence in the future, their faith in themselves, and their difference from their feebler neighbours—a difference as of an iron wedge in a lump of clay—made them, to use a modern phrase, class-conscious. Like the modern proletarian, who feels that, whatever his personal misery and his present disappointments, the Cause is rolled forward to victory by the irresistible force of an inevitable evolution, the Puritan *bourgeoisie* knew that against the chosen people the gates of hell could not prevail. The Lord prospered their doings.°

The conception to which it appealed to bridge the gulf sprang from the very heart of Puritan theology. It was that expressed in the characteristic and oft-used phrase, "a Calling". The rational order of the universe is the work of God, and its plan requires that the individual should labour for God's glory. There is a spiritual calling and a temporal calling. It is the first duty of the Christian to know and believe in God; it is by faith that he will be saved. But faith is not a mere profession, such as that of Talkative of Prating Row, whose "religion is to make a noise". The only genuine faith is the faith which produces works. "At the day of Doom men shall be judged according to their fruits. It will not be said then, Did you believe? but, Were you doers, or talkers only?" The second duty of the Christian is to labour in the affairs of practical life, and this second duty is subordinate only to the first. "God", wrote a Puritan divine, "doth call every man and woman... to serve him in some peculiar employment in this world, both for their own and the common good. ... The Great Governor of the world hath appointed to every man his proper post and province, and let him be never so active out of his sphere, he will be at a great loss, if he do not keep his own vineyard and mind his own business".

From this reiterated insistence on secular obligations as imposed by the divine will, it follows that, not withdrawal from the world, but the conscientious discharge of the duties of business, is among the loftiest of religious and moral virtues.

Richard H. Tawney, "Religion and the Rise of Capitalism", 1926

The Quakers

In the England of today the church has found itself included in the critical examination of all previously held social values and standards of personal behaviour. Serious questioning is going on within the Church itself on its real faith and its true role and message in a rapidly changing world.

A numerically small group, the "Society of Friends", usually called Quakers, is making an increasingly relevant contribution to this re-thinking by its emphasis on simplicity and the deeply-held belief that there is "that of God" in every man.

Whereas the Roman Catholic faith is based on the authority of the Church, and for most Protestants the final authority is the Bible, Quakers, whilst respecting the rich heritage from the past, and finding great inspiration in the Bible, believe that they must follow the "Inner Light" of the spirit of God in their own lives.

The Quakers have no paid ministers or priests; they observe no outward sacraments such as Holy Communion or Baptism; they are not bound by fixed creeds or doctrines; they have no predetermined order of service, but meet for worship on a basis of silence. Any member of the group can rise to speak or pray if he or she feels they have a message for the meeting; they practise full equality between men and women. From the earliest days of their formation in the 17th century, Quakers have been deeply concerned for the sufferings of mankind; above all, they have steadfastly refused to fight in wars. "We utterly deny all outward wars and strifes and fightings with outward weapons ... for we certainly know and testify to the World that the Spirit of Christ which leads us into all Truth will never move us to fight and war against any man with outward weapons, neither for the kingdom of Christ nor for the kingdoms of this world." This is a quotation from "A declaration from the harmless and innocent people of God, called Quakers", addressed to King Charles II in 1660, a time of great persecution of the Quakers and all dissenting religious groups.

Though they did not fight, they have always been ready to help and relieve the misery and privations of the victims of war. In every movement for social reform the Quakers have provided pioneers—in fighting slavery, in urging the humane treatment of prisoners and of those suffering from mental illness, in housing improvement, in creating better industrial working conditions, and many other forms of service. All these practices are explained by the central belief of the Quakers that in every man and woman God has planted the capacity to respond to His spirit; therefore all men are members of God's family, and as such have to be treated with love and consideration. Those who do the will of the Father are brethren of Jesus Christ; therefore the Quakers are Christians although they are not baptized.

The Anglican prelate Dean Inge wrote about them: "The Quakers, of all Christian bodies, have remained nearest to the teaching and example of Christ."

Eric Priestman, Special Contribution for "Britain and America"

New England Calvinism and Anglicanism

American religious culture originated in Calvinist New England. Even today the nation's moral standards and criminal codes largely reflect the Puritan values of seventeenth and eighteenth century Calvinism. Some of the major aspects of Calvinist dogma and church structure relevant to our consideration of competition among religious cultures in the market place of public issues are the following:

1. *The wickedness of man.* Orthodox Calvinism was obsessed with the dogma of original sin. Men were inherently evil and, with the exception of a few whom God selected to save, were doomed to damnation. This obsession with the inherent fallibility of all men did imply a concept of egalitarianism which was an important part of New England's heritage to American democracy.

2. *Compulsion and election.* It follows from this that the idea that men should be free in matters of faith and morals was alien and repugnant to New England Calvinism. If man were free to choose, he would invariably choose error and evil. Election belongs exclusively to God; the obligation of man is to obey the word of God as communicated through the church. It is well known that the Puritans came to America not to establish religious liberty but to secure freedom of worship for themselves alone. They had no hesitation in imposing upon articulate dissenters the same persecution that they had suffered at the hands of the Anglican Church.

3. *Church and state.* For the same reasons, the concept of separation of church and state was alien and repugnant to New England Calvinism. The Congregationalist Church of Massachusetts was the last of all American churches to become disestablished, and when separation was finally achieved in 1833 it was against the desires of the church.

4. *Man's purpose in life.* Man's sole purpose in life was the glorification of God. Whatever detracted from man's efforts and activities in the pursuit of this end was necessarily evil. Happiness, as the term is generally understood, if not intrinsically evil was certainly not the aim of life.

5. *Austerity and simplicity.* The Puritan mind abhorred pomp, pageantry, and ornateness. Puritan church services centered on the sermon and eschewed all rites and ritual.

6. *The moral standards.* Puritan moral standards were the strictest of all among the tributaries to American culture. The principal evils were lewdness, covetousness, anger, untruthfulness, Sabbath-breaking, vanity, gossiping, and idleness.

As Congregational Calvinism was the established church in New England, so Anglicanism was the established church in Virginia and the Southern Colonies. However, while Calvinism played a tremendous role in shaping American cultural patterns, the contributions of Anglicanism were comparatively insignificant. The religion and culture of Anglicanism after the disappearance of early Calvinist influence, fitted well the needs of the Southern plantation aristocracy (as they had fitted the needs of the Tudor and Stuart aristocracies), and whatever influence Anglicanism might have on American culture vanished along with the disappearance of the plantation aristocracy.

Leo Pfeffer, "Creeds in Competition", 1958

Protestantism in the U.S.A.

America is a Protestant country, not formally Protestant—that is, a majority of its population are not enrolled members of some Protestant denomination—but it is Protestant in a far deeper sense than a mere statistical statement can prove. The whole background of American history, with local exceptions in Maryland, Louisiana, California, and New Mexico, is Protestant; the attitude of Catholics and Jews is profoundly affected by this saturation of the national life in the Protestant tradition. That tradition is hard to define, but it is impossible not to recognize it. It emphasizes preaching rather than the sacraments, the Bible rather than church organization, and, since the middle of the nineteenth century, good works, or in modern terms "service", rather than doctrine. The identification of "sanctity" with "success", attributed by some historians to the early Calvinists, can be more safely attributed to modern American popular religion.

Secular and religious views of life are mingled; religion helps to make men "good", i.e., honest and non-criminal, and to diminish adolescent indiscipline, so it is supported by financial contributions, sometimes by personal service, and by advertisements calling attention to its benefits in the local press, paid for by the local business community. The government, however, gives no funds to churches. The separation of church and state is a cardinal American principle. The Constitution of the United States protects the freedom of the American people to choose their own church and religious faith, and to worship according to their own consciences. The First Amendment to the Constitution states:

"Congress shall make no law respecting an establishment of religion, or prohibiting the free exercise thereof."

In ethical questions, where powerful interests are not too clearly antagonized, American public opinion is still profoundly affected by the leaders of Church opinion and by slogans and ideals which revive memories of the national religious tradition. This is perfectly well known to politicians and to all who attempt to influence the public mind; from the Bible and from popular hymns come the best raw materials for mass emotion.

The American contribution to religious variety in modern times has been marked by the national optimism and the national belief that most important events in religion, as in other departments of life, now occur in America. At one end of the scale is Christian Science, in many ways a legitimate extension of the development of New

England religion, at the other end such odd cults as that of "Father Divine", a successful cult of a God incarnate in a living American negro, a cult not confined to negroes. Still important in the West are the Mormons, whose basic belief is that the North American continent had its place in the central Christian history long before the coming of Columbus.

The main organ of coherence among the immigrants is the churches. The Lutheran churches and colleges were, and to some extent are, forces retarding the complete assimilation of German and Scandinavian immigrants; they help, at least, to preserve the language and the culture of the mother country.

America is overwhelmingly Protestant, and still more overwhelmingly Christian. Organized religion still plays a greater part than it does in any other great industrial state. What "Christianity" means in this context is hard to define. But it does mean that the majority of the American people have an emotional, if not intellectual, attachment to absolute values, that they believe that things are right or wrong, not merely profitable or pleasant, or the reverse. They may not agree, in any given instance, as to what is the right thing to do, but they do agree that "righteousness exalteth a nation".

"Righteousness" nearly always takes an active form. The way of Martha, not the way of Mary, is the American way of religion. Contemplative religious orders do not flourish on American soil; but all churches make great play with statistics of numbers, of schools, colleges, orphanages, hospitals, social services of all kinds. On such figures they base their successful claim to be free from taxation, their claim to be an indispensable part of a healthy American society. And, despite criticism from the Left, despite the decline of dogmatic belief among the young, the American people wishes all Churches well, as long as they do not thrust before it doctrines that offend American optimism and do not, in the name of morals, attempt to enforce by law standards of conduct too completely unlike those obeyed by the average citizen. The churches are in retreat on some fronts; they have been defeated over prohibition, over Sunday observance, over many minor moral questions. They are perplexed by doctrinal difficulties and by the increasing indifference of the laity to doctrine. But deep in the American mind is a belief that his is God's Own Country.

Denis W. Brogan, "U.S.A., An Outline of the Country, its People and Institutions", 1941

XII Humanity

The Unity of European Culture

I °want to make a little clearer what I mean when I use the term "culture". Like "democracy", this is a term which needs to be, not only defined, but illustrated, almost every time we use it. And it is necessary to be clear about what we mean by "culture", so that we may be clear about the distinction between the material organisation of Europe, and the spiritual organism of Europe. If the latter dies, then what you organise will not be Europe, but merely a mass of human beings speaking several different languages. And there will be no longer any justification for their continuing to speak different languages, for they will no longer have anything to say which cannot be said equally well in any language: they will, in short, have no longer anything to say in poetry. I have already affirmed that there can be no "European" culture if the several countries are isolated from each other: I add now that there can be no European culture if these countries are reduced to identity. We need variety in unity: not the unity of organisation, but the unity of nature.

By "culture", then, I mean first of all what the anthropologists mean: the way of life of a particular people living together in one place. That culture is made visible in their arts, in their social system, in their habits and customs, in their religion. But these things added together do not constitute the culture, though we often speak for convenience as if they did. These things are simply the parts into which a culture can be anatomised, as a human body can. But just as a man is something more than an assemblage of the various constituent parts of his body, so a culture is more than the assemblage of its arts, customs, and religious beliefs. These things all act upon each other, and fully to understand one you have to understand all. Now there are of course higher cultures and lower cultures, and the higher cultures in general are distinguished by differentiation of function, so that you can speak of the less cultured and the more cultured strata of society, and finally, you can speak of individuals as being exceptionally cultured. The culture of an artist or a philosopher is distinct from that of a mine worker or field labourer; the culture of a poet will be somewhat different from that of a politician; but in a healthy society these are all parts of the same culture; and the artist, the poet, the philosopher, the politician and the labourer will have a culture in common, which they do not share with other people of the same occupations in other countries.

Now it is obvious that one unity of culture is that of the people who live together and speak the same language: because speaking the same language means thinking, and feeling, and having emotions, rather differently from people who use a different language. But the cultures of different peoples do affect each other: in the world of the future it looks as if every part of the world would affect every other part. I have suggested earlier, that the cultures of the different countries of Europe have in the past derived very great benefit from their influence upon each other. I have suggested that the national culture which isolates itself voluntarily, or the national culture which is cut off from others by circumstances which it cannot control, suffers from this isolation. Also, that the country which receives culture from abroad, without having anything to give in return, and the country which aims to impose its culture on another, without accepting anything in return, will both suffer from this lack of reciprocity.

There is something more than a general exchange of culture influences, however. You cannot even attempt to trade equally with every other nation: there will be some who need the kind of goods that you produce, more than others do, and there will be some who produce the goods you need yourselves, and others who do not. So cultures of people speaking different languages can be more or less closely related; and sometimes so closely related that we can speak of their having a common culture. Now when we speak of "European culture", we mean the identities which we can discover in the various national cultures; and of course even within Europe, some cultures are more closely related than others. Also, one culture within a group of cultures can be closely related, on different sides, to two cultures which are not closely related to each other. Your cousins are not all cousins of each other, for some are on the father's side and some on the mother's. Now, just as I have refused to consider the culture of Europe simply as the sum of a number of unrelated cultures in the same area, so I refused to separate the world into quite unrelated cultural groups; I refused to draw any absolute line between East and West, between Europe and Asia. There are, however, certain common features in Europe, which make it possible to speak of a European culture. What are they?

The dominant force in creating a common culture between peoples each of which has its distinct culture, is religion. Please do not, at this point, make a mistake in anticipating my meaning. This is not a religious talk, and I am not setting out to convert anybody. I am simply stating a fact. I am not so much concerned with the communion of Christian believers to-day; I am talking about the common tradition of Christianity which has made Europe what it is, and about the common cultural elements which this common Christianity has brought with it. If Asia were converted to Christianity tomorrow, it would not thereby become a part of Europe. It is in Christianity that our arts have developed; it is in Christianity that the laws of Europe have—until recently—been rooted. It is against a background of Christianity that all our thought has significance. An individual European may not believe that the Christian Faith is true, and yet what he says, and makes, and does, will all spring out of his heritage of Christian culture and depend upon that culture for its meaning. Only a Christian culture could have produced a Voltaire or a Nietzsche. I do not believe that the culture of Europe could survive the complete disappearance of the Christian Faith. And I am convinced of that, not merely because I am a Christian myself, but as a student of social biology. If Christianity goes, the whole of our culture goes. Then you must start painfully again, and you cannot put on a new culture ready made. You must wait for the grass to grow to feed the sheep to give the wool out of which your new coat will be made. You must pass through many centuries of barbarism. We should not live to see the new culture, nor would our great-great-great-grandchildren: and if we did, not one of us would be happy in it.

To our Christian heritage we owe many things beside religious faith. Through it we trace the evolution of our arts, through it we have our conception of Roman Law which has done so much to shape the Western World, through it we have our conceptions of private and public morality. And through it we have our common standards of literature, in the literatures of Greece and Rome. The Western World has its unity in this heritage, in Christianity and in the ancient civilisations of Greece, Rome and Israel, from which, owing to two thousand years of Christianity, we trace our descent. I shall not elaborate this point. What I wish to say is, that this unity in the common elements of culture, throughout many centuries, is the true bond between us. No political and economic organisation, however much goodwill it commands, can supply what this culture unity gives. If we dissipate or throw away our common patrimony of culture, then all the organisation and planning of the most ingenious minds will not help us, or bring us closer together.

The unity of culture, in contrast to the unity of political organisation, does not require us all to have only one loyalty: it means that there will be a variety of loyalties. It is wrong that the only duty of the individual should be held to be towards the State; it is fantastic to hold that the supreme duty of every individual should be towards a Super-State. I will give one instance of what I mean by a variety of loyalties. No university ought to be merely a national institution, even if it is supported by the nation. The universities of Europe should have their common ideals, they should have their obligations towards each other. They should be independent of the governments of the countries in which they are situated. They should not be institutions for the training of an efficient bureaucracy, or for equipping scientists to get the better of foreign scientists; they should stand for the preservation of learning, for the pursuit of truth, and in so far as men are capable of it, the attainment of wisdom.

Thomas Stearns Eliot, "Notes towards the Definition of Culture", 1948

Individuality

There has been a time when the element of spontaneity and individuality was in excess, and the social principle had a hard struggle with it. The difficulty then was to induce men of strong bodies or minds to pay obedience to any rules which required them to control their impulses. To overcome this difficulty, law and discipline, like the Popes struggling against the Emperors, asserted a power over the whole man, claiming to control all his life in order to control his character—which society had not found any other sufficient means of binding. But society has now fairly got the better of individuality; and the danger which threatens human nature is not the excess, but the deficiency, of personal impulses and preferences. Things are vastly changed since the passions of those who were strong by station or by personal endowment were in a state of habitual rebellion against laws and ordinances, and required to be rigorously chained up to enable the persons within their reach to enjoy any particle of security. In our times, from the highest class of society down to the lowest, every one lives as under the eye of a hostile and dreaded censorship. Not only in what concerns others, but in what concerns only themselves, the individual or the family do not ask themselves—what do I prefer? or, what would suit my character and disposition? or, what would allow the best and highest in me to have fair play, and enable it to grow and thrive? They ask themselves, what is suitable to my position? what is usually done by persons of my station and pecuniary circumstances? or (worse still) what is usually done by persons of a station and circumstances superior to mine? I do not mean that they choose what is customary in preference to what suits their own inclination. It does not occur to them to have any inclination, except for what is customary. Thus the mind itself is bowed to the yoke: even in what people do for pleasure, conformity is the first thing thought of; they like in crowds; they exercise choice only among things commonly done; peculiarity of taste, eccentricity of conduct, are shunned equally with crimes: until by dint of not following their own nature they have no nature to follow: their human capacities are withered and starved: they become incapable of any strong wishes or native pleasures, and are generally without either opinions or feelings of home growth, or properly their own. Now is this, or is it not, the desirable condition of human nature?°

It is not by wearing down into uniformity all that is individual in themselves, but by cultivating it, and calling it forth, within the limits imposed by the rights and interests of others, that human beings become a noble and beautiful object of contemplation; and as the works partake the character of those who do them, by the same process human life also becomes rich, diversified, and animating, furnishing more abundant aliment to high thoughts and elevating feelings, and strengthening the tie which binds every individual to the race, by making the race infinitely better worth belonging to. In proportion to the development of his individuality, each person becomes more valuable to himself, and is therefore capable of being more valuable to others. There is a greater fulness of life about his own existence, and when there is more life in the units there is more in the mass which is composed of them. As much compression as is necessary to prevent the stronger specimens of human nature from encroaching on the rights of others cannot be dispensed with; but for this there is ample compensation even in the point of view of human development. The means of development which the individual loses by being prevented from gratifying his inclinations to the injury of others, are chiefly obtained at the expense of the development of other people. And even to himself there is a full equivalent in the better development of the social part of his nature, rendered possible by the restraint put upon the selfish part. To be held to rigid rules of justice for the sake of others, develops the feelings and capacities which have the good of others for their object. But to be restrained in things not affecting their good, by their mere displeasure, develops nothing valuable, except such force of character as may unfold itself in resisting the restraint. If acquiesced in, it dulls and blunts the whole nature. To give any fair play to the nature of each, it is essential that different persons should be allowed to lead different lives. In proportion as this latitude has been exercised in any age, has that age been noteworthy to posterity. Even despotism does not produce its worst effects, so long as individuality exists under it; and whatever crushes individuality is despotism, by whatever name it may be called, and whether it professes to be enforcing the will of God or the injunctions of men.

Having said that the individuality is the same thing with development, and that it is only the cultivation of individuality which produces, or can produce, well-developed human beings, I might here close the argument: for what more or better can be said of any condition of human affairs than that it brings human beings themselves nearer to the best thing they can be? or what worse can be said of any obstruction to good than that it prevents this? Doubtless, however, these considerations will not suffice to convince those who most need convincing; and it is necessary further to show, that these developed human beings are of some use to the undeveloped—to point out to those who do not desire liberty, and would not avail themselves of it, that they may be in some intelligible manner rewarded for allowing other people to make use of it without hindrance.

In the first place, then, I would suggest that they might possibly learn something from them. It will not be denied by anybody, that originality is a valuable element in human affairs. There is always need of persons not only to discover new truths, and point out when what were once truths are true no longer, but also to commence new practices, and set the example of more enlightened conduct, and better taste and sense in human life. This cannot well be gainsaid by anybody who does not believe that the world has already attained perfection in all its ways and practices. It is true that this benefit is not capable of being rendered by everybody alike: there are but few persons, in comparison with the whole of mankind, whose experiments, if adopted by others, would be likely to be any improvement on established practice. But these few are the salt of the earth; without them, human life would become a stagnant pool. Not only is it they who introduce good things which did not before exist; it is they who keep the life in those which already exist.

John Stuart Mill, "On Liberty and Considerations on Representative Government", 1859

The Indestructibility of the United Nations

The need for the United Nations is so strong and so deep that it is for all practical purposes indestructible. The U.N. can be destroyed, of course, by a third world war. But we may be sure that the survivors would re-create something very like the U.N. The League of Nations, which was destroyed between the two world wars, was revived as the United Nations after the second world war. Does this not mean that the need for such an organization is so persistent that while a great war can demolish the tree, the roots are deep and cannot be killed?

What, we may ask ourselves, is the nature of this need which is the vital principle of the United Nations? It is not to be found, I think, in any of the specific provisions of the charter which was written at Dumbarton Oaks and adopted in San Francisco. Nor does the vital principle reside in the controversial peacemaking and peacekeeping activities, such as the Congo and the Gaza strip. Nor does it reside in the good works of the United Nations, which are invaluable and numerous. The vital principle of the United Nations is the enduring need for a meeting place where the governments can, whenever they choose to do so, talk privately about anything.

There are, to be sure, other important functions which the U.N. performs. One of them is that it provides a public forum in which the weak nations can talk to the great powers and get back some kind of accounting. Although the debates in the General Assembly do not produce the purest candor or the highest wisdom, and are in fact often ignorant and foolish, it is better that the grievances and accusations be brought into the open than that they should be left to fester in the dark.

But, while the public forum is useful and indeed necessary, the indispensable activity of the United Nations is what goes on privately and off the record. It goes on in the corridors and lounges of the U.N., at private lunches and dinners and cocktail parties, some of them in the U.N. itself and often in private homes. Delegates often complain that the incessant rounds of parties and gatherings are exhausting, and no doubt they are, especially if the delegate does not ration his food, his drink and his time. But those who are involved in this coming and going and getting together are powerful officials. As they can meet without benefit of newspaper publicity or television, this facility is indispensable to the peace of the world.

There is no other place where conversation is possible at any time of the day or night among the contending and quarreling peoples of the world. Only at the U.N. do the Pakistanis and the Indians, the Greeks and the Turks, the Arabs and the Israelis, the Chinese and the Russians and the Americans, the Saigonese and the Viet Cong and the North Vietnamese have a network of communications, either direct or indirect, which can be made supersecret or boldly open as and when they choose.

91 African Delegates in the UNO Delegates' Lounge

This network provides an element which, while it has always been indispensable in the conduct of diplomacy, has become rare and difficult under the white lights of modern publicity and of democratic government. This indispensable element is the ability to try out proposals without being publicly committed to them, of letting them be accepted or amended or rejected without public debate, without any need to explain them or justify them if they do not work. This was the way the beginning of the end of the Korean War was initiated—over Martinis in the delegates' lounge of the United Nations. The end of the Berlin blockade also was initiated by private talks in the lobby.

I am not meaning to say, of course, that the clandestine activity at the United Nations is a kind of benevolent conspiracy which will ensure the peace of the world. But I am persuaded that, though the dangerous issues are not being resolved at the U.N., the network of communications is a great shock absorber in the conflicts which threaten us.

Walter Lippmann in "Newsweek", 1965

Excerpts from the Universal Declaration of Human Rights, 1948

Art. 1 All human beings are born free and equal in dignity and rights. They are endowed with reason and conscience and should act towards one another in a spirit of brotherhood.

Art. 2 Everyone is entitled to all the rights and freedoms set forth in this Declaration, without distinction of any kind, such as race, colour, sex, language, religion, political or other opinion, national or social origin, property, birth, or other status.°

Art. 3 Everyone has the right to life, liberty, and the security of person.

Art. 5 No one shall be subjected to torture or to cruel, inhuman, or degrading treatment or punishment.

Art. 7 All are equal before the law and are entitled without any discrimination to equal protection of the law. All are entitled to equal protection against any discrimination in violation of this Declaration and against any incitement to such discrimination.

Art. 9 No one shall be subjected to arbitrary arrest, detention, or exile.

Art. 10 Everyone is entitled in full equality to a fair and public hearing by an independent and impartial tribunal, in the determination of his rights and obligations and of any criminal charge against him.

Art. 18 Everyone has the right to freedom of thought, conscience, and religion; this right includes freedom to change his religion or belief, and freedom either alone or in community with others and in public or private, to manifest his religion or belief in teaching, practice, worship, and observance.

Art. 19 Everyone has the right to freedom of opinion and expression; this right includes freedom to hold opinions without interference and to seek, receive, and impart information and ideas through any media and regardless of frontiers.

Art. 23, 1. Everyone has the right to work, to free choice of employment, to just and favourable conditions of work, and to protection against unemployment.

2. Everyone, without any discrimination, has the right to equal pay for equal work.

3. Everyone who works has the right to just and favourable remuneration, ensuring for himself and his family an existence worthy of human dignity, and supplemented, if necessary, by other means of social protection.

4. Everyone has the right to form and to join trade unions for the protection of his interests.

Art. 25, 1. Everyone has the right to a standard of living adequate for the health and well-being of himself and of his family, including food, clothing, housing, and medical care and necessary social services, and the right to security in the event of unemployment, sickness, disability, widowhood, old age, or other lack of livelihood in circumstances beyond his control.

2. Motherhood and childhood are entitled to special care and assistance. All children, whether born in or out of wedlock, shall enjoy the same social protection.

"Yearbook of the United Nations 1948/49", 1950

Excerpts from the UNESCO Constitution

The Governments of the States parties to this Constitution on behalf of their peoples declare:
    that since wars begin in the minds of men, it is in the minds of men that the defences of peace must be constructed;
    that ignorance of each other's ways and lives has been a common cause, throughout the history of mankind, of that suspicion and mistrust between the peoples of the world through which their differences have all too often broken into war;
    that the great and terrible war which has now ended was a war made possible by the denial of the democratic principles of the dignity, equality and mutual respect of men, and by the propagation, in their place, through ignorance and prejudice, of the doctrine of the inequality of men and races;
    that the wide diffusion of culture, and the education of humanity for justice and liberty and peace are indispensable to the dignity of man and constitute a sacred duty which all the nations must fulfil in a spirit of mutual assistance and concern:°
    For these reasons, the States parties to this Constitution, believing in full and equal opportunities for education for all, in the unrestricted pursuit of objective truth, and in the free exchange of ideas and knowledge, are agreed and determined to develop and to increase the means of communication between their peoples and to employ these means for the purposes of mutual understanding and a truer and more perfect knowledge of each other's lives;
    In consequence whereof they do hereby create the United Nations Educational, Scientific and Cultural Organization for the purpose of advancing, through the educational and scientific and cultural relations of the peoples of the world, the objectives of international peace and of the common welfare of mankind for which the United Nations Organisation was established and which its Charter proclaims.

"Unesco-Publications 367", 1945

Excerpts from J. F. Kennedy's Message on the Peace Corps, March 1, 1961

Throughout the world the people of the newly developing nations are struggling for economic and social progress which reflects their deepest desires. Our own freedom, and the future of freedom around the world, depend, in a very real sense, on their ability to build growing and independent nations where men can live in dignity, liberated from the bonds of hunger, ignorance, and poverty.
    One of the greatest obstacles to the achievement of this goal is the lack of trained men and women with the skill to teach the young and assist in the operation of development projects—men and women with the capacity to cope with the demands of swiftly evolving economies, and with the dedication to put that capacity to work in the villages, the mountains, the towns, and the factories of dozens of struggling nations.
    The vast task of economic development urgently requires skilled people to do the work of the society—to help teach in the schools, construct development projects, demonstrate modern methods of sanitation in the villages, and perform a hundred other tasks calling for training and advanced knowledge.

To meet this urgent need for skilled manpower we are proposing the establishment of a Peace Corps—an organization which will recruit and train American volunteers, sending them abroad to work with the people of other nations.

This organization will differ from existing assistance programs in that its members will supplement technical advisers by offering the specific skills needed by developing nations if they are to put technical advice to work. They will help provide the skilled manpower necessary to carry out the development projects planned by the host governments, acting at a working level and serving at great personal sacrifice. There is little doubt that the number of those who wish to serve will be far greater than our capacity to absorb them.°

Most heartening of all, the initial reaction to this proposal has been an enthusiastic response by student groups, professional organizations, and private citizens everywhere—a convincing demonstration that we have in this country an immense reservoir of dedicated men and women willing to devote their energies and time and toil to the cause of world peace and human progress.

Among the specific programs to which Peace Corps members can contribute are: teaching in primary and secondary schools, especially as part of national English language teaching programs; participation in the worldwide program of malaria eradication; instruction and operation of public health and sanitation projects; aiding in village development through school construction and other programs; increasing rural agricultural productivity by assisting local farmers to use modern implements and techniques. The initial emphasis of these programs will be on teaching.°

Because one of the greatest resources of a free society is the strength and diversity of its private organizations and institutions much of the Peace Corps program will be carried out by these groups, financially assisted by the Federal Government.

Peace Corps personnel will be made available to developing nations in the following ways:

1. Through private voluntary agencies carrying on international assistance programs.
2. Through overseas programs of colleges and universities.
3. Through assistance programs of international agencies.
4. Through assistance programs of the United States government.
5. Through new programs which the Peace Corps itself directly administers.°

In all instances the men and women of the Peace Corps will go only to those countries where their services and skills are genuinely needed and desired.°

Length of service in the Corps will vary depending on the kind of project and the country, generally ranging from two to three years. Peace Corps members will often serve under conditions of physical hardship, living under primitive conditions among the people of developing nations. For every Peace Corps member service will mean a great financial sacrifice. They will receive no salary. Instead they will be given an allowance which will only be sufficient to meet their basic needs and maintain health. It is essential that Peace Corps men and women live simply and unostentatiously among the people they have come to assist. At the conclusion of their tours, members of the Peace Corps will receive a small sum in the form of severance pay based on length of service abroad to assist them during their first weeks back in the United States.

John F. Kennedy, "Public Messages, Speeches and Statements", 1962

Text Sources and Acknowledgements

Agriculture/2000. Ed. by the U.S. Department of Agriculture. U.S. Government Printing Office, Washington, D.C. 1967 (pp. 93, 156). *America and Britain.* Three Volumes in One. Ed. by Prof. P. Sargant Florence. G. Harrap, London 1946 (pp. 7, 54). *American Colloquy.* Ed. by L. Lief and D. Hawke. The Bobbs-Merrill Co., Indianapolis 1963 (p. 67). *American History told by Contemporaries.* Vol. II. Macmillan, New York/London ⁶1950 (p. 73). *American Newsletters for Teachers of English in Germany.* U.S. Information Center, Stuttgart, Issue No. 19, 1965 (p. 134), Issue No. 17, 1964 (p. 201). *American Women.* U.S. Information Agency, Bad Godesberg n. d. (p. 88). *Australian Panorama.* Office of the High Commissioner for Australia, London 1968 (p. 117). *The Beauty of Britain.* Introduction by J. B. Priestley. B. T. Batsford, London 1962 (p. 10). Bernstein, L.: *The Joy of Music.* Simon & Schuster, New York 1959 (p. 185). Block, G. D. M.: *About the Conservative Party.* Conservative Political Centre, London 1965 (p. 106). Braddell, D.: *How to look at Buildings.* 1932 (p. 170). Braun, W. v.: *Space Frontier.* Holt, Rinehart and Winston, New York 1963; © 1963, 1964, 1965, 1966, 1967 by W. v. Braun. Reprinted by permission of Holt, Rinehart and Winston, Inc., Publishers, New York (p. 161). *Britain, An Official Handbook.* Her Majesty's State Office, London 1968 (p. 28). Brogan, D. W.: *U.S.A., An Outline of the Country, its People and Institutions.* Oxford University Press, London/New York/Toronto 1941 (p. 211). Bromhead, P.: *Life in Modern Britain.* Longmans, Harlow ⁶1968 (pp. 30, 44, 204). Brooke, R.: *Letters from America.* Sidgwick & Jackson, London 1916 (p. 63). Burke, E.: *Speeches and Letters on American Affairs.* Introduction by P. McKevitt. Dent & Sons, London 1955 (p. 98). *Collier's.* P. F. Collier, New York 1955 (p. 55). *Collier's Yearbook 1967.* Crowell, Collier and Macmillan, New York 1967 (p. 65). *Constitutional Documents II, IV, V.* Historical Association, London n. d. (pp. 95, 95, 96). Conton, W.: *The African.* Heinemann, London 1966 (African Writers Series, 12) (p. 128). Creighton, Th. H.: *American Architecture.* R. B. Luce, Washington, D.C. 1964; used by permission of David McKay Co., Inc., New York (p. 180). Darwin, C.: *The Origin of Species.* Introduction by W. R. Thompson. Repr. ed. Dent & Sons, London 1956 (p. 147). *A Documentary History of the United States.* An expanded edition by R. D. Heffner. The New American Library, New York 1965 (Mentor Book) (pp. 131, 132, 133). Eliot, T. S.: *Notes towards the Definition of Culture.* Faber & Faber, London 1962 (Fabers' paper covered editions) (p. 213). *English Historical Documents.* Ed. by C. Douglas. Vol. IX. Eyre & Spottiswoode, London 1955 (p. 131). *Esquire.* New York, July 1966 (p. 41). *The Funnies—An American Idiom.* Ed. by D. M. White and R. H. Abel. Colliers-Macmillan, London 1963 (p. 188). *The Guardian.* London, January 1, 1973; reprinted by permission (p. 109). *Harper's Magazine.* New York, July 1967 (p. 12). Heyer, P.: *Architects on Architecture. New Directions in America.* Walker & Co., New York 1960 (p. 183). Herling, J.: *Labor Unions in America.* R. B. Luce, Washington, D.C. 1964; used by permission of David McKay Co., Inc., New York (p. 143). *Higher Education in the U.S.A.* U.S. Information Service, London 1964 (pp. 80, 81). Howes, H. W.: *Presenting Modern Britain.* G. Harrap, London 1966 (pp. 29, 32). *The Inaugural Addresses of the American Presidents. From Washington to Kennedy.* Annotated by D. N. Lott. Holt, Rinehart and Winston, New York 1961 (p. 144). Inge, W. R.: *England.* Rev. ed. E. Benn, London 1953 (p. 24). Johnson, S.: *Preface to Shakespeare with Proposals for Printing the Dramatic Works of William Shakespeare.* Oxford University Press, London 1957 (p. 195). Kennedy, J. F.: *A Nation of Immigrants.* Rev. and enl. ed. Harper & Row, New York 1964; © 1964 by Anti-Defamation League (Abridgement of pp. 64–67) (p. 69). Kennedy, J. F.: *Containing the Public Messages, Speeches and Statements of the President.* U.S. Government Printing Office, Washington, D.C. 1962 (p. 220). King, M. L.: *Stride toward Freedom.* Harper & Row, New York 1958 (hardbound edition); © by M. L. King, 1958 (Abridgement of pp. 189–191, 196–197) (p. 75). Lerner, M.: *America as a Civilization.* Simon & Schuster, New York 1957 (p. 151). *Life—Atlantic Edition.* Amsterdam, October 1965 (p. 57), June 1966 (p. 113),

March 1968 (p. 126), December 1965 (p. 157), June 1966 (p. 198). Lilienthal, D. E.: *This I do believe*. Harper & Row, New York 1949; © by Harper, 1949 (Abridgement of pp. 45-48) (p. 150). *The Listener*. London, February 1948 (pp. 99, 121). Locke, J.: *The Second Treatise of Government*. Ed. by T. P. Peardon. Liberal Arts Press, New York 1952 (p. 97). *London Calling—European Edition*. London, January 1967 (p. 40), 1950 (pp. 101, 136), 1949 (pp. 169, 206), May 1966 (p. 174). *Look at America*. New York 1947 (p. 59). *Manchester Guardian Weekly*. Manchester, February 1968 (p. 76), December 1966 (p. 122). Mill, J. St.: *On Liberty and Considerations on Representative Government*. Ed. with an introduction by R. B. McCallum. B. Blackwell, Oxford 1948 (p. 215). *Milton's Prose Writing*. Introduction by K. M. Burton. Dent & Sons, London 1958 (p. 24). *National Geographic*. Vol. 130, No. 6. National Geographic Society, Washington, D.C. 1966 (p. 163). Newman, J. H.: *On the Scope and Nature of University Education*. Dent & Sons, London 1943 (p. 25). *Newsweek*. New York; © Newsweek, Inc., December 1966 (p. 186), October 1965 (p. 217). *The New York Times Magazine*. New York; © by The New York Times Co., October 1967 (p. 72); reprinted by permission. *The Observer*. London, September 1967 (p. 167). Orwell, G.: *Shooting an Elephant and Other Essays*. Secker & Warburg, London 1950 (p. 46). Pfeffer, L.: *Creeds in Competition*. Harper & Row, New York 1959; © 1959 by Harper & Row (Abridgement of pp. 25-26) (p. 210). Priestley, J. B.: *All about Ourselves and Other Essays*. Heinemann, London 1956; reprinted by permission of A. D. Peters & Co., London (p. 18). *Proceedings upon the Unveiling of the Statue of Baron v. Steuben...* Comp. by G. H. Carter. Printed under the Direction of the Joint Office on Printing of the Congress of the United States, Washington, D.C. 1911 (p. 133). Ribicoff, A., and Newman, J. O.: *Politics: The American Way*. Allyn & Bacon, Boston 1967; © 1967 by Allyn & Bacon, Inc., reprinted by permission of Allyn & Bacon, Inc. (pp. 139, 141). Ruskin, J.: *Sesame and Lilies. The Two Paths, The King of the River*. Dent & Sons, London 1944 (Everyman's Library Texts) (p. 197). Sampson, A.: *Anatomy of Britain today*. Hodder & Stoughton, London 1965 (pp. 38, 51). Sanderson, I. T.: *This Treasured Land*. G. P. Putnam's Sons, New York 1966 (p. 86). Seeley, J. R.: *The Expansion of England*. Macmillan & Co., London 1931 (p. 110). *Shakespeare in a Changing World*. Ed. by A. Kettle. Lawrence & Wishart, London 1964 (p. 195). Shaw, G. B.: *Plays Pleasant and Unpleasant*. Vol. 2. Constable, London 1952; reprinted by permission of The Public Trustee and The Society of Authors, London (p. 25). Shelley, P. B.: *Selected Poetry, Prose and Letters*. Ed. by A. S. B. Glover. Nonesuch Press, London 1951 (p. 196). Simonds, W. A.: *Edison—His Life, his Work, his Genius*. The Bobbs-Merrill Co., New York 1934; © 1934 by the Bobbs-Merrill Co., Inc., reprinted by permission of the publishers (p. 148). Smith, E.: *A Guide to English Traditions and Public Life*. Oxford University Press, London ²1955 (p. 33). *Sport and the Community. The Report of the Wolfenden Commission on Sport 1960*. Central Council for Physical Recreation, London 1961 (p. 46). Steinbeck, J.: *America and Americans*. The Viking Press, New York 1966; © 1966 by J. Steinbeck. All rights reserved. Reprinted by permission of The Viking Press, Inc. (p. 200). *The Sunday Times*. London, July 30, 1967 (p. 129). Tawney, R. H.: *Religion and the Rise of Capitalism*. Penguin Books, Harmondsworth 1964 (Pelican Books) (p. 207). Teller, E., and Latter, A. L.: *Our Nuclear Future—Facts, Dangers and Opportunities*. S. G. Phillips, New York 1958; © 1958 by S. G. Phillips, Inc., reprinted by permission (p. 159). Thackeray, W. M.: *The Works of W. M. Thackeray... in 26 Volumes*. Vol. 25. J. Murray, London 1911 (Centenary Edition) (p. 174). Thurber, J.: *Vintage Thurber*. H. Hamilton, London 1963; © by H. Hamilton, London (p. 90). *Time*. New York, September 1966 (p. 61), May 1967 (p. 114). *The Times*. London, March 21, 1973; reprinted by permission (p. 21). Trevelyan, G. M.: *History of England*. 3rd ed. with minor corrections. Longmans, Harlow 1959 (p. 205). *The Twentieth Century Magazine*. London, July 1961 (p. 177). *UNESCO-Publications 367*. 1945 (p. 220). *U.S. News & World Report*. Washington, D.C., February 24, 1964; © 1964 by U.S. News & World Report, Inc., reprinted by permission (p. 153). Wade, D.: *Our Aim and Purpose*. Published by Liberal Publication Department, London ⁴1967 (p. 104). *The Washington Post*. Washington, November 1967 (p. 165). Wilkinson, A.: *In your Own Words*. BBC, London 1967 (p. 190). Wilson, H.: *The Relevance of British Socialism*. Weidenfeld & Nicolson, London 1964 (p. 103). Wilson, J. D.: *The Essential Shakespeare*. Cambridge University Press, London 1946 (pp. 172, 191, 193). *Wireless Bulletin from Washington*. No. 42. U.S. Information Service, Washington, D.C. 1968 (p. 79). *Yearbook of the United Nations 1948/49*. Columbia University Press, New York 1950 (p. 219).

Sources of Illustrations

Archiv für Kunst und Geschichte, Berlin (No. 78). Australian News and Information Bureau, London (No. 47). British Travel Association, London (Nos. 6, 14, p. 6). Camera Press, London (No. 8). Canadian Embassy, Bonn (No. 46). J. Allan Cash, London (Nos. 29, 45, 66, 67). Central Office of Information, London (Nos. 3, 5, 11, 18, 41, 79, 90). Paul Gerhard Deker, Stuttgart (No. 76). dpa-Bilderdienst, Frankfurt am Main (Nos. 1, 4, 27, 48, 72, 84, 87). FOX photos ltd., London (No. 15). Fremdenverkehrsamt der USA, Frankfurt am Main (Nos. 26, 74). Gernsheim Collection, Humanities Research Center, The University of Texas at Austin (No. 42). Harper & Row, Inc., New York (No. 40). Historisches Porträtarchiv, Berlin (No. 50). Institut für Meteorologie und Geophysik der Freien Universität Berlin (No. 61). laenderpress, Düsseldorf (Nos. 7, 9, 62, 68). K. Lehnartz, Berlin (Nos. 25, 36, 70). Manchester Guardian, London (No. 23). National Portrait Gallery, London (No. 77). Paul Popper Ltd., London (Nos. 2, 16, 20, 21, 49, 57, 58, 89, 91). Punch Publications, London (No. 19, pp. 27, 178, 179, 180). Simon & Schuster, Inc., New York (p. 188). Süddeutscher Verlag, München (Nos. 10, 85). Staatsbibliothek Berlin, Bildarchiv [Handke] (Nos. 59, 80). Ullstein Bilderdienst, Berlin (Nos. 22, 69, 71). USIS, Bad Godesberg (Nos. 28, 30, 31, 32, 33, 34, 35, 38, 39, 52, 53, 54, 55, 56, 60, 73, 75, 81, 82, 83, 86, 88, p. 132). Velhagen & Klasing, Berlin (Nos. 17, 24, 37, 43, 44, 51, 63, 64, 65, p. 168).

Cover

British Travel Association, London (front cover, left; back cover, left). K. Lehnartz, Berlin (front cover, right; back cover, right).

Colour Plates

AEG-Telefunken, Frankfurt am Main (No. XI). British Travel Association, London (Nos. II, VIII). Reg Butler (No. XV). Lynn Chadwick (No. XVI). dpa-Bilderdienst, Frankfurt am Main (No. VI). Fremdenverkehrsamt der USA, Frankfurt am Main (No. IV). E. Klawitter, Berlin (No. I). R. Lindenberger, Jugenheim (Nos. IX, X). Henry Moore (Nos. XIII, XIV). National Gallery, London (No. XIX). Pan American World Airways, Berlin (No. V). Paul Popper Ltd., London (Nos. III, VII). M. Rosenthal, Berlin (No. XVIII). A. Schwolow, Berlin (No. XII). Tate Gallery, London (No. XVII).